Beyond the Stars II

Beyond the Stars II:
Plot Conventions in
American Popular Film

Edited by
Paul Loukides
and
Linda K. Fuller

Bowling Green State University Popular Press
Bowling Green, Ohio 43403

Dedication

This one is for Nora, Cindy and Jason with love and gratitude.

Paul Loukides

This volume on plot conventions owes my research on the baseball genre to Eric Fuller who, by indisputable account was the best third baseman that Milton Academy ever had; he is also, after 25+ years of marriage, an outstanding right-hand man.

Linda K. Fuller

Contents

Introduction
Plot Conventions in American Popular Film

While some movie critics decry the use of stock plot devices within new films, most recognize that conventional narrative devices are as old as storytelling itself. Aristotle spoke confidently of such dramatic conventions as the "scene of recognition" and the "reversal," with a sure sense that his audience would recognize the conventions of the Greek drama. In like fashion, any regular movie-goer recognizes such stock plot elements as instant antipathy that leads to romance, Cinderella transformations, the forceful kiss that melts resistance, last round rallies to victory, arming scenes, the spy within, sweet vengeance, monsters set loose by human failings, mistaken jealousies resolved by last minute clarifications, etc.

Yet even though the most casual film-goer recognizes dozens of narrative conventions, the literature of film outside of genre studies offers surprisingly little in the way of focused cataloguing, description, or analysis of these basic storytelling components of the American popular film tradition. While formulaic plot elements have been well delineated in studies of the most formalized and ritualized genres like the gangster film, the Western, and the horror film, there has been surprisingly little work which has focused on plot conventions used across the various genres, or widely shared in films of mixed genre like the space Western or the Sci-fi romantic comedy. Equally surprising is how little attention has been paid to the dynamics of the birth and evolution of plot conventions.

As useful and as illuminating as the traditional genre approach to popular film has been, most films—including those nominally within a given genre—mix their formulaic elements in ways that are less precisely patterned than "classic" genre films. In both "classic" genre films and those films of mixed modes, the conventions which permeate and dominate American popular film can be described as either: 1) conventions of character, 2) conventions of plot, 3) conventions of the material world, 4) conventions of locale or setting, and 5) thematic or ideological conventions.

Within traditional genre studies, the most highly ritualized of the genres like the Western, horror, or gangster genres, show a close conformity of elements across each of the five dimensions of filmic conventions. To take but one example, the central character of the Western is a puritan hero; the Western plot works toward the ritualized shoot-out; the horse and the

1

gun are the material focus of the hero's world; frontier towns and wilderness form the requisite locales. Ideologically, the Western endorses individualistic capitalism in which broad social needs (law and order) are met out of the efforts of the individual hero acting in his own self-interest.

The study of the conventional dimensions of film, whether of characters, narrative devices, material objects, locales, or themes and motifs, provides the student of popular culture a means of examining the most fundamental cultural assumptions of American movie makers and movie audiences. Conventions of plot, like all other filmic conventions, are highly revealing of cultural values and beliefs. Within the order of movie conventions, certain patterns of behavior are assumed to be part of the fixed or natural order of the world. The gunfighter, driven past endurance, will best the villain in a fair fight, no matter what the odds; the homely young woman who wears glasses and keeps her hair in a bun will not become more homely when she takes off her glasses and shakes her hair free. Rocky will not lose his fight by boozing it up the night before the championship bout. Because plot conventions are, in themselves, indexes of cultural assumptions about the physical and social world and how it should or must function, scholarship which focuses on the birth, evolution, or obsolescence of individual plot conventions offers the opportunity to examine the interrelationship between the movements of popular film and changes in the social mileau.

A systematic appraisal of the relationship between popular film and the cultural values of American society must doubtless wait until a much more exhaustive cataloguing of the conventions of popular film is available. However, an examination of stock narrative devices both within and without the framework of film genre is critically important to our understanding of the relationship between film and society.

What this book should help demonstrate is the immense amount of cultural information to be gained by examining narrative conventions in American popular film. Further, this collection of essays is intended to suggest that the systematic analysis of stock plot devices outside of any concern for genre may afford the popular culturist a more reliable index of cultural values and beliefs than those given by using genre as a starting point. To take only a single example, the much noted—and variously explained—decline of the Western genre film may be of less cultural interest than the persistence and evolution of most of its component conventions in other kinds of films. The symbolic value of the six-gun and the expanses of the Southwest transcend the Western as cultural icons. The shootout, whether on the streets of a classic Western town, or in the trash-filled alleys of a contemporary urban setting, retains its ritualistic dimensions.

* * *

In editing *Beyond The Stars II*, it has proven useful to make some distinction between narrative conventions which dominate or control the plot or structure of the film and those which serve a subsidiary role in the unfolding of the basic plot. Although it is tempting to use the traditional theatrical terms of "plot" and "scene" to describe greater and smaller stock plot devices, it seems more useful to think of them as strategic or tactical narrative devices. As any student of military history knows, the distinction between strategy and tactics tends to blur as the scale of tactical consideration grows. In like fashion, some narrative conventions used as tactical devices in a number of films serve important strategic roles in others. While the vocabulary used to describe various story conventions may seem a minor issue at best, the lack of terminology for describing various narrative functions emphasizes that the work contained in this collection is part of a yet evolving field of study.

That even minor (i.e., tactical) narrative conventions are revealing of cultural values is well demonstrated in the work on lesser stock devices done here by Rick Shale, Ann Boswell, and Brooks Robards. Shale's analysis of song interludes in the screwball comedies of the 1930s reveals—among other things—how quickly American popular music, particularly songs made popular by earlier films, was assimilated and used in later films as emblems of community. Self-consciously borrowed from contemporary popular culture, the songs in screwball comedies are used as minor plot devices which help reveal potential for action on the part of the main characters at the same time as they demonstrate the unifying force of the artifacts of popular culture— both songs and movies.

Although the wedding sequences discussed in Ann Boswell's paper, "The Pleasure of Our Company," range in length from the very brief wedding episode in *The Graduate* to the two hour wedding of Robert Altman's *The Wedding*, most movie weddings serve as tactical narrative devices which reveal social and interpersonal relationships. The frequent use of wedding scenes in films suggests that both film makers and film audiences are highly attuned to the social values revealed in this commonplace socio/religious ritual.

Brooks Robards' discussion of the uses of dream sequences in popular film ("California Dreaming") documents the longevity of this very popular narrative device, while at the same time clarifying the relatively narrow range of uses to which this device is put. Could it be that the dream sequences' direct and universal relationship to every audience member's personal experience helps to explain why dream sequences found their form and function early in film history and have remained virtually unchanged?

A variant of that same question might be asked about the uses of Christmas in American movies. Greg Metcalf, in "Have Yourself a Cinematic Christmas," constructs a convincing argument that even in the 1980s virtually all cinematic uses of Christmas reflect one or more of the narrative strands and thematic motifs of Dickens' *A Christmas Carol*. Although the particular manifestations of alienation, greed and redemption vary across the thirty films Metcalf cites from *Gremlins* to *Die Hard*, it is clear that American audiences continue to endorse the narrative conventions of the Dickens' tale.

While changes in American society do seem to affect the particular details of our Christmases and our dreams collectively, the form and function of dream and Christmas sequences appears to be relatively constant. The same cannot be said of the tactical-strategic plot convention of interracial love examined by Carlos Cortes in "Hollywood Interracial Love." Cortes' tracing of the varieties of interracial love through 75 years of film history and scores of films suggests quite how responsive popular movies can be to evolutionary changes in American social attitudes.

The overt racism that allowed the threat of miscegenation to be used as a stock plot device for more than fifty years no longer permeates American films or American social institutions; on the other hand, that films continue to reflect a great deal of social unease in matters of race is reflected in the typical movie pattern of mixed couples being composed of white males and ethnic women, rather than ethnic males and white women.

In like fashion, John Lenihan's analysis of "Movie Images of American Politics" closely documents how the most popular film images of the workings of the American political process very clearly reflect changes in the American political mood from the populist swing of the 1930s to post-Watergate America.

In somewhat different mode, Ralph Donald's essay, "Conversion as Persuasive Convention in American War Films," documents how the plot device of the conversion of a primary or secondary character has served as a mainstay of both pro-war and anti-war films from the patriotic swell of the 1940s to the disillusionment of Vietnam.

Clinton Sanders, a sociologist interested in the role of both producers and consumers in the life of movie conventions, examines the wide range of stock narrative devices used within even as formal a genre as the classic horror film. From Sanders' perspective, the fundamental definition of genre revolves around plot conventions and variations.

Other writers, like Gary Hoppenstand, Garyn Roberts, Linda K. Fuller, and Roy Vestrich, who are concerned with documenting the narrative strategies of a wide variety of films, also focus their attention on the core plot premise(s) and the ways in which formalized or ritualized stories recur and reoccur in a variety of guises. Roberts' essay on 1950s science fiction invasion films outlines the uses of revelation, demonstrations of human weaknesses, and cautionary scenes within the invasion film. Linda Fuller presents "'The Triumph of the Underdog' in Baseball Films" and shows how that basic plot device dominates baseball comedies, baseball melodramas and even baseball biographic films across decades and scores of films. Gary Hoppenstand, in his essay on the Supernatural Sit-Com and the plot convention of the ghost comedy, traces the uses of "lively spirits" and other "other worldly forces" in comedy from the Topper films of the 1930s to *Beetlejuice* and *High Spirits*. Roy Vestrich, in "The Culture Clash Comedies of the 1980s," looks at more than a dozen films premised on having a yuppie hero confront an alien culture or subculture.

While many of the essays contained within this volume might be viewed as dealing with established genres or defining new genres, or sub-genres, it is perhaps more useful to think of them simply as works which help us understand how important a role both tactical and strategic conventions of plot are to popular film and to our understanding of the interplay of events in American society and the world of popular film.

The best of the literature of film genres has always been carefully focused on the description and analysis of the component conventions of the genres. This collection is premised on the idea that an analysis of American popular film which uses that same concern for filmic conventions without regard for genre *per se* rewards the student of popular culture with new insights into the workings of American popular film.

If this book does no more than provoke others to document and examine the ritualized narrative devices (or other conventions) of American film, it will have succeeded in one of its goals; if, in addition, the essays contained in this volume help illuminate some small portion of American popular culture, then this work will have achieved its most important goal.

Paul Loukides

The Pleasure of Our Company:
Hollywood Throws A Wedding Bash

Parley Ann Boswell

Everybody's got problems—take a look at this wedding.
> Father of the groom (Frank Costellano),
> *Lovers and Other Strangers* (1970)

Now, if there's nothing else, I'd like to go to my daughter's wedding.
> Don Corleone (Marlon Brando),
> *The Godfather* (1972)

Stanley T. Banks (Spencer Tracy) is slumped in his armchair in the middle of his living room, which is cluttered with the debris of what seems to have been a lavish party. He massages his aching feet, lifts his head wearily, and addresses his audience: "I would like to say a few words about weddings." He will say more than a few words, of course, before he has finished telling his audience how it feels to be the father of the bride. For his audience, Stanley's story about his daughter's wedding serves as a means to an end. The tale of his life as an American father includes a plot device as traditional to American film as his daughter's ceremony is to American culture: the wedding celebration.

As he takes us through his version of his daughter's courtship and engagement, and as we experience Kay Banks' (Elizabeth Taylor's) elaborate traditional wedding in *Father of the Bride*, we begin to realize that what Stanley is really telling us is not the simple story of how his daughter became married, but of how he had to adapt to changes in his life which he didn't fully understand. We become aware early in the movie that this is really *his* story. He confides to us:

Someday in the far future, I may be able to remember [my daughter's wedding] with tender indulgence, but not now. I always used to think that marriage was a simple affair—boy and girl meet, they fall in love, get married, they have babies, eventually the babies grow up and meet other babies and fall in love and get married, and on and on and on. Looked at that way, it's not only simple, it's downright monotonous. But I was wrong. I figured without the wedding.

6

Through his often exasperated voice-overs and his grimaces, we sense Stanley's reluctance to understand or accept his daughter's choices. Although he tells his story in a whimsical, humorous way, we understand that he is trying to define the world he lives in, a world where he is trying to survive life—and parenthood—in a post-World War II suburban environment where much of what he experiences rings false to him, and where he is sure of nothing.

Father of the Bride was certainly not the first American movie to include a wedding celebration scene.[1] American audiences have been the honored guests at innumerable weddings in Hollywood movies since the 1920s. From dramas to comedies, from musicals to horror movies, Hollywood has provided us with a variety of marriage celebrations. We have watched elopements, lavish fairy-tale affairs, and interrupted ceremonies. We have seen couples marry in the midst of war, in Western cowtowns, in ancient cathedrals, and in the backs of cars. As audiences, we have experienced these weddings as opening scenes, as flashbacks, and as concluding scenes.

A wedding celebration—on film or otherwise—combines ceremony with idiosyncrasy. Because of this contrast of the universal with the serendipitous, weddings are well suited to the complicated nature of storytelling through film. Depending on the directors' motives and choices, audiences experience a variety of powerful responses to the weddings we see on film. We can be standing at the altar with the wedding party, or among the other invited guests, or as detached outsiders when we see weddings on film, and where we are in relation to the marrying couple helps us to identify conflict or resolution. We either cringe with embarrassment at the spectacle before our eyes, or we feel some sense of doom, or we rejoice. We recognize both universal truths and unique characteristics of whatever culture is being presented to us. We begin to distinguish tradition from fad and institution from intuition.

As plot devices, wedding celebrations serve as significant gauges to how we will interpret and judge characters and circumstances—indeed, entire cultures—in the movies. Through weddings, we can identify any number of significant, sometimes powerful, aspects of the worlds being presented to us. Director Vincente Minnelli's *Father of the Bride*, as light-hearted as it might have appeared to be when it was released in 1950, represents one of the first Hollywood productions to use the wedding celebration as a plot device that helped the audience to identify characteristics of a segment of American culture.

In his study of American films of the 1950s, Douglas Brode discusses how the traditional wedding we see in this film is used to expose to the audience a set of conflicting images: "...while [*Father of the Bride*] lovingly portrayed the people and their foibles, it mixed that tenderness with a satiric point of view on middle-class customs that, at moments, was almost savage" (28). This film "set the pace for many films that followed" because it was "the first American film to be set, quite clearly, in suburbia" (28).

Since the 1950s, and especially since the 1960s, the rise of American suburban culture has become an easy and popular target among Hollywood filmmakers, and weddings have served as an effective kind of "ammunition" most often used to attack the hypocrisies of that segment of American society. There may be no better way to understand the power of the wedding celebration as plot device that to look at how films since *Father of the Bride* use weddings to highlight what Hollywood sees as the superficial vulgarity of the middle and upper middle classes in American society.

One of the most memorable wedding scenes from an American film is a wedding that we do not celebrate, that of Elaine Robinson (Katharine Ross). When Benjamin Braddock (Dustin Hoffman) intrudes on Elaine's traditional wedding near the end of *The Graduate*, we see this fiasco from several different perspectives. We watch with Elaine while Benjamin, standing crucifix-like, screams for her from the balcony of the church. We stand with Benjamin above and watch the wedding party and Elaine's parents mouthing threats and curses at Benjamin. We see Elaine run out of the church while Benjamin jams the door behind her, and our parting shot is of Benjamin, in his street clothes, and Elaine, in her bridal gown, sitting tentatively at the back of a public bus moving away from the church and from us.

In the spirit of *It Happened One Night* and *The Philadelphia Story*, *The Graduate* concludes with a bride defying the tradition of her own wedding ceremony by deserting her groom. Also like the brides in these comedies of the 1930s, Elaine Robinson leaves behind a comfortable, predictable, upper class life. What distinguishes the interrupted wedding in *The Graduate*, however, is that we are not convinced of the reasons for Elaine's decision to run away with Benjamin. We recognize self-knowledge and true love in Claudette Colbert's and Katharine Hepburn's characters; in both films, the families of the brides fully endorse the rebellion. We recognize ambiguity, confusion, and possibly anger in Elaine Robinson. Does she love Benjamin? We're not sure, but we know that she loathes her mother, the infamous Mrs. Robinson (Anne Bancroft). We understand the intensity with which she hates her mother, and her mother's way of life, most pointedly by her choice to disrupt her own wedding.[2]

Several other Hollywood films of the 1960s use wedding celebration scenes to help us identify conflict between generations or clashes among several sets of social values in American culture. As in the *The Graduate*, other wedding scenes help up to sympathize with characters who are only on the periphery of the weddings, or who really do not "fit in" to the socio-economic classes presented to us. We watch these celebrations through the eyes of the "outsiders," and we see what they see. Segments of American culture are defined for us as contradictory, hypocritical, and vulgar.

Goodbye Columbus (1970) and *The Heartbreak Kid* (1972), movies which came out shortly after *The Graduate,* include blatantly vulgar wedding scenes, and both of these films expand the wedding scenes to include lengthy reception scenes. In a sense, they allow us to see the wedding reception which Elaine Robinson did not have.

Neil Klugman (Richard Benjamin), has chosen to spend his summer vacation away from his library clerking position and with the suburban family of his girlfriend, Radcliffe coed Brenda Patimkin (Ali McGraw). Neil's "bookish ways" and urban mentality have caused trouble between Brenda and her parents, yet he has reluctantly agreed to attend the wedding of Brenda's brother, Ron (Michael Marlin), and his new bride, Harriette (Gail Ommerle). By the time of the wedding scene, we have been prepared for a clash of value systems. We know that Neil is independent of his family and somewhat worldly—he lives and works in a city environment and he has served time in the army. We also know that he does not share many of the values of Brenda's suburban, nouveau riche family. When we attend the traditional wedding with Neil, we understand that he is skeptical of many of the values and institutions which the Patimkins hold dear. When we attend the wedding reception, we see more vividly the aspects of the Patimkins' way of life which appall Neil.

Our first image of the wedding reception is a shot of a liver pâté duck being beheaded. With one violent gesture, the father of the groom (Jack Klugman) shoves the entire pâté head into his mouth. From that point on, we are subjected to any number of shots of celebrating guests at various stages of imbibing, eating, and dancing to excess. The women are dressed in sequins which glitter and clash before our and Neil's eyes; the men are talking about business profits and the value of real estate.

We are uncomfortable at this reception, for reasons which have very little to do with the actual wedding. In fact, the bride and groom are not particularly important to us, except to further our response that this is a group of people who, compared to Neil, seem limited and have shallow ideas. Ron Patimkin, ex-basketball star at Ohio State University, has proved himself to be a mental midget, and his bride, on finding out that Neil is a library clerk, responds vacuously that "it must be nice to get first-crack at all of the best-sellers." We are allied with Neil, isolated with him in horror at the vulgarity and superficiality of the world of the Patimkins. When Neil's and Brenda's relationship dissolves in the next (and final) scene, we are not surprised, nor particularly disappointed. The wedding reception has served to assure us that neither Neil nor we want to be part of the world of Brenda Patimkin.

In *The Heartbreak Kid,* a film which has much in common with both *The Graduate* and *Goodbye Columbus,* we meet Leonard (Charles Grodin) just before he marries Lila (Jeannie Berlin). After their small, traditional Jewish wedding in New York City, they head for a honeymoon in Miami

Beach. When Lila becomes bedridden because of acute sunburn, an irritated and irritable Leonard goes out on the beach alone where he meets Kelly (Cybill Shepard), a wealthy young coed on vacation with her parents. Leonard leaves Lila (we never see her again after her ordeal in Miami), and he follows Kelly and her family back to her hometown in Minnesota. From this point on, Leonard's quest is to woo and win the beautiful Kelly, despite (or perhaps because of) the differences in their backgrounds. After painful attempts to be accepted by Kelly and her possessive father (Eddie Albert), Leonard *does* marry Kelly. Just as we were when he married Lila, we are in attendance at his second wedding.

As soon as we see the elegant Kelly on the arm of her silver-haired father, walking down the aisle of what looks to be a large Protestant church, we are reminded of Lila, in one of the first scenes of the movie, walking clumsily between her parents, the three of them negotiating their way toward Leonard among narrow rows of folding chairs. When we hear the band at Kelly's and Leonard's wedding playing "Close To You," we are reminded that a smaller, less skilled dance band played this same song at Lila's and Leonard's wedding. We remember that the guests at the first wedding danced and sang "Hava Nagila"; at the second wedding, the guests want to know about Leonard's profession (he has none), and they discuss business deals and finances.

The Heartbreak Kid combines the young-man-who-will-stop-at-nothing aspect of *The Graduate* with the young-man-from-the-wrong-side-of-town story from *Goodbye Columbus*. What distinguishes *The Heartbreak Kid* from these other movies is that unlike Benjamin and Neil, who are not "members of the wedding," Leonard, the character to whom the audience is most closely allied, marries not once, but twice. By watching *two* wedding celebration scenes, we begin to see the contrasts between the world Leonard has forsaken and the world he has entered. The final scene of this movie shows Leonard sitting on a sofa during his reception, discussing his aspirations with two bored thirteen-old wedding guests. We have heard him discussing the same topic at least twice before at this wedding, and, as all of his adult listeners did, his young listeners get up and leave him sitting alone at his own wedding. Leonard is truly the odd man out.

We are embarrassed and worried for him. After all, we are the only guests who have been to both of Leonard's weddings, and, at the end of the film, we are also the only guests who might even begin to understand the confused, ridiculous world that Leonard has made for himself. We have had the opportunity to compare Leonard's urban Jewish culture of New York City to the suburban waspish culture into which he finally marries, and we cringe. The weddings are very different, but Leonard is the same. We realize that poor Leonard cannot win.[3]

The Heartbreak Kid is not the only Hollywood production to use twice the plot device of the wedding celebration. Several other movies open and close with wedding scenes, including *It Happened One Night, The Palm Beach Story, Private Benjamin,* and *Mystic Pizza.* As in *The Heartbreak Kid,* this symmetrical "bracketing" of wedding scenes lets us compare characters and situations in ways which we could not do without the combination of ceremony and circumstance that two weddings allow.

A pair of weddings in one film can serve several functions. In *It Happened One Night,* we recognize true love by seeing the bride leave her own wedding a second time—this time for Clark Gable. In *The Palm Beach Story,* a mystery is cleared up for us by watching a wedding ceremony for the second time. And in two of the most recent movies to employ this device, *Private Benjamin* and *Mystic Pizza,* we become aware of great changes in certain characters by watching their weddings. Not uncharacteristic of many films made in the 1970s and 1980s, we can gauge growth in female characters by watching opening and closing wedding scenes.

Judy Benjamin's first wedding is an elegant, joyous affair. She seems happy enough; her biggest concern at her reception is that the upholsterer she hired has covered her new husband's ottoman with the wrong fabric. We quickly realize, however, that Judy's world is not as bright as it first appears. During her reception, her attorney husband (Albert Brooks) leaves her to take care of some business on the phone, and her father expresses more interest in a televised sports event than he does in Judy. When her groom dies on their wedding night, and she is faced with major decisions about her future, Judy begins to understand what we have understood since her wedding celebration scene. She is a victim in a world that has been defined for her by men, to whom she is truly nothing more than a princess.

We experience life in the army with Private Benjamin, and we finally travel with her to France, where she experiences a loving relationship with a wealthy young Frenchman (Armand Assante). She consents to marry him, and we are all ready for the second-chance happy ending we know that Judy deserved at the beginning of the film. However, for reasons that seem all to familiar to her (and to us), Judy leaves the scene of her own wedding. She recognizes that she does not need to be married to be happy, that she is capable of making her own major life decisions and of determining her own way of life. When she runs off into the beautiful French landscape, throwing her wedding veil into the air, we celebrate with her. Through her rejection of her marriage, we see how much Judy has grown. The contrast of the two weddings in *Private Benjamin* is perhaps the most effective plot device of the film. This contrast allows us to recognize Judy's "coming of age."

We have a similar response to the second wedding of Jojo (Lili Taylor) in *Mystic Pizza.* Her first wedding ceremony is interrupted because, out of desperation and nervousness, she faints at the altar. She later confesses to her two friends Daisy (Julia Roberts) and Kat (Annabeth Gish) that she panicked during the wedding. She is not ready to become the wife of her fisherman boyfriend until he understands that she wants to maintain her own identity and have her own brand of freedom.

Jojo's is only one of three stories of the "coming of age" process in *Mystic Pizza*. Yet, just as we are exposed to Jojo's conflict *first*, so we see the resolution of her problem with her boyfriend as the *last* scene in the film, her second—and successful—wedding celebration. When Jojo finally marries Billy, we feel a comfortable sense of closure for her and for her friends, both of whom have come to terms with their own sets of conflicts. Daisy has reached an understanding with her rich, immature boyfriend and Kat has acknowledged that, despite the broken heart she has suffered because of her one-night encounter with her married employer, she really does want to attend college. It is the final joyous celebration of Jojo's wedding where we, along with the three young women, acknowledge that they have learned a great deal by the end of the film.

The final wedding scene in *Mystic Pizza* illustrates another way in which wedding celebrations are used as plot devices in movies: they make the audience aware of the cultural boundaries of a film. Jojo, Daisy, and Kat are all "locals" who work in a pizza parlor in the resort town of Mystic, Connecticut, and throughout the film, there is a "subtext" which involves the conflict between the local Portuguese-American working class culture of these young women, and the upper class clientele—those waspish creatures who "summer" on the coast. The audience resolves this conflict at the same time that we resolve the others in the movie, in the final wedding celebration scene. We watch all three women and their friends and families participate in dances and sing songs which may be foreign to us, unless we know about Portuguese culture. Whether we understand Portuguese or not, we recognize that Jojo, Daisy, and Kat have a rich heritage and that their lives in Mystic have a depth and a texture which go well beyond the pizza parlor where they work.

Other American films include wedding scenes which serve to portray and define character and ethnicity for the audience. The opening scenes of *The Godfather* and *The Deer Hunter* illustrate the power of wedding scenes to help an audience identify character, distinguish relationships among characters, and recognize ethnic and social dimensions of the films. Like the two American epics in which they appear, these wedding celebration scenes are themselves epic. They are the means by which we are prepared for the compelling, sometimes overwhelming, worlds of these films.

Connie Corleone (Talia Shire) has just been married, and her family is hosting a lavish reception on the grounds of their compound. We meet the entire Corleone family at this reception, and our first impressions of them and their way of life are significant. The entire reception sequence (one of the longest of any film: twenty-five minutes) is a series of cuts from inside the house, where Connie's father, Don Corleone (Marlon Brando), is taking care of business in his office, to the festivities outside. We are forced to adjust our eyesight to watch this sequence because the contrast between what goes on inside and what goes on outside is visually stunning. The Don's office is dark, with Venetian blinds barely cracked, and every time we move back to the reception, we are in the bright sunlight of the Corleone estate.

We must, of course, adjust more than our eyesight as we try to understand the world of Don Corleone and his family. During this series of wedding reception scenes we are introduced to any number of conflicts, and we begin to identify characters and their individual conflicts in terms of their behavior during the celebration. The Don spends most of his time granting favors to his Sicilian-American friends; among these favors on his daughter's wedding day is the promise to make a group of young thugs "suffer." Sonny Corleone (James Caan) spends part of the day with one of his sister's bridesmaids enjoying a quick sexual encounter in an upstairs bedroom of the Corleone home while his wife sits at the reception outside. And Michael Corleone (Al Pacino), the returned war hero still in military uniform, spends his afternoon trying *not* to represent himself as a member of the Corleone "family." He tells his naive, waspish girlfriend, Kay Adams (Diane Keaton), "That's my family, Kay, not me."

During this opening wedding party sequence we begin to judge the strengths and weaknesses of the members of the Corleone family and the power of the family itself. Vito Corleone is proud, commanding, and at the same time, a "family man" who glides gracefully across the dance floor with his daughter. Sonny is guided by passion, and he makes rash decisions. His timing is never quite right, as we note when the family attorney (Robert Duvall) has to knock on a bedroom door to summon Sonny to his father's office during Sonny's afternoon liaison with the bridesmaid. And Michael seems genuinely different from the other Corleones in the opening sequence. We not only learn that he is a veteran, but that he is bright and worldly in a way that none of his relatives are. We also recognize, even before he makes his first appearance, that he is his father's favorite son.

These are significant character traits among the Corleone *men* which we can identify only because of a marriage celebration of a female Corleone. It is not insignificant that the Corleone *women* remain outside the house, away from the Don's work, throughout the scene. The Corleone women are presented to us as "outsiders" within the structure of the film. Vito Corleone's nameless wife dances with her husband, sings a Sicilian song with the band, but never says one line. We see Connie only from distances, always dancing or laughing or posing for wedding pictures. Of the Corleone women, only Kay, (the ethnic "outsider" whom Micheal insists on including in the Corleone family photo,) speaks more than a few lines, and she only then asks questions.

Just as we establish character traits for the Corleone men in this sequence, we also acknowledge the absence of strong female characters—in the world of the Corleones, women are mothers, wives, daughters, and sexual objects who are silent shadows, or who behave in ways which complement their men. Through the opening wedding scene, we realize that these celebrating women help us to establish a paradigm for *The Godfather*. The Corleone men celebrate their religious traditions and cultural heritage while they defy or distort them; they espouse family values while they destroy families; they both value and abuse their women, just as they value and abuse the world outside of their compound.[4]

Seth Cagin and Phillip Dray point out in their study of American films, *Hollywood Films of the Seventies*, that the "trajectory of the Corleones in America is measured by traditional ceremonies of faith" (186). Both the opening wedding scene and the closing baptism/gangland murder scene attest to the importance of these ceremonies to our understanding of *The Godfather*. The ceremonies, particularly the long wedding celebration scene where doors are closed more than once against women, children, and wedding guests, represent "a signal motif of the film...the shutting away of Christian ethics in the name of power, revenge or greed" (187). The Corleone world is a closed one, and any viewing audience understands the potential power of secrecy and darkness after attending Connie Corleone's sunny wedding party.[5]

The Deer Hunter begins with a lengthy sequence of scenes (over an hour) which includes a Ukrainian Orthodox wedding ceremony. Like *The Godfather*, the audience is able to delineate relationships and define conflict because of this celebration scene. By the time this long wedding celebration ends, we are aware that groom Steven (John Savage) and his two best friends, Mike (Robert DeNiro) and Nick (Christopher Walken), are to leave for Vietnam on the following day. By the time the party ends, and Nick says to Mike, "If anything happens over there, don't leave me, man," we have been assured, by attending this long wedding celebration scene, that something *will* happen.

Also like the beginning of *The Godfather*, the wedding sequence in *The Deer Hunter* allows us to see behaviors in characters, and often we are the *only* wedding guests to notice these behaviors. We are privy to any number of secrets which will become increasingly important to us as the story moves away from its Pennsylvania setting and to Vietnam. We notice that although Nick and Mike are very close, there seems to be a tension between them, particularly concerning Nick's fiancée, Linda (Meryl Streep). Both men are attracted to her, and during the wedding reception, the "significant looks" which pass between her and Mike do not go unnoticed by either Nick or the audience. Only *we* notice the drops of red wine which fall on bride Angela's (Rutanya Alda's) white bodice during the couple's ritual drink from the double wine vessel. We recognize that this close-up of her stained bodice is for our benefit, and we sense doom for Steven and Angela.[6]

We see the women who belong to the men of *The Deer Hunter* most often in the first sequence, just as we see the Corleone women in *The Godfather*, and we recognize that they (particularly Linda and Angela) have all of the marks of victims. Also like *The Godfather*, it is through the women that we understand much of the dynamic between and among the men. Certainly Linda, first Nick's fiancée and later Mike's tentative lover, stands out to us during the wedding scene as a significant character, not just because we see that both men are attracted to her, but because she represents a sort of a "bridge" to us—a connection between the two soldiers and their hometown, a fusion of Old World and New World, 1960s values. While the wedding party is preparing for the wedding near the beginning of the film, Linda is beaten by her drunken immigrant father (not insignificantly, while she is wearing her bridesmaid's gown). She packs a bag and moves temporarily into her boyfriend's home. To us, she has chosen a very twentieth-century American approach to her problem. Uneasy with her role as maid of honor in a traditional Ukrainian ceremony—she has some trouble carrying the wedding crown for Angela—Linda is more comfortable sitting at the reception drinking beer.

During this very long wedding sequence there are many more details which will haunt us later. The three friends, Mike, Nick and Steven, try to carry on a brazen conversation with a uniformed Green Beret who will not look at them, and whose only response to them is "fuck it." At those later points in the movie when all three of these now-soldiers isolate themselves—Steven in the hospital, Mike in his motel room, and Nick in the gambling dens of Saigon—we will remember this lone Green Beret's isolation during the festivities.[7]

As the film moves into the Vietnam sequences, and the three friends are first held prisoner and then separated in their attempts to escape, we will remember that Steven has always seemed more delicate than Mike and Nick and that he has depended on the strength of his two friends. After we finally see the paraplegic Steven in the hospital, we may remember that he clumsily fell to the floor while he was doing an Ukrainian dance at his wedding, or we may remember Nick's parting advice to Steven as the couple left for their honeymoon —"hang tough"—when we watch Steven being lifted from the Vietnam jungle into a helicopter.

The wedding celebration scene in *The Deer Hunter* helps, then, to educate us about the world that Steven, Mike, and Nick are leaving. After we have moved through this scene with them, we understand what is important to them, and because of this scene, we also understand aspects of their characters that they cannot understand. Mike displays a tendency to isolate himself, even during the wedding reception; Nick takes small risks, constantly pushing himself into situations, and Steven seems naive and fragile.

We are not particularly celebratory at the conclusion of this sequence, which attests to the power of this wedding celebration in *The Deer Hunter*. We have gotten to know these characters and their families, and they all seem doomed. After the party is over, Mike laments to Nick as the two of them sit in the darkness of the Pennsylvania night, "Everything's going so fast." Nick doesn't seem to understand this comment, but we do. We have spent a long, festive day with these men, and we now anticipate that "things" will go even faster for them.[8]

Although these may represent two of the most distinctively powerful wedding scenes in American film, the opening scenes of *The Godfather* and *The Deer Hunter* share characteristics as plot devices with many other contemporary American films. Both *Prizzi's Honor* and *Heartburn* open with wedding scenes. Because of these first scenes, we are introduced to the cultures of these movies. The opening wedding scenes in these films serve another purpose as well. In these films we meet characters who themselves are introduced to each other for the first time in opening wedding scenes (Jack Nicholson and Kathleen Turner in *Prizzi's Honor*, and Jack Nicholson and Meryl Streep in *Heartburn*).

Like both epics, we come to know families during other wedding scenes, as in *Lovers and Other Strangers*, *Prizzi's Honor*, and *The Accidental Tourist*. The sense of doom we feel toward certain characters in *The Deer Hunter* and *The Godfather* we also feel in other wedding scenes, among them the wedding of the ill-fated, wealthy wheat rancher Sam Shepard and opportunist Brooke Adams in *Days of Heaven*, and the wedding of two Jewish citizens of 1933 Berlin, Marisa Berenson and Fritz Wepper, in *Cabaret*.

No matter where, why, or for how long we attend a wedding in a movie, from *It Happened One Night* to *Working Girl*, wedding celebration scenes represent one of the most versatile and most often used of film devices. Although—or perhaps *because*—weddings can be incorporated so flexibly as plot devices, they are rarely the subjects themselves of American movies (even Stanley Banks' story is about himself, not about his daughter's wedding). Robert Altman's *A Wedding* is one of the only American films in which the wedding celebration represents the entire plot of the film. In its uneven (and perhaps unsuccessful) expansion of this plot device into a full-length treatment, *A Wedding* finally proves just how valuable and necessary the device really is to other films and to audiences.

The aspects of American culture which other wedding scenes bring to our attention—especially vulgarity and hypocrisy—make us painfully uncomfortable in *A Wedding*, which presents us with a pointed caricature of a wedding day. The officiating priest is senile. The bride (whose name is "Muffin" and whose parents are "Snooks" and "Tulip") has braces on her teeth. Her groom has impregnated her sister/maid of honor, "Buffy." During the reception, the groom's grandmother dies, and his mother, an elegant, erratic heroin addict married to a lecherous doctor, leaves the reception to be "medicated."

Like several other Altman films, *A Wedding* is complicated and yet plotless; it is an accumulation of conversations and vignettes which the audience must struggle to distinguish. When we watch this movie, we are attending a two-hour wedding celebration from beginning to end. Unfortunately, although we are with this wedding party for two hours, we never really know much about the couple, and we are among families and guests we may not particularly like. At its worst, *A Wedding* becomes a tedious, perhaps cruel parody of an upper middle class American wedding, and we respond with indifference. However, at its best moments, it is valuable because it is also an elaborate parody of many other wedding scenes in American film.[9]

As valuable or amusing as *A Wedding* might be, we do not need to watch a simulated wedding celebration in its entirety in order to understand the value of weddings to American film. We have seen countless marriage ceremonies created by Hollywood, and especially since *Father of the Bride*, we have come to realize that weddings bring us into the films we are watching in ways that challenge and delight us. When we attend weddings in movies, we know what is expected of us as viewers. We know, for instance, that a wedding will indicate much more to us about the plot than merely the marital status of two of the characters. We may guess that a wedding will introduce us to individual characters or will educate us about the traditions of groups which we need to know. And we will always anticipate that a wedding celebration will signal a beginning, an ending, a conflict, or a twist of plot.

To watch weddings in American movies is to be exposed to lost, changing, or plural traditions in our culture.[10] We see ceremonies and parties which represent our expectations—and Hollywood's projection of those expectations—at their best and at their worst, at their ugliest and at their most glorious. We learn to gauge our own responses to cultural values, to the concepts of family, love, loyalty, or belief, by watching other groups responding to these same concepts when they gather to celebrate marriage on film.

In American films, weddings are not only traditional plot devices; they are signs on a map which help guide us through the complexities of the films we see. Stanley Banks tried to tell us this when he confided to us after his daughter's wedding: we cannot take these celebrations for granted. If we "figure without the wedding," we may get lost.

Notes

[1]There are no full-length studies of wedding celebrations in American film. However, there are several discussions of the particular wedding scenes discussed in this essay, including Brode's essay on *Father of the Bride*. There are also helpful essays on related topics: romantic comedy in Harvey, and the comedy of remarriage in Cavell. For other related general discussions see Haskell and Maio.

I thank the following for their help: S. and C. Carey, L. Coleman, K. Hutson, P. Loukides, B. Searle, N. Workman.

[2]The best discussions of the interrupted (or peculiar) weddings of the 1930s and 40s are in Cavell and Harvey. There are many good discussions of *The Graduate*, among them Alpert, in *"The Graduate* Makes Out," and Cagin and Dray, who point out very aptly the problems we might have with Benjamin's and Elaine's final scene: "They don't know where they are going and neither do we, and we have been given no reason to believe they will manage adulthood any differently than their parents" (32).

[3]There are significant discussions of ethnicity in both *Goodbye Columbus* and *The Heartbreak Kid* in Erens, *The Jew in American Cinema*. Erens points out that the wedding reception scene in *Goodbye Columbus* "drew heavy criticism for its poor taste and shades of anti-Semitism," but she makes a solid case for the value of the scene: "The chaos and commotion, the abundance of food, the noise, all of these are accurate and neither innately positive or negative . . ." (275).

[4]Although there are certainly women characters in *The Godfather*, Molly Haskell refers to this film—I think accurately—as a "womanless melodrama"(23).

[5]We can consider *The Godfather* to be epic in terms of the number of publications devoted to it, also. Among the best are the following: Cagin and Dray, Ray, Kolker, and Yates.

[6]Wood describes the "spilt wine" scene as one of the "great poetic moments where the tension crystalizes" because the audience is allowed to "put things together": "the moment anticipates the blood of Vietnam and Steven's loss of his legs," and the moment also allows us to see Steven's "split allegiance" between Angela and his male friends (283).

[7]Wood cites this scene as a "second great poetic moment" in the film; he compares the Green Beret in the bar to the Ancient Mariner: ". . . though he has returned to America, [he] is no longer 'of' it" (283).

[8]There are many good essays on *The Deer Hunter*. Wood's is particularly helpful because he includes a lengthy discussion of each sequence of scenes in the film. Other helpful studies include Boyd, *"The Deer Hunter*: The Hero and the Traditions"; Cagin and Dray, Hellman's chapter, "Epic Return"; and Wilson's chapter, "Derealizing Vietnam: Hollywood." Two helpful general discussions of Vietnam war movies are Adair, and Auster and Quart.

[9]In his chapter on Altman, Kolker points out the "It is difficult not to be angry with [*A Wedding*] . . . Its cleverness always threatens to become smugness, a smugness that is always at the expense of its characters, and finally at ours" (328). I agree with his assessment that, despite the value of this film as' part of the body of work of a gifted director, the movie ultimately "only makes us smirk" (329). Other discussions of *A Wedding* are in Thomson and in McGilligan's biography of Altman, *Robert Altman: Jumping Off the Cliff.*

[10]As must be apparent by this point, the wedding scenes included in this discussion share one other characteristic with which I am uncomfortable, but must acknowledge:

they represent the traditions of only a few of the cultures of the United States. There are few wedding scenes which appear in *Hollywood* productions, from 1930 to the present, which reflect any ethnic group, religious group, or race other than those which represent white, Judeo-Christian, middle or upper middle classes. Although we sometimes see married couples from other ethnic or racial groups, the *absence* of their marriage traditions in Hollywood productions seems to be the norm. This "silence" tells us much more about the choices made by Hollywood during the last sixty years than it does about wedding scenes, and deserves to be studied (at least) on its own terms.

For good general discussions of racial politics and Hollywood productions, see Cripps, "The Death of Rastus: Negros in American Films Since 1945," and Horowitz, "Hollywood's Dirty Little Secret."

Works Cited

Adair, Gilbert. *Vietnam on Film: From "The Green Berets" to "Apocalypse Now".* New York: Proteus, 1981.

Alpert, Hollis. "*The Graduate* Makes Out." In Arthur F. McClure, ed. *The Movies: An American Idiom: Readings in the Social History of the American Motion Picture.* Cranbury, New Jersey: Associated University Presses, Inc. 1971.

Auster, Albert and Leonard Quart. *How the War was Remembered: Hollywood and Vietnam.* New York: Praeger, 1988.

Boyd, David. "*The Deer Hunter*: The Hero and the Tradition." *Australian Journal of American Studies* 1 (1980): 41-51.

Brode, Douglas. *The Films of the Fifties.* Secaucus, New Jersey: The Citadel Press, 1976.

Cagin, Seth and Philip Dray. *Hollywood Films of the Seventies: Sex, Drugs, Violence, Rock 'n' Roll & Politics.* New York: Harper & Row, 1984.

Cavell, Stanley. *Pursuits of Happiness: The Hollywood Comedy of Remarriage.* Cambridge: Harvard University Press, 1981.

Cripps, Thomas R. "The Death of Rastus: Negroes in American Films Since 1945." In Arthur F. McClure, ed. *The Movies: An American Idiom: Readings in the Social History of the American Motion Picture.* Cranbury, New Jersey: Associated University Presses, Inc., 1971.

Erens, Patricia. *The Jew in American Cinema.* Bloomington: Indiana University Press, 1984.

Harvey, James. *Romantic Comedy in Hollywood, from Lubitsch to Sturges.* New York: Alfred A. Knopf, 1987.

Haskell, Molly. *From Reverence to Rape: The Treatment of Women in the Movies.* Chicago: University of Chicago Press, 1987.

Hellman, John. *American Myth and the Legacy of Vietnam.* New York: Columbia University Press, 1986.

Horowitz, Joy. "Hollywood's Dirty Little Secret." *Premiere* (March 1989): 56-64.

Kolker, Robert Phillip. *A Cinema of Loneliness: Penn, Kubrick, Coppola, Scorsese, Altman.* New York: Oxford University Press, 1980.

Maio, Kathi. *Feminist in the Dark: Reviewing the Movies.* Freedom, California: The Crossing Press, 1988.

McGilligan, Patrick. *Robert Altman: Jumping Off the Cliff*. New York: St. Martin's Press, 1988.

Ray, Robert B. *A Certain Tendency of the Hollywood Cinema, 1930-1980*. Princeton: Princeton University Press, 1985.

Thomson, David. "The Lives of Supporting Players." *Film Commentary* (November-December 1989): 32-34.

Wilson, James C. *Vietnam in Prose and Film*. Jefferson, Missouri: McFarland, 1982.

Wood, Rubin. *Hollywood from Vietnam to Reagan*. New York: Columbia University Press, 1986.

Yates, John. "*Godfather* Saga: The Death of a Family." In Michael T. Marsden, John G. Nachbar, and Sam L. Grogg Jr., eds., *Movies as Artifacts: Cultural Criticism of Popular Film*. Chicago: Nelson-Hall, 1982.

Filmography

1934	*It Happened One Night*	Dir. Frank Capra
1940	*The Philadelphia Story*	Dir. George Cukor
1942	*The Palm Beach Story*	Dir. Preston Sturges
1950	*Father of the Bride*	Dir. Vincente Minnelli
1967	*The Graduate*	Dir. Mike Nichols
1969	*Goodbye Columbus*	Dir. Larry Peerce
1970	*Lovers and Other Strangers*	Dir. Cy Howard
1972	*Cabaret*	Dir. Bob Fosse
1972	*The Godfather*	Dir. Francis Coppola
1972	*The Heartbreak Kid*	Dir. Elaine May
1978	*Days of Heaven*	Dir. Terrence Mallick
1978	*The Deer Hunter*	Dir. Michael Cimino
1978	*A Wedding*	Dir. Robert Altman
1980	*Private Benjamin*	Dri. Howard Zieff
1985	*Prizzi's Honor*	Dir. John Huston
1986	*Heartburn*	Dir. Mike Nichols
1988	*Working Girl*	Dir. Mike Nichols
1988	*Mystic Pizza*	Dir. Donald Petrie
1989	*The Accidental Tourist*	Dir. Lawrence Kasdan

Hollywood Interracial Love:
Social Taboo as Screen Titillation

Carlos E. Cortés

"Miscegenation (sex relationship between the white and black races) is forbidden." So reads Section II, Rule 6 of Hollywood's 1930 Motion Picture Production Code (the Hays Code), which prescribed U.S. movie content from 1934 until the mid-1960s. Resting beneath rules II-4 ("Sex perversion or any inference to it is forbidden") and II-5 ("White slavery shall not be treated") and poised above rule II-7 ("Sex hygiene and venereal diseases are not proper subjects for theatrical motion pictures"), the "miscegenation rule" formally encoded the established informal Hollywood practice—using the interracial love plot convention to preach against this industry-proclaimed social deviation while simultaneously employing it to titillate moviegoers (Stanley and Steinberg, 80-93).

Since the beginning of motion pictures, American moviemakers have consciously addressed or casually injected this theme—exploring it, exploiting it, and manipulating it. Interracial love's very status as a societal taboo and, for a period, as Code-forbidden fruit (even though it had long been a social reality), made it a plot convention with special power to titillate, disturb, and antagonize. According to film critic Michael Wood:

> Movies bring out...worries without letting them loose and without forcing us to look at them too closely. They trot around the park in the half-light. ...It seems to be enough for us if a movie simply dramatizes our semi-secret concerns and contradictions in a story, allows them their brief, thinly disguised parade (Wood, 16).

Movies have used interracial love to manipulate personal phobias, probe psychological recesses, critique social practices, and sometimes attack legal statutes. In its continuities and changes, consistencies and variations, this plot convention has occasionally suggested or revealed the status and reality of interracial love in the United States. More often, however, it has provided glimpses, often unintended glimpses, into pervasive American angsts, concerns, and tensions.[1]

21

Hollywood's interracial love stock convention has passed through three main phases. First came the pre-Code period, from the beginning of film until the 1930 completion and 1934 industry-wide adoption of the Hays guidelines. Second came the era of the Hays Code, which ruled Hollywood until the mid-1950s and then slowly, agonizingly declined until its demise in the late 1960s. Third came the post-Hays years, beginning with the 1968 adoption of Hollywood's new multi-lettered movie rating system.

In dealing with and manipulating the theme of miscegenation, Hollywood has extended a centuries-old literary tradition. For example, Shakespeare addressed it in *Othello*. The love between Othello, the heroic Moor, and Desdemona provides a weapon for the villainous Iago, who wounds Desdemona's father by goading him that "an old black ram is now tupping your white ewe."

Throughout the pre-movie era, American writers regularly dealt with miscegenation (as threat and reality) in geographical genres that might be categorized as Easterns, Westerns, and Southerns. Easterns embraced so-called "Indian captivity narratives," which often contained sensationalistic revelations by real or fictitious abducted white women concerning their lives (including their sex lives) among the Indians. Westerns, too, abounded with tales of Indian captivity, but they also expanded the ethnic dimensions of the miscegenation theme by adding the sexual threat of Mexican men, usually the *mestizo* (mixed blood) offspring of Indian-white relations. Finally, in Southerns, black men served as the interracial sexual threat. (Surveys conducted for Gunnar Myrdal's 1944 classic, *An American Dilemma: The Negro Problem and Modern Democracy*, asked southern whites what discriminatory lines were most important to maintain. Their most common answer—"the bar against intermarriage and sexual intercourse involving white women.") (Myrdal, 60). The perceived sexual threat to white women by colored men ("colored" defined by mainstream American racial perceptions, not by genetics or categorical "objectivity"), then, served as a plot convention in nineteenth-century American literature. [2]

However, the reversing of genders brought a fundamental change in this popular plot convention. In contrast to their non-white brethren, colored women in U.S. literature often served as interracial sexual conveniences, particularly for young white men going through their sexual rites of passage (after all, boys, at least white ones, will be boys). Yet, while white men had access to colored (black, brown, red, or yellow) women, such fictional liaisons almost always proved transitory, usually ending sadly.

Therefore, when movies came into existence, they could draw upon a long popular literary tradition. Colored men had become consistent sexual threats, often resorting to force in their lustful pursuits. Colored women had become readily available sexual conveniences, who seldom achieved permanent interracial bliss. As early movies mindlessly adopted and casually adapted this literary legacy, colored sexual threats and sexual conveniences leaped from the printed page to movie screens.[3]

Silent Screen Interracial Love: The Convention Develops

Screen visualization of interracial love involved additional complications. In particular, it raised three thorny questions. First, for movie purposes, who was white and who was colored? Second, what should be the basic parameters of the miscegenation plot convention? Third, what variations could filmmakers employ and what limits could they test within the convention?

In practical movie terms, whiteness and coloredness did not always emerge clearly. With the popular beliefs of mainstream white Americans as the guiding principle, the movie categorization of coloreds evolved in the following general pattern. African-Americans were colored, along with black Africans and mixed-blood mulattos. Asian-Americans were colored (also Asians, Eurasians, and Pacific Islanders). Native Americans (American Indians) were colored, along with "half-breeds" (although those with lesser amounts of Indian ancestry sometimes played white on screen). Movie Arabs, too, fell into this racial twilight zone.

Latinos presented an even more complex challenge. Most Mexicans, the preponderant U.S. Latino population during the early movie era, enjoyed mixed racial ancestry, principally white and Indian. But some Latinos came from pure or heavily European descent. So to what racial agglomeration did Latinos belong, white or colored? Hollywood soon answered—"both." Indianized or Africanized Latinos were colored; Europeanized ones were white (usually inaccurately labeled as "Spanish" to differentiate them from colored "Mexicans"). For screen Latinos, physical appearance and stated (or implied) ancestry became the racial dividing line. Within the interracial love plot convention, "Spanish" Latinos played white, while "Mexicans" usually functioned as colored, thereby permitting the screen co-existence of the Latin lover (white) and the lecherous Latino greaser (colored).

Rapidity of racial categorization proved particularly critical during the early days of moviemaking. In ten-minute one-reelers, filmmakers had little opportunity to develop plot or character subtleties. Established stereotypes, reified by popular literature, provided convenient shortcuts to reach movie audiences—colored men lusting after white women and white men sowing their wild oats with colored women.

Film titles also helped condition audience reactions. Titles told viewers when to expect Latinos to provide interracial sexual threats (*The Girl and the Greaser*, 1913) or sexual conveniences (*How Porto Rican Girls Entertain Uncle Sam's Soldiers*, 1899). As for Indian-white love relations, a stream of movies—*Comata, the Sioux* (1909), *A Romance of the Western Hills* (1910), *The Chief's Daughter* (1911), and *The Squaw Man* (1914)—combined audience titillation with moral lecturing on the inappropriateness and tragic consequences of interracial liaisons. By the mid-1910s, Hollywood had solidified the two basic miscegenation conventions.

Two 1915 films both epitomized these themes and helped to invest them with iconic significance. In that year, D. W. Griffith's classic Southern, *The Birth of a Nation* (based on *The Clansman*, Thomas Dixon's novel/play about the Civil War and Reconstruction South) exploded onto movie screens, featuring the inflammatory manipulation of the miscegenation threat. In one climactic moment, a white southern belle leaps to her death from a cliff rather than suffer the advances of a black man. In the face of pressure from the National Association for the Advanced of Colored People, Griffith reportedly cut several other scenes of blacks pursuing and sometimes catching white women (Kirby, 121). But never fear! A stock element of the plot convention involved the timely arrival of the white male hero to rescue the racially/sexually-threatened damsel. In *Birth of a Nation*, the Ku Klux Klan becomes the hero, saving the city (by implication, the south and even the entire nation) from the black menace, symbolized as a sexual threat.

That same year, *The Cheat* dramatized the colored sexual threat of Asians, in the person of wealthy, lascivious Japanese immigrant businessman Hishuru Tori, played by the popular Japanese-American actor, Sessue Hayakawa. Spurned by a white woman, Tori *brands* her! But, like blacks in *Birth of a Nation*, like Indians and Mexican "greasers" in myriad westerns, the Asian upstart ultimately receives his comeuppance, being beaten and nearly lynched by an enraged white courtroom mob.

Upset with being asked to play so many stereotypically lustful, villainous Asians, Hayakawa formed his own film company. Usually set in Japan, his movies gently explored interracial love, almost always involving a white man and a Japanese woman, such as in two 1920 features, *Locked Lips* and *Breath of the Gods*. Hayakawa's films typified the gender-reversal flip-side of the screen miscegenation theme—that colored women felt a magnetic attraction to and sometimes preference for white men.

Basic guidelines were developing within American filmdom's interracial love stock convention. "Spanish" Latinos functioned as white. Colored men sexually threatened white women, who spurned their advances and waited for white men to save them. White men could cross the color line with Indian, Asian, and Latin women, although usually for transitory satisfaction and with generally unhappy results. In the case of African-Americans, the screen color line became nearly impermeable (although white plantation owners had historically permeated it with regularity).

In only rare instances did silent movies bend the convention. For example, in the acclaimed 1926 film, *The Vanishing American*, love develops between a Navajo man and a white reservation teacher. However, as regularly occurred in interracial love films, death comes to the rescue. The Navajo dies fighting for his people against an unscrupulous Indian agent, thereby providing filmmakers with a convenient resolution for the love affair.

Sometimes movies appeared to break the convention, only to later expose the illusion. In *The Sheik* (1921), Rudolph Valentino's Ahmed Ben Hassan abducts a white woman, but the movie finally reveals that he is really a European, not an Arab. According to a *New York Times* reviewer, "You won't be offended by having a white girl marry an Arab either, for the Sheik really isn't a native of the desert at all" (Michalek, 4).

Running until the late 1920s, the Silent era developed three major parameters for screen interracial love. It created a movie working definition of white and non-white. It established a screen gender gap—love between white men and colored women became transitorily permissible, while colored men provided sexual threats to white women. And it erected a screen pecking order for interracial love, with Latinos requiring the most careful internal differentiation, Asians, Indians, and Arabs enjoying some flexibility, and African-Americans becoming the least likely to cross interracial barriers.

The Codification of Interracial Love

Then came the Hays Code. In 1922, former Republican Postmaster General Will Hays became president of the Motion Picture Producers and Distributors of America. Selected by Hollywood to provide a buffer against governmental and public criticism, Hays sought to create a system of industry self-regulation. However, he encountered opposition from studio moguls as he tried to impose his rural Protestant moral standards on film content.

In 1930, Hays commissioned the writing of a Motion Picture Production Code—content guidelines for what Hollywood movies should teach and not teach viewers. At first filmmakers only selectively followed the Code. But increasing threats of federal censorship and growing public pressure, including the 1934 establishment by Catholic bishops of the Legion of Decency to evaluate movies, impelled Hollywood to choose self-censorship via the Code as a lesser evil. So in 1934 the studios reluctantly agreed to submit scripts to the industry's Production Code Administration, whose suggestions had to be followed for a film to earn a Code Seal of Approval, increasingly de rigueur for exhibition.

The Hays Code listed acceptable and unacceptable plot conventions, including the miscegenation prohibition. The fact that interracial love and marriage occurred in the United States took a back seat to the Hays bunch's conviction that Hollywood should teach their inappropriateness. In general, they should not occur; if they occur, they should be punished.

Moreover, both Hollywood's informal traditions and Code formal guidelines reflected other socio-economic factors. Racial bigotry was alive and well in the United States, including a widespread (although not universal) white taboo against interracial love (Hernton). Some states outlawed miscegenation (the U.S. Supreme Court did not invalidate such laws until 1967). Finally, not wanting to offend white southern moviegoers, whom

Hollywood feared would not patronize films about blacks, studios operated on a self-imposed "southern veto" of movie content.[4]

Although the Code's miscegenation rule specified black and white, Hollywood applied the rule with variations to other colored groups, while using Hollywood's traditional gender double standard as a further informal guideline. After all, Code or no Code, taboos make titillating screen material. So filmmakers skirted the borders of the Code-hardened convention, teasing audiences with touches or hints of interracial love.

The Bitter Tea of General Yen (1933) employed sexual fantasizing. A white American woman becomes simultaneously repelled by and attracted to the magnetic Chinese warlord, General Yen. Then one night he breaks into her bedroom. However, another Yen, masked and in western clothes, intercedes and saves her, for which she kisses him. Before anything more can happen, she awakens, realizing she has had a "nightmare."

Bordertown (1935), too, reached the sexual edge before stopping. Chicano casino owner Johnny Ramirez proves dangerously attractive to two Anglo women. Not to worry; of course it won't last. One woman goes crazy, the other dies in an automobile accident...proper punishment for defying interracial frontiers.

But when filmmakers reversed the genders, the Code became more porous. White men occasionally crossed the interracial line, at least transitorily. Moreover, this usually occurred at a safe geographical distance from the United States, such as in the South Pacific.

In *Bird of Paradise* (1932), for example, an American sailor (Johnny) and a Polynesian princess (Luana) fall in love, although Luana is betrothed to a native prince. However, Johnny's American determination and ingenuity prevail, as he abducts the willing princess during their wedding ceremony and they (implicitly) consummate their love. Yet 1930s' screen interracial affairs do not end happily. Johnny ultimately leaves on an American ship while Luana sadly returns to her people, sacrificing love to lift the curse of an erupting volcano!

With the arrival of World War II, Hollywood transformed the miscegenation plot convention into a patriotic appeal to galvanize public support for the war effort. Historically, to strengthen public wartime resolve, nations have used propaganda to degrade the enemy and suggest the calamitous results of an enemy victory (Keen). During World War II, film industries worldwide played a critical role in this process. For Hollywood, the interracial sex convention provided an ideal vehicle. In the Pacific, the United States confronted Japan, its only racially-different enemy. Movies portrayed Japanese soldiers as being dedicated to rape as well as to military victory, with American nurses in the Phillippines facing this threat in films like *So Proudly We Hail!* (1942) and *Cry Havoc* (1943). In fact, Hollywood's version of World War II sometimes made it seem as if the United States were fighting a Pacific war mainly to protect military nurses.

The post-World War II era ushered in a new dimension in American filmmaking. Having focused for four years on evils abroad, filmmakers turned their crusading zeal to evils at home, including the blight of anti-ethnic bigotry. Once again that increasingly chameleon-like plot convention, interracial love, became a message-carrying vehicle. However, screen tradition survived even as movies used the theme to explore racism.

The traditional themes of sexual threat and convenience remained. Indians continued to lust for white women, for example, provoking John Wayne to devote years looking for his Comanche-abducted niece in *The Searchers* (1956). According to Indian-hater Ethan (Wayne), "Living with Comanches ain't being alive."

The minority sexual threat even moved from the old west into modern urban America. In *Trial* (1955), a white teenage girl drops dead from a heart attack while she and a young Chicano are kissing and fondling. With the town superheated over this interracial incident—he *must* have been forcing himself on her—the sheriff barely prevents a lynching. Placed on trial for murder, the boy is saved through the efforts of a dedicated Anglo lawyer and the sensitive decision of an African-American judge.

Less fortunate is black Tom Robinson, wrongfully accused of attempting to rape a white woman in the 1962 film adaptation of Harper Lee's novel, *To Kill a Mockingbird*. Despite an impassioned defense by a white lawyer, the all-white southern jury convicts Tom. Panic-stricken and rightfully fearing a lynching, Tom tries to escape and is killed.

Tradition also survived alongside social critique when genders were reversed. The "love-em-and-leave-em" convention continued, although colored females gained improved stature. In the 1952 western masterpiece, *High Noon*, a series of Anglos cohabit with (but do not marry) small-town Mexican entrepreneur Helen Ramirez. Admired for her business acumen but scorned for her ethnicity, Ramirez embodies strength and intelligence...but also tragedy. Appropriately, according to convention, the Anglo town marshal dumps her and marries a white blonde.

Sometimes filmmakers made interracial marriage the central issue. That most formidable screen taboo, black-white love, began to receive attention, most notably in the 1949 *Pinky*. A southern mulatta, Pinky goes north to study nursing. So light-skinned that she passes there for white, Pinky falls in love with a white doctor. When she goes home to visit her mother, the doctor follows, discovers her secret, but still begs Pinky to marry him and move north. However, instead she decides to dedicate her life to running a clinic and nursing school for young black women.

Pinky uses interracial love to critique racism, yet it ultimately conforms to Hollywood tradition and the Code convention against interracial love by having Pinky choose to stick to her own race. Even director Elia Kazan expressed some concern:

I'm worried because people might think we're saying Negroes and whites shouldn't marry. We solve this story in personal terms. This particular boy and girl shouldn't get married....But we don't mean the story to be true of all people with colored and white skins ("Zanuck," 25).

In still another way the movie pulled punches. The filmmakers cast a popular white movie star, Jeanne Crain, as Pinky, thereby adding another fantasy layer for white viewers, their main audience, and making it easier for those moviegoers to identify with Pinky's humiliating experiences (Jones, 110-120). (Hollywood has consistently cast whites performers as non-white characters, but rarely the reverse.) Despite Hollywood's apprehensions, *Pinky* became one the year's top-grossing movies...even drawing sizable southern audiences, casting further doubt on the rationality of the industry's informal southern veto (Campbell, 55-56).

At times screen interracial marriages occurred, although seldom without complications. Screen black-white marriage remained virtually non-existent, but whites occasionally married other coloreds—almost always involving white men and colored women. Yet interracial marriage still usually spelled "trouble."

In *Giant* (1956), plucky Chicana nurse Juana Villalobos marries the son of powerful Texas rancher Jordan (Bick) Benedict. Yet despite the Benedict name, Juana is denied service at a high-class hotel beauty salon. However, the film ends with a hopeful metaphor, as Bick's two grandsons, one blonde, one mestizo brown, lie together in a crib on top of a black-and-white sheet.

The complications of love between white Americans and Japanese dominate the 1957 *Sayonara*, with marriage leading to tragedy. When the Air Force reassigns an American airman but denies permission for his Japanese wife to accompany him, they commit dual suicide rather than be separated. But *Sayonara*, too, ends on a note of hope as another American airman, a decorated war hero, decides to marry a Japanese actress.

White man-Indian woman relations, generally enveloped by interracial conflict, achieved the broadest spectrum of post-war screen exposure. The 1950 *Broken Arrow* simultaneously celebrates interracial love and suggests its probable tragic consequences, as a white man marries an Apache princess, who is killed soon thereafter (by white racists, of course). Along with death, the sufferings of racially-mixed off-spring provided the most common unhappy results. The 1954 *Broken Lance* featured a white-Indian marriage, this time involving a Comanche princess (few screen white men marry Indians who are not princesses). Yet their mixed-blood son faces racism both from the young man's all-white half-brothers of his father's first marriage and from local townspeople, including the father of the white woman he loves. Other films, such as the 1952 *The Big Sky* and the 1955 *The Indian Fighter*, use white man-Indian princess marriages as Sayonara-style hopeful conclusions, thereby avoiding the issue of whether or not they and their off-spring encounter later interracial problems.

Most post-war interracial marriage films involved two elements that made them more acceptable to the Hays bunch and, presumably, to American audiences. First, love generally occurred either in distant lands or in the distant past, providing an avenue of escapism rather than a role model for contemporary behavior. Second, they injected the element of social class—if a white man marries an Indian, for example, she should be a princess.

Even adaptations of Broadway hit musicals generally followed the basic post-war plot convention—racism critiqued, but interracial love leading to unhappiness. The 1951 film version of Jerome Kern's *Show Boat* used the tragic marriage convention. When anti-miscegenation laws wreck light-skinned mulatta Julie's marriage to a white man, she ultimately plunges into alcoholism.

The 1958 movie adaptation of *South Pacific* features dual World War II interracial dilemmas. Should sweet, bubbly "cockeyed optimist" Navy Ensign Nellie Forbush marry French planter Emile De Becque, even after she discovers that he had been married to a Polynesian and has two mixed-blood children, or should she wash him right out of her hair? Should handsome U.S. Navy Lieutenant Cable marry a beautiful Polynesian girl? Forbush and Cable ponder their dilemmas together in song:

> You've got to be taught to be afraid
> Of people whose eyes are oddly made
> And people whose skins are a different shade.
> You've got to be carefully taught.

The musical resolved Cable's moral quandary with the standard screen solution—he is killed by the Japanese. But Cable's death also shocks Nellie into accepting marriage to De Becque. After all, he isn't Polynesian; he merely married one.

The dilemma of interracial love even moved musically into urban America with the 1961 screen version of *West Side Story*. Polish-American Tony and Puerto Rican Maria try to make a go of it in the midst of interethnic turf warfare. Maria even disregards the musical warning of her friend, Juanita, to "Stick to your own kind, one of your own kind." This leads, of course, to tragedy—a Puerto Rican shoots Tony, whose death magically brings the gangs together as they join to carry his body away.

By the 1960s, filmmakers increasingly challenged the Hays Code, including the miscegenation rule. That ultimate taboo, black-white love, received special examination. In the 1965 *A Patch of Blue*, a kind African-American man befriends a blind white girl, who falls in love with him. One day she surprises him by passionately kissing him and asking him to make love to her, but he knows better and refuses. Viewing the kiss one studio executive reportedly opined, "There goes Alabama," referring to the movie's assumed southern unsuitability.

In 1964, the sensitive low-budget *One Potato, Two Potato* ventured into new ground by portraying a successful, loving marriage between a black man and a white woman. Of course, she pays a penalty. Her white ex-husband contests her for custody of their children and wins.

Finally, in 1967, with the Hays code in tatters, Stanley Kramer struck the final blow against the miscegenation rule with his *Guess Who's Coming to Dinner?*. The dilemma—an African-American man and a white woman want the blessing of both sets of parents before they marry. At first the parents oppose them, but finally they all come around to accepting the couples' decision, after a long afternoon and evening of haggling. The film suggests that all six (four parents and two children) will live happily ever after, even to the point of enjoying an interracial dinner.

The Post-Hays Code Era

In 1968, Hollywood laid to rest the moribund Hays Code, replacing it with a multiple lettering system (currently G, PG, PG-13, R, and X). This included the burial of the anti-miscegenation rule. Onscreen interracial love and sex, which had gained an increased and more diversified presence in post-war American movies, now lost their codified illegitimacy.

Moreover, the collapse of the Code occurred simultaneously with other changes, both societally and within the film industry. The Civil Rights movement had shaken the nation, challenging bigotry, discriminatory laws, and inequitable institutions while myriad ethnic pride movements arose. Colored Americans were becoming a growing proportion of the population, spurred both by higher minority (as contrasted to non-minority) birthrates and by large-scale immigration from Latin America and Asia. Moreover, white flight to the suburbs was eroding much of the traditional downtown movie house audience, with blacks and Latinos taking up the slack. Finally, racial intermarriage was on the rise (an estimated 40 percent of Japanese-Americans and one-third of U.S. Latinos now marry outside of their own groups, while the Census Bureau reported more than 200,000 black-white marriages by 1988).

Eager for new themes to take advantage of the civil rights-spawned interest in race relations, the growth in ethnic pride, and the increase of minority moviegoers, Hollywood experienced a short-lived ethnic flip-flop. No longer did white heroes ride to the rescue of threatened white women; now colored heroes (usually African-Americans) whipped white villains. Although the ethnic flip-flop lasted only briefly and colored villains soon returned to the screen (take, for example, the recent rash of Latino drug dealers), colored heroes have continued to prosper.

The ethnic flip-flop shook the interracial love plot convention, as new adaptations provided enlightening glimpses into both new American realities and the changing American psyche. Particularly suggestive have been three variations of screen interracial love and sex: as a symbol of progress toward social equity; as an expression of colored power; and as an embodiment of pluralism within evolving American sexual mores, particularly concerning sexual preferences.

Interracial love became a theme for proclaiming the need for racial equality. Black-white love now led the way. White men develop loving relationships with black women in films ranging from the 1970 *The Landlord* to the 1987 *Fatal Beauty*, while in the 1972 *Fat City* a black man loves and cares for an unfaithful, alcoholic white woman. Mixed offspring also fare better. In *Carbon Copy* (1981), a white father, who years before had engaged in a love affair with a black woman, suddenly discovers that he has a half-black teenage son when the young man appears at his home. After a period of shock and conflict, they grow to accept and even "bond" with each other.

White men fall in love with Indian women in the old west (the 1972 *Jeremiah Johnson* and the 1980 *The Mountain Men*), with Eskimo women in the far north (the 1974 *The White Dawn*), and with native Hawaiian women (the 1987 *North Shore*), while in modern America white women fall in love with Indian men without being abducted (the 1966 *Johnny Tiger* and the 1972 *When the Legends Die*). Anglo men regularly fall in love with and sometimes marry Latinas in screen modern America (the 1980 *Gloria*, the 1986 *Touch and Go*, and the 1987 *Extreme Prejudice*). Reverse genders— in the 1979 *Walk Proud* a white girl helps a young Chicano outgrow his misdirected youth gang loyalty, while in the 1987 *La Bamba* another white girl provides Chicano rock-and-roller Ritchie Valens with the inspiration for one of his biggest hits, "Donna." Anglo-Asian love predictably flourishes in distant places (the 1987 *Captive Hearts*) and in distant times (the 1988 *Young Guns*), but it also occurs in the contemporary United States. In the 1985 *Year of the Dragon*, a Chinese-American female television reporter helps to redeem a violence-prone Polish-American police officer.

In the two post-Hays decades, interracial love has pervaded American movies. But although the screen gender gap has narrowed, it still remains. The vast majority of love relations—whether they occur in the past or in the present, in the United States or in other nations—still involve white men and colored women.

While many recent movies have used interracial love to suggest progress toward interracial understanding, in other cases they have been used to proclaim colored power through interracial sex. This occurred particularly during the brief ethnic flip-flop era. Some of the so-called "blaxploitation films" of the early 1970s featured black studs, like the street-smart, drug-dealing *Superfly* (1972), who dominated white men and women alike. Screen

Latinos, too, sometimes used sex to demonstrate ethnic power. In *Scarface* (1983), Cuban-American drug lord Antonio Montana tries to gain social acceptability by acquiring a blonde Anglo wife. Male black slaves remained sexual titans, but in a new function—on the sixtieth anniversary of *The Birth of a Nation*, the horrendous, exploitative 1975 *Mandingo* transformed them from sexual threats into unwilling sexual conveniences for white women.

Occasionally, the traditional theme of colored sexual threat reappears. In *Bad Boys* (1983), Chicago Latino Paco Moreno rapes a white girl, but he receives his punishment—a brutal prison-ward beating by her boyfriend. In the ludicrous 1981 *Tarzan, the Ape Man*, a huge black African prepares to sexually assault terror-stricken Bo Derek, but Tarzan swings to the rescue. Indian men lust for white women in *Ulzana's Raid* (1972), Chinese men abduct them in *Big Trouble in Little China* (1986), and Arabs chase them in *Paradise* (1982)—but whites continue to emerge victorious.

Moreover, as movies increasingly presented diversity of sexual preference, interracial love gained admission into non-traditional gender combinations. It spread into movies about homosexuality, whether involving male gays (*The Boys in the Band*—1970 or *Norman . . . Is That You?*—1976) or lesbians (*Working Girls*—1987). It spread into pornography, such as the 1983 soft-porn cult classic *Eating Raoul*, in which the Chicano title role burglar takes up with an Anglo woman, although she does help her husband kill Raoul in the end. Name the genre. In the last two decades, interracial love has probably left its mark.

A final variation of interracial love (although seldom interracial sex) has emerged in the form of male-bonding movies, where interracial pals often emit stronger screen vibes together than they do with their women. (In his review of the 1989 *Lethal Weapon 2*, which features black policeman Danny Glover and his white partner, Mel Gibson, *Newsweek*'s David Ansen wrote, "The real love story here is between the cops—the subsidiary romance between Gibson and Patsy Kensit, playing a wan 'good' South African, feels half-hearted.") (Ansen, 53). Black-white buddies (*Skin Game, Nighthawks, White Knights*, and, *48 HRS.*), Latino-white buddies (*Freebie and the Bean* and *Cobra*), Indian-white buddies (*Young Guns* and *The Legend of the Lone Ranger*), and Asian-white buddies (*The Karate Kid* and *The Goonies*) now grace the screen.

The Dirty Harry movies have become almost role models of cross-categorical bonding. Harry Callahan, the reluctant affirmative action cop, finds himself unwillingly paired with a Chicano (*Dirty Harry—1971*), a woman (*The Enforcer—1976*), and a Chinese-American (*The Dead Pool—1988*). Each movie follows the same pattern—first Harry scorns his assigned partners, then he grows to admire them in spite of himself, and finally becomes saddened when they get either killed or mangled by the villain, leaving Harry to finish the job alone.

Conclusion

As the 1990s begin, interracial love not only has become common in American movies, but it has even entered daytime television soaps. No longer do filmmakers have to tiptoe around the theme or handle it with delicacy. Unfortunately, exploitation of interracial love has become prominent within the old plot convention. In particular, movies now use colored men as monuments to interracial virility, both in melodramas (such as *Mandingo*) or in comedies like the tasteless 1984 *Sixteen Candles*, in which a white girl has an affair with an oversexed Chinese exchange student with the oh-so-clever name of Long Duk Dong (she calls him The Donger).

Moreover, tragedy continues to stalk interracial love relationships. Symptomatic is the 1987 *China Girl*, an updated *West Side Story* (or *Romeo and Juliet*) about a Chinese immigrant girl and an Italian-American boy. Their love is buffeted by neighborhood warfare as an expanding Chinatown encroaches on a traditional Italian-American neighborhood. Almost predictably, as it has since the beginning of movies, death resolves the film— a Chinese hood shoots and kills both of the young lovers.

Even as variations appear, plot conventions persist. But so do social taboos and societal realities. In August, 1989, in the Bensonhurst section of Brooklyn, a 16-year-old African-American named Yusuf Hawkins was killed by whites. According to some reports, they were angry because they thought Hawkins and his black companions were friends of a local white girl who had said she was going to date blacks and Latinos.

Notes

[1]Much of the evidence for this article comes from my Ethnicity and Foreignness in Film Computer Data Bank in the University of California, Riverside, Department of History's Laboratory for Historical Research. I would like to thank my exceptional research assistant, Thomas Thompson, for his collaboration in the development of the Data Bank. For a methodological discussion of my film research, see Carlos E. Cortés, "The History of Ethnic Images in Film: The Search for a Methodology," in *Ethnic Images in Popular Genres and Media*, special issue of *Melus, The Journal of the Society for the Study of the Multi-Ethnic Literature of the United States*, XI, 3 (Fall, 1984), 63-77.

[2]"Colored" in this essay refers to individuals or groups that have been categorized as non-white in American history or culture (primarily by mainstream white American perceptions or official government labeling).

[3]For my book-in-progress on the history of the U.S. film treatment of interracial love, I have so far examined more than 400 films incorporating the theme.

[4]Thomas Cripps, "The Myth of the Southern Box Office: A Factor in Racial Stereotyping in American Movies, 1920-1940," in James C. Curtis and Louis L. Gould (eds.), *The Black Experience in America: Selected Essays* (Austin: University of Texas Press, 1970), 116-144, challenges the validity of Hollywood's vision of this so-called southern market.

Works Cited

Ansen, David. "Gibson and Glover Return: 'Lethal Weapon 2' serves up sadism with a smile." *Newsweek*, July 17, 1989, p. 53.

Campbell, Russell. "The Ideology of the Social Consciousness Movie: Three Films of Darryl F. Zanuck." *Quarterly Review of Film Studies*, III (Winter, 1978), pp. 49-71.

Hernton, Calvin C. *Sex and Racism in America*. New York: Grove Press, 1965.

Jones, Christopher John. "Image and Ideology in Kazan's *Pinky*." *Literature/Film Quarterly*, IX, 2 (1981), pp. 110-120.

Keen, Sam. *Faces of the Enemy: Reflections of the Hostile Imagination*. New York: Harper & Row, 1986.

Kirby, Jack Temple. "D. W. Griffith's Racial Portraiture." *Phylon*, XXXIX (June, 1978), pp. 118-127.

Michalek, Laurence. "The Arab in American Cinema: A Century of Otherness." *The Arab Image in American Film and Television, Cineaste* Supplement, XVII, 1 (1989), pp. 3-9.

Myrdal, Gunnar. *An American Dilemma: The Negro Problem and Modern Democracy*. New York: Harper & Brothers, 1944.

Stanley, Robert H. and Steinberg, Charles S. *The Media Environment: Mass Communications in American Society*. New York: Hastings House, 1976.

Wood, Michael. *America in the Movies*. New York: Basic Books, 1975.

"Zanuck Made Movie Despite Criticism of Racial Theme." *Ebony* (September, 1949), p. 25.

Filmography

1915	*The Birth of a Nation*	Dir. D. W. Griffith
1915	*The Cheat*	Dir. Cecil B. DeMille
1920	*Breath of the Gods*	Dir. Sessue Hayakawa
1920	*Locked Lips*	Dir. Sessue Hayakawa
1921	*The Sheik*	Dir. George Melford
1925	*The Vanishing American*	Dir. George Seitz
1932	*Bird of Paradise*	Dir. King Vidor
1933	*The Bitter Tea of General Yen*	Dir. Frank Capra
1935	*Bordertown*	Dir. Archie Mayo
1943	*Cry Havoc*	Dir. Richard Thorpe
1943	*So Proudly We Hail!*	Dir. Mark Sandrich
1949	*Pinky*	Dir. Elia Kazan
1950	*Broken Arrow*	Dir. Delmer Daves
1951	*Show Boat*	Dir. George Sidney
1952	*The Big Sky*	Dir. Howard Hawks
1952	*High Noon*	Dir. Fred Zinnemann
1954	*Broken Lance*	Dir. Edward Dmytryk
1955	*The Indian Fighter*	Dir. Andre de Toth
1955	*Trial*	Dir. Mark Robson
1956	*Giant*	Dir. George Stevens
1956	*The Searchers*	Dir. John Ford

1957	*Sayonara*	Dir. John Ford
1958	*South Pacific*	Dir. Joshua Logan
1961	*West Side Story*	Dir. Robert Wise
1962	*To Kill a Mickingbird*	Dir. Robert Mulligan
1964	*One Potato, Two Potato*	Dir. Larry Peerce
1965	*A Patch of Blue*	Dir. Guy Green
1966	*Johnny Tiger*	Dir. Paul Wendkos
1967	*Guess Who's Coming to Dinner?*	Dir. Stanley Kramer
1970	*The Boys in the Band*	Dir. William Friedkin
1970	*The Landlord*	Dir. Hal Ashby
1972	*Fat City*	Dir. John Huston
1972	*Jeremiah Johnson*	Dir. Sydney Pollack
1972	*Superfly*	Dir. Gordon Parks Jr.
1972	*When the Legends Die*	Dir. Stuart Millar
1974	*The White Dawn*	Dir. Philip Kaufman
1975	*Mandingo*	Dir. Richard Fleischer
1976	*Norman...Is That You?*	Dir. George Schlatter
1979	*Walk Proud*	Dir. Robert Collins
1980	*Gloria*	Dir. John Cassavetes
1980	*The Mountain Men*	Dir. Richard Lang
1981	*Carbon Copy*	Dir. Michael Schultz
1981	*Tarzan, the Ape Man*	Dir. John Derek
1982	*Eating Raoul*	Dir. Paul Bartel
1982	*Paradise*	Dir. Stuart Gillard
1983	*Bad Boys*	Dir. Rick Rosenthal
1983	*Scarface*	Dir. Brian De Palma
1984	*Sixteen Candles*	Dir. John Hughes
1985	*Year of the Dragon*	Dir. Michael Cimino
1986	*Touch and Go*	Dir. Robert Mandel
1986	*Working Girls*	Dir. Lizzie Borden
1987	*Captive Hearts*	Dir. Paul Almond
1987	*China Girl*	Dir. Abel Ferrara
1987	*Extreme Prejudice*	Dir. Walter Hill
1987	*Fatal Beauty*	Dir. Tom Holland
1987	*La Bamba*	Dir. Luis Valdez
1987	*North Shore*	Dir. William Phelps
1988	*Young Guns*	Dir. Christopher Cain

Conversion as Persuasive Convention
in American War Films

Ralph R. Donald

Alone and disgraced, the young soldier awaits the fate of all accused of cowardice under fire: court-martial, followed by imprisonment or the firing squad. But circumstances allow him to escape. Instead of skulking off to safety and oblivion, the soldier decides to return to the front. There, he rejoins his company, fights and dies heroically, redeeming himself. Through the years, in scenarios such as James Cagney's performance in *The Fighting 69th*, (1940), Hollywood war films possessed no peer in the use of the conversion convention. In the conversion's simplest form, soldiers initially fail to give their all to the fight; however, later in the picture, these men (and, occasionally, women), encounter circumstances that convince them to repent. Newly converted, they take up the struggle for some military objective with a commitment bordering on fanaticism. Often these regenerate characters become heroes in the process.

As main plots and subplots, these conversions provided pro-war models for America's moviegoing citizenry during wartime, and object lessons in team play and patriotic action between wars. In more recent years, however, war films (especially Vietnam War films) have inverted the American mythic landscape to such a degree that conventional conversions occur in reverse: the initially faithful, "gung ho" soldier becomes disenchanted with the war, and converts from a crusading zealot to a faded, disillusioned veteran bent solely on personal and/or small group survival rather than victory for his country's forces.

This essay examines both polarities of this convention, a process that results in making a dramatic decision to subjugate one's personal needs, wants, and well-being to that of his/her country. But regardless of which pole of the convention one discusses, seven main classifications of conversions appear to occur with the greatest regularity:

1. From rugged individualist to team player,
2. From selfish to selfless,
3. From immature to mature,
4. From coward to hero,
5. From unconcerned about the issues and effects of the war to concerned,

6. From anti-military to pro-military,
7. From pacifist to pro-war.

Rugged Individualist to Team Player

One of the most important tasks of narrative feature film war propaganda, or war propaganda in general, is to create identifiable role models through whom filmmakers create or reinforce important values. Especially in World War II, when American pro-war propaganda films experienced their heyday, the government knew it needed to overcome an ingrained American trait: stubborn individuality. Audiences had to be shown that although in peace time "doing one's own thing" was an acceptable, even praiseworthy, American entrepreneurial virtue, team play and regimentation are more desirable goals in wartime.

In John Ford's *They Were Expendable*, (1945), John Wayne portrays a typical example of the rugged individualist faced with a conversion decision. Tired of no-glory milk runs in the P.T. boats to which he was assigned, Wayne wants a transfer. He's convinced that his ambitions can only be served if he is reassigned to a destroyer, where he can make a name for himself. He even goes so far as to fill out a transfer application, but tears it up when he hears about the Japanese attack on Pearl Harbor. His ambition and search for glory must wait. Similarly, Robert Montgomery, Wayne's P.T. boat squadron commander, is frustrated by his admiral's unwillingness to use P.T.'s on combat missions. On one occasion, the admiral, in a prototypical World War II pep talk, uses a sports analogy to remind Montgomery of the need for teamwork. "You and I are professionals: If the manager says 'sacrifice,' we lay down a bunt, and let somebody else hit the home runs." Duly chastised, Montgomery adjusts his attitude.

Similarly, in *Crash Dive* (1943), Tyrone Power is resentful for being transferred to submarine service, especially since he has recently made a name for himself in P.T. boats, his favorite naval craft. But, through various espirit de corps-building experiences on board the submarine, the hardheaded Power finally realizes that each kind of naval craft has a valuable and equal role in the team effort to win the war. At the conclusion, with patriotic music rising in the background, Power recites a litany of naval craft, from P.T.'s to battleships to carriers, extolling their individual contributions to team victory.

In *The Fighting Seabees* (1944), John Wayne once again plays a rugged individualist, a salty civilian construction contractor who refuses to play ball by the Navy's rules. While Wayne's men are building an airstrip for the Navy in the Pacific, the Japanese attack. Ignoring orders to stay in a shelter while Naval personnel repel the invaders, Wayne and his men attack the enemy. But due to their lack of discipline and training, many of these construction workers are killed and wounded. Repentant, Wayne assists the Navy in setting up a new branch of the service, a construction battalion, which, as their anthem says, can both build *and* fight. Later, Wayne, now a naval officer, and his men are building another base. Ever hard-headed, he disobeys orders, and leads a sortie against Japanese snipers instead of guarding valuable oil tanks. Realizing that he has once again erred on the side of individuality, Wayne once again repents. He brings his men back to the oil tanks, engages the enemy, and in so doing, sacrifices his life.

Both James Cagney in *Captains of The Clouds* (1942) and Forrest Tucker in *Sands of Iwo Jima* (1949) represent a character type whose individualism and initial unwillingness to submit to authority result in ruin for their comrades. Witnessing the folly of their actions, both also mend their ways. Cagney, a skillful and experienced Canadian bush pilot, ignores flying regulations with which he disagrees, causing a crash and injuries to a flying student. He is cashiered from the Royal Canadian Air Force. Later, Cagney engages in a drunken flying stunt that causes the death of one of his best friends. To assuage his guilt, Cagney assumes a false identity and joins a group of civilian pilots ferrying bombers to England. Attacked en route by a German fighter, the unarmed bombers prove to be easy prey. But Cagney uses his bush pilot skills to maneuver the enemy plane into a fatal mid-air collision with his bomber, thus saving the rest of the flight.

As typified by *Captains Of The Clouds*, the Hollywood formula for a seriously delinquent character's redemption calls for either his death, or at least a serious wound or two. In *Sands of Iwo Jima* (1949), Tucker is more fortunate: a marine sharing a foxhole with two buddies on a Japanese-held island, Tucker volunteers to fetch ammunition for the others. Returning with these essentials, he is sidetracked by another marine's offer to share some hot coffee. An undisciplined individualist and the squad troublemaker, Tucker neglects his friends, dallying for ten minutes to savor his coffee. During this time, Tucker's buddies run out of ammunition, and are overrun by the Japanese. One is killed, the other badly wounded. When he realizes what he has done, Tucker totally reforms, and for the rest of the picture accepts the need for strict discipline and training with no complaints. Having learned the hard way, he becomes a model marine, an example to the rest.

A character quite similar to Tucker is the role played by Ann Sothern in *Cry Havoc!* (1943). A streetwise woman, less than pristine by her own self-definition, Sothern has a problem with authority figures, especially if it means "takin' orders from dames." She comes into direct conflict with her regimented, by-the-book boss, played by Margaret Sullivan. But eventually, Sothern softens toward her superior, accepts (albeit begrudgingly) Sullivan's authority and the need for discipline, and becomes a productive member of their nurse's aide team.

Unlike Cagney and Tucker, the individualistic actions of Edmund O'Brien's "China tramp" character in *Fighter Squadron* (1948) are not responsible for the deaths of any of his comrades. Experience as a Flying Tiger in China and has given him both superior skills, a long line of swastikas painted on the nose of his plane, and an extremely independent attitude.

O'Brien has no use for authority, and continually presents his superiors with the decision whether to court-martial him for ignoring standing orders or add another oak leaf cluster to his chest of medals. Eventually, O'Brien's commanding officer is promoted, and the reluctant individualist is asked to change roles: from rule-breaker to rule-maker. O'Brien asks his boss, Colonel Buckley (John Rodney), if he can be passed over for command, but Rodney will have none of it. In the quintessential "grow up and get with the program" speech, Rodney lays is on the line to O'Brien:

Buckley: [You were] a cute kid lieutenant in Honolulu. But you wanted to be a rover boy. Threw up your commission and went to China. That was your meat. Play it high, wide and handsome. Voluntary missions. Plaster 'em. Think of nobody but yourself. Fun, sure: We used to do that in the Eagle Squadron. But you've made this war your private, three-ring circus, and I've taken the rap for you, and now you can pay me back! Listen, this is *my* outfit: I want every man in it to have the best fighting chance to come out alive. To keep 'em on their toes, strict rules, split-second timing. Now are you gonna do it, or are you going to go on flying for Ed Hardin? Or can't you take it?

Faced with his own irresponsibility, O'Brien agrees to accept command, and the responsibilities that go with it. O'Brien enforces discipline, and, to the amazement of his fellow flyers, does not rescind the strict rules and regulations of his predecessor. Although he criticized them earlier, once O'Brien views them from the perspective of the commander's chair, he realizes that they are important and necessary.

Similarly, Randolph Scott in *Bombardier!* (1943) is a pilot extremely set in his ways, refusing to accept the notion that team play in a bomber requires the pilot to relinquish command and control of the plane to the bombardier during the actual bombing run. Scott naturally clashes with his tough-as-nails, by-the-book commander, Pat O'Brien, a perfect dramatic foil to Scott's happy-go-lucky character. Unwilling to cooperate, Scott is grounded for a time. Finally, realizing he has been wrong, the flyer repents and becomes an enthusiastic supporter of bombardier training. In the climax, Scott is shot down in a bombing raid over Nagoya, and is captured by the Japanese. He escapes, and sets fires around the target area to help the bombardiers he helped train find their mark. Ironically, Scott himself is killed in the ensuing air raid.

There is very little difference between the aforementioned characters and newer incarnations, such as Richard Gere's officer cadet in *An Officer and A Gentleman* (1982). Symbolized by the motorcycle he rides, Gere plays a loner. To ride with him, Debra Winger must hop aboard his cycle; in other words, she can only join with Gere on his terms. But regardless of her affection for him, he proves to be only out for himself, uncaring about his girlfriend or his fellow cadets. From the start, drill instructor Louis Gossett recognizes Gere's character weakness, and confronts him it.

Eventually, through Gossett's goading and his interplay with Winger and his fellow cadets, Gere learns to care for others, and to work with the group as a team member. Regardless of era, these films state clearly that individualism must take a back seat to the needs of the military organization.

Selfish To Selfless

There is great similarity between John Carroll in *The Flying Tigers* (1942) and the characters in the previous section. Like Edmund O'Brien and James Cagney, Carroll plays a veteran pilot not used to taking orders, very short on teamwork and discipline. But Carroll provides a bridge from the previous category to this one because of his motivation: Primarily, he's a modern-day bounty hunter out strictly for the money paid to Flying Tigers for each Japanese plane they shoot down. Unlike the other Tigers, who, like Texan Jimmy Dodd, agree that "Where I come from there doesn't have to be a bounty on a rattlesnake to kill him," Carroll is selfish and is only motivated by money. He abandons wingmen if he can shoot down another plane, takes reckless chances, and endangers others, all for money. But when he sees the results of Japanese bombing of an orphanage, his outlook widens. And when his irresponsibility causes the death of a fellow Tiger, Carroll repents, and takes on an expiative suicide mission.

Similarly, three 1943 film heroes—George Montgomery in *China Girl*, Alan Ladd in *China*, and Ward Bond in *Hitler: Dead or Alive*—are concerned solely with money at the outset of their adventures. Montgomery, a salty photojournalist, is out to document the war for fame and a tidy profit, and, like Carroll, is unconcerned about what is happening to the Chinese people he photographs. Ladd sells truckloads of gasoline to anyone who will pay, Chinese guerrillas or the Japanese. When both protagonists experience the love of Eurasian women (Gene Tierney and Loretta Young, respectively), and witness first-hand Japanese atrocities committed against Chinese civilians, they set aside profits and personal safety and join the Chinese guerrillas.

In *Hitler: Dead or Alive*, a particularly silly grade-B gangster caper film, Ward Bond is an underworld "big-shot" who, along with two other hoodlums, accepts a million dollar contract let by a rich American industrialist to assassinate or kidnap Adolph Hitler. At first only concerned with the money, Bond witnesses a Nazi "blood purge," the killing of innocent women and children. Horrified, he rejects the opportunity to kill Hitler. Instead, Bond tries no negotiate an end to the war in return for the *fuhrer*, whom he has kidnapped. This altruistic attempt fails, and Bond is killed. But in memory of Bond's attempt, the industrialist nonetheless "pays off" the gangster by donating a million dollars worth of planes to the war effort.

When the litany of characters "only out for themselves" is read, first and foremost is Humphrey Bogart in *Casablanca* (1942). But unlike Bond, Ladd, and Montgomery, Bogart began as an unselfish supporter of losing causes in Spain and Ethiopia. Only after his abortive love affair with Ingrid Bergman does Bogart, as the phlegmatic Rick, adopt his famous "I stick out my neck for nobody" attitude. But in the well-known story, his love for Bergman and sense of duty to Paul Henried's democratic cause overcome his selfish stance; Henreid welcomes Bogart back to the fight. As a bonus, Bogart's example even converts the corrupt Claude Rains to the Free French side.

Anthony Quinn in *Back to Bataan* (1945) and, in a later film, Kirk Douglas in *The Heroes of Telemark* (1965), are other interesting permutations of the "fella only out for himself" faced with circumstances that confound their personal philosophies. Quinn plays the grandson of a famous Filipino guerrilla fighter. Quinn resents being recruited by John Wayne to help inspire Filipinos to stand up to the oppressive Japanese occupation force. He wants nothing more than to disappear from sight with his fiancée and ignore the entire war. But Wayne and Quinn's fiancée cajole him into helping. Finally he witnesses something that makes him come around: One night on a beach, Quinn witnesses hundreds of Filipino men, women and children risking their lives just to unload arms and supplies from a submarine for use in the guerrilla effort. Ashamed, Quinn commits to fighting to the end, and soon after bravely leads a successful guerrilla attack on a vital Japanese stronghold.

In *The Heroes of Telemark*, Kirk Douglas is a playboy physicist blithely ignoring the war in Nazi-occupied Norway. While Norwegian resistance fighters press the war against the Germans, Douglas prefers to romance female lab assistants at the university. Richard Harris, a resistance fighter, presses Douglas reluctantly into service to help evaluate microfilmed evidence of Nazi heavy water production in Norway. Realizing that the Germans are close to creating an atom bomb, Douglas gives up his neutrality and joins in a series of operations designed to destroy the Germans' ability to produce heavy water. Character exposition throughout the film shows that Douglas cares for no one but himself. Typical of his values, he would rather bomb an entire town, killing many civilians, than risk his life in a commando raid on the town's heavy water factory. But witnessing the self-sacrifice of the Norwegian resistance, and confronted with his self-centeredness by his ex-wife, Douglas gradually changes. In the climax, he chooses to risk his life to save civilians on a soon-to-be-destroyed ferry boat which he has sabotaged.

Immature to Mature

There are different kinds of maturity required of soldiers in battle: putting away childish things and assuming the responsibilities of men, changing from inexperienced young civilian-soldiers into seasoned veterans, and growing up to the point that they can accept responsibility both for their actions and for those of others.

In the category of leaving childhood behind, Farley Granger in *The Purple Heart* (1944) and Robert Walker in *Bataan* (1943) are typical examples. Granger and Walker are the requisite youths found in every World War II combat film's array of stock characters. Granger, a sheltered rich kid, and Walker, a wide-eyed innocent from the midwest, find themselves in harm's way. Granger is a bomber crewman captured and put on trial by the Japanese for so-called "war crimes," and Walker is a member of a doomed squad tasked with denying the Japanese the use of a bridgehead on Bataan. Both are forced to shed their naiveté and their Pollyanna outlooks. Both learn the savagery of their enemy, and both respond to their situations with bravery and grim resolve. As often occurs to youthful members of combat units, both youngsters are ultimately killed. However, in these two instances, none of the protagonists survive.

Some war films feature another kind of naive young soldier, the kind who is not destined to die. This character may show some signs of maturation as the film goes on, but the purpose behind the character is to show how war changes the youngsters who survive into seasoned soldiers. Two examples from World War II are Richard Jaeckel in *Guadalcanal Diary* (1943) and Marshall Thompson in *Battleground* (1949). Tom Quill provides an updated version of the same character in the Vietnam saga, *Hamburger Hill* (1987). In *Guadalcanal Diary*, Jaeckel, a fuzzy-cheeked teenage Marine treated more like a son or kid brother by the older, more seasoned members of his platoon, must learn the ways of war by hard experience. For example, he is wounded when he recklessly exposes himself to sniper fire to retrieve a souvenir, a samurai sword. When Jaeckel recuperates and returns to the fight, he, also, has the sad eyes, if not the whiskers, of a much older man.

In *Battleground*, Thompson, as a new replacement in his squad, is at first ignored and ridiculed: He quickly learns that new men have a higher mortality rate, so the veterans prefer not to get to know them until they have proven themselves and become more likely survivors. Little by little, Thompson's civilian ideas and attitudes, as well as his naiveté, are replaced with hard, cold, professionalism and fatalism. By the end of the film, Thompson, cigarette dangling from his mouth, has the same glazed expression, reduced expectations and weary step as the other veterans, as they march down the road toward a welcome rest.

Tom Quill in *Hamburger Hill* is a particularly irritating new replacement in a platoon soon to return to a particularly hot sector in Vietnam, the Ashau Valley. No matter how many times veterans advise him to forget all the useless, unimportant things he was taught in advanced infantry training, Quill's dim character repeatedly drives everyone crazy with dumb questions about them. Also an insensitive, self-centered individual, Quill eventually learns to care for others. He finally realizes that what is worth remembering in-country is simple: only one thing counts: your squad and your buddies. Eventually, this sinks in, and Quill becomes a useful, sensitive member of the squad.

James Brown in *Corvette K-225* (1943), Henry Fonda in *The Immortal Sergeant* (1943), and Robert Ryan in *Flying Leathernecks* (1951) all possess the same problem: Their immaturity keeps them from assuming and coping with the responsibilities of soldiers responsible for the lives of other soldiers. Brown is a young sub-lieutenant on a corvette, who is ridden hard by skipper Randolph Scott. The unseasoned young officer can't understand why Scott is so hard on him for little errors in judgement, inattention to details, etc. Eventually, Brown learns that each of these details can mean the difference between success or failure, life and death. Soon, Brown changes his attitude, and accepts the need to carry out his responsibilities in a grown-up manner.

In *The Immortal Sergeant*, Fonda is not young: Both in and out of the service, his failure to be assertive, to take decisive action about anything, would in today's slang brand him a wimp. He even refuses a commission in the British Army to avoid responsibility. But when his sergeant, Thomas Mitchell, dies, Fonda finds himself in charge of a desperate mission in the middle of the North African desert. Assuming Mitchell's wisdom and attitudes, Fonda leads his men through their perilous mission simply by doing things the way he thinks the old sergeant would. Successful and a hero, sporting an officer's battlefield commission, Fonda realizes he does indeed possess the potential for leadership and decisive action.

Robert Ryan's character in *Flying Leathernecks* is both similar and dissimilar to Fonda's: Ryan, a marine fighter squadron executive officer, believes he is seasoned and mature enough to command, and desires it. But Ryan displeases his boss, John Wayne, who sees him as unwilling to make tough decisions, too chummy with his pilots to enforce discipline, and too sensitive to the men's feelings. Initially Ryan discounts these criticisms simply as differences in leadership style and continues to believe that he is ready for command. But Wayne continues to point out his weaknesses, and when the time comes to relinquish command, passes him over. Finally Ryan begins to take Wayne's ideas more seriously. On another tour, the two are once again assigned as commander and executive officer. Ryan mends his ways, and learns to make tough decisions unpopular with the men. Wayne is wounded, and is to be evacuated and reassigned. He realizes that Ryan is now ready for command, and this time recommends him for promotion.

Coward to Hero

In Act III of *Julius Caesar*, Shakespeare wrote, "Cowards die many times before their deaths; the valiant never taste death but once." Films depicting various wars have always managed to deal with those who faced fear and mastered it. War propaganda must address the subject of fear, and supply its audiences with reasons sufficient to convince peaceful men to engage in mortal combat. Patriotism, responsibility, revenge, espirit de corps, and other motivations are provided as justification for risking one's life. Object lessons about fearful men are most helpful: That is why one of the most often heard stock conversations in combat films is the one in which a soldier new to combat is surprised to discover that the old sarge, or the captain is scared too, "and anyone who says he ain't scared is a liar or a fool."

In two occupied-country war films, Charles Laughton in *This Land is Mine* (1943) and Roman Bohnen in *The Edge of Darkness* (1943) portray men for whom courage is a foreign concept. Although an adult in his forties, Laughton's character is a mamby-pamby mama's boy, afraid of everything, especially guns and violence. But he lives in occupied France during World War II, and Nazi atrocities and allied air raids are common occurrences. A schoolteacher, Laughton is ashamed of himself, because he is a poor example to his students, who show no respect and ridicule him. But when his headmaster and mentor, who had urged him to become a positive example to his students, is shot by the Nazis as a reprisal for resistance activities in the area, Laughton becomes both enraged and courageous. He openly speaks out against the enemy, urging the townspeople to join the fight and engage in resistance and sabotage. His students now look on him with pride and admiration. Just before the Germans lead him out of his classroom to be shot, he reads the French Declaration of the Rights of Men to his pupils. When he is gone, he leaves a classroom full of new young zealots for the cause of freedom.

Roman Bohnen plays a shopkeeper in occupied Norway in *The Edge of Darkness*. Unlike Laughton, he has always been vocal in his hate for the Germans, and imagines himself as a soldier shooting all of them. But Bohnen's character is all bluster and talk: In a face-to-face confrontation with a group of derisive German troops, he has the opportunity to bravely tell the Nazis what he thinks of them. But he becomes so frightened he can say nothing. The message of the film is that although as individuals, people are hard pressed to stand up to such an invader, if everyone stands together, they can prevail. So when the whole village rises up as one against the Nazis, Bohnen takes his place among the men, picks up a rifle, and realizes his daydreams: He joins his fellow townspeople in the extermination of the entire German garrison.

Woody Strode in *Pork Chop Hill* (1959), James Cagney in *The Fighting 69th*, and Hugh Marlowe in *Twelve O'Clock High* (1949) have one thing in common: each has committed acts of cowardice, each man's deeds are known to their commanders, and each must choose between either court-martial or some expiative act of bravery. Strode's and Cagney's situations are quite similar, although the former fights in Korea and the latter in the trenches of France during World War I. Also, both have displayed cowardice under fire and are under arrest. Their motivations, however, are quite different: Strode, a black soldier and a draftee, sees Korea as a white man's war, and refuses to die for the causes of an oppressor race. Cagney boasts of the medals he'll win and the many Germans he will kill. But when the time comes, Cagney turns "yellow." Both men's experiences eventually cause them to reconsider. Both witness the deaths of many of their friends, both are challenged by other soldiers to be true to the memory of these men, and both finally decide to rejoin the war and take their chances with fate. Cagney dies, but Strode survives the experience.

Marlowe in *Twelve O'Clock High* is a similar case. A pilot in World War II, he is the executive officer of a bomber group. When General Gregory Peck takes over the group, he finds that Marlowe has been avoiding hazardous missions for months and has discharged scant few of his responsibilities as group executive officer. Peck gives Marlowe two choices: to be court-martialed for cowardice and dereliction of duty, or accept a unique punishment: Command of a bomber to be called the Leper Colony, in which "every foul-up and goof-off" crewman in the group would be transferred to do penance. Marlowe chooses the Leper Colony. In the months that follow, he distinguishes himself in dozens of dangerous missions. Finally, although suffering excruciating back pain from a flak wound the previous day, Marlowe chooses not to miss out on an important mission. Later, in traction in the hospital, Marlowe is visited by Peck, who tacitly assures him that all is forgiven: He has done his duty.

Unconcerned to Concerned

This category of character conversion is quite similar to the selfish-selfless conversion, since in these scenarios concern with one's self is often tied to a singular lack of concern for anything else. Certainly, Alan Ladd in *China* and George Montgomery in *China Girl* both were principally concerned with money and fame, but the needless slaughter of the Chinese had as much to do with their conversion to the cause as did the encouragements of Loretta Young and Gene Tierney. This section will discuss other non-ideologically-committed types whose personal observations convince them to join the fight with vigor and commitment.

Tyrone Power in *A Yank in the R.A.F.* (1941), Ronald Reagan in *International Squadron* (1941), and Robert Stack in *Eagle Squadron* (1942) portray three similar characters in three nearly identical pictures who undergo nearly identical conversions, practically down to their final outcomes. Stack joins the R.A.F. for adventure, fame, and to be able to wear a tailored uniform while chasing women. Like Reagan and Power, Stack has no real sense of what the war is really about, nor does he care to learn. Power and Reagan are both hired to ferry bombers from the U.S. to England. Power enlists in the R.A.F. to stay close to Betty Grable, and Reagan joins up when he witnesses a small child killed in an air raid. All three become more and more committed to the war effort as they observe the devastation caused by the blitz. But unlike Power and Stack, our future president continues his irresponsible behavior. A fellow flyer is killed because Reagan is busy womanizing, causing him finally to repent. As does John Carroll in *Flying Tigers*, Reagan atones by taking on a suicide mission and dying a heroic death. Stack and Power fare better. They also take on life-threatening missions and do heroic deeds—but both survive, and return to their women, whom, incidentally, they both have wooed away from British flying officers. It seems that although England was our ally in war, Hollywood made sure that when it came to love, it was *America uber alles*.

Tallulah Bankhead in *Lifeboat* (1944) and Henry Hull in *Objective Burma* (1945) play journalists more interested in filing sensational stories than in the issues and outcomes of the war. Instead of helping victims of a U-Boat attack into her lifeboat, Bankhead takes movies, and curses when John Hodiak accidentally knocks her camera into the water. Hull, slightly anti-military, bored, and mainly concerned with a good story, accompanies Errol Flynn on a paratrooper raid into Japanese-held territory. Despite their wishes to remain onlookers, both characters cease to be objective chroniclers and become active participants in events. The demure Bankhead ultimately joins the others in savagely killing their Nazi lifeboat-mate in reprisal for the murder of a wounded man. Hull witnesses the remains of American troops brutally tortured by the Japanese. Losing his customary worldly cool, Hull, wild-eyed and shaking, shouts, "Stinking little savages! Wipe 'em out! Wipe 'em off the face of the earth!"

Even series pictures such as the Sherlock Holmes and Tarzan films joined in the propaganda battle during World War II. In one such film, *Tarzan Triumphs* (1943), the ape man, played by Johnny Weissmuller, enacts what amounts to an anti-isolationist allegory. Tarzan wants no part of a conflict between countries, so when a company of German paratroops occupies a tiny African principality nearby, he takes no action. The issues of the outside world have no meaning to the jungle dweller. But when the Germans make the mistake of threatening his family, Tarzan wakes up to the fact that the Nazis are a threat to everyone. Practically single-handed, Tarzan kills the entire German company, and liberates the oppressed principality.

Antimilitary to Military

Many jokes have been made through the years about the ineptitude of the military establishment. From the notion that "military intelligence" is an oxymoron to the stereotype of the militarist as an ideologically-rigid warmonger, the Armed Forces have been easy prey for their detractors. But especially when the nation is at war, it is important for a government to try to put the best face possible on its fighting forces. The character conversions in this section attempt to do just that.

Carl Harbord's character in *Sahara* (1943), David Niven's in *The Guns of Navarone* (1961) and John Agar's in *Sands of Iwo Jima* are all examples of a stock intellectual humanist character. Initially antimilitary, he either converts to military thinking or at least consents to the need for military-mindedness in wartime. In *Sahara*, Harbord is a British soldier who finds himself in the middle of the desert under the command of American Sergeant Humphrey Bogart. From the outset, Harbord, nicknamed "the professor" for his erudite remarks, makes it clear that he dislikes authority and sergeants, especially Yank NCO's. Often Harbord opposes Bogart's military ruthlessness. But the script uses these opportunities to allow Bogart to demonstrate the strategic wisdom of the sacrifices he asks them to make. Similarly, David Niven provides a critical counterpoint for Gregory Peck's military authority figure in *Navarone*. Objecting to Peck's ruthless task-orientation, Niven, in civilian life a college professor, joins Harbord in voicing the humanistic, anti-military point of view. Both ultimately are faced with decisions: in Harbord's case, to flee or to fight the Germans to the death, buying time for their comrades at El Alemein; with Niven's, to attempt a desperate, probably suicidal assault on the Nazi's heavily-guarded guns. But both have learned sufficiently from role models Bogart and Peck to realize that there are times when one must simply put away one's sense of humanism and morality and concentrate on the greater good: in this case, achieving the military objective.

John Agar portrays the son of a "blood and guts" marine colonel, but he marches to a different ideological drummer. Agar objects to Sergeant John Wayne's sense of military expediency and Wayne's loyalty to Agar's estranged father, under whom Wayne served. But in the heat of battle, Agar, like Niven and Harbord, discovers that Wayne's way of doing things is necessary for survival and victory. When Wayne is killed, Agar, having become a true-blue "gyrene," assumes both Wayne's command and Wayne's persona, enthusiastically leading his men onward up Mount Suribachi.

Both William Bendix in *Wake Island* (1942) and John Garfield in *Air Force* (1943) are counting the days until their hitches in the service end. Bendix serves in the Marines on Wake Island, and Garfield is a machine gunner on a B-17 crew. In each case, the films begin a few days before the Japanese sneak attack on Pearl Harbor. Bendix plans to return to civilian life and forget about everything the service stands for. His only regret is that he must say good-bye to his friend and tent-mate, Robert Preston. In *Air Force*, Garfield, soured on the Air Corps because he was washed out of pilot training, turns a deaf ear to bomber crew chief Harry Carey's sermons about the advantages of a career as an enlisted man. The unhappy Garfield just wants out, and is counting the days until his enlistment ends. Then each hears the news of Pearl Harbor. Benedix, already in civilian clothes, has only to board the clipper plane for home, and he's free and safe. Instead, he chooses to reenlist, and ends up fighting and dying in a foxhole alongside his buddy Preston. When Garfield hears the news, he is furious with the Japanese, and vows revenge. He becomes a loyal, team-oriented crew member, responsible for a number of downed enemy planes and other heroic acts.

Anti-war to Pro-war

"Thou shalt not kill" is a commandment at odds with the essentials of warfare, creating in the citizenry moral misgivings that propagandists must dispel. Films with anti-war to pro-war conversions attempt to rationalize the need to break the "thou shalt not kill" commandment in wartime. Both Gary Cooper in *Sergeant York* (1941) and Patrick Wolfe in *Beach Red* (1967) wrestle with this conflict, and find ways to rationalize their behavior. Cooper plays the real-life character Alvin York, a violent man and a crack shot, who converts to Christianity and becomes a pacifist. Wolfe is a minister's son who believes that, "there's got to be another way, or what's the point?" But in a bloody assault on a Japanese-held island, Wolfe witnesses the grisly deaths of several of his friends. Likewise, Cooper, in the trenches of World War I, watches many of his buddies die. Both put away their religious ideals and their humanism for another, more peaceful epoch. Both take up the sword, rationalizing what they must do. Cooper explains that he kills Germans to save American lives, and Wolfe decides that killing Japanese is simply a matter of self-defense, for they will surely kill him if he doesn't shoot first. Through these rationales, each finds an uneasy peace with himself.

Similarly, Clinton Greyn in *Raid on Rommel* (1971) and Richard Fraser in *The Edge of Darkness* portray men of peace, one a doctor drafted into the army, and the other a minister caught up in a war delivered to the doorstep of his church. Both refuse to understand or condone killing, but cannot just sit back and watch: Like Cooper and Wolfe, they are forced to make a decision. Greyn is repulsed by the awful waste of human life war represents, and he is especially opposed to the mission of the film, which quite likely means death or capture for all. Since they will wear German uniforms to get through enemy lines, capture also means being shot as a spy. But Greyn is also compelled by his oath as a physician to care for wounded men. Also, Richard Burton, in charge of the operation, convinces Greyn that many allied lives will be lost if their mission to destroy a battery of German guns is a failure. This logic is sufficient for Greyn, who agrees to the mission.

In *The Edge of Darkness*, Fraser, a minister, initially opposes the townspeople's uprising against the Germans. He reminds them of God's commandments, and refuses to participate. But as the days go on, German atrocities apparently convince Fraser that when God said, "Thou shalt not kill," He meant killing Germans to be an exception. A few moments before all the village leaders are to be executed in the town square, the minister opens fire on the Germans from the Church belfry with a submachine gun. This sparks the townspeople's revolt and the extermination of the entire Nazi garrison.

In *The Green Berets* (1968), John Wayne uses similar logic and arguments to persuade a liberal, antiwar journalist (David Janssen) that American intervention in Vietnam is justified. Throughout this work of absolute nonsense, Wayne purports to show Janssen savage Viet Cong atrocities against civilians which must be avenged. Plus, Janssen witnesses the South Vietnamese working with the Americans to liberate their country. This causes Janssen to set aside his non-interventionist, pacifist attitudes and commit himself to a campaign of slanted reporting designed to convince America that continued belligerence is justified.

Conversion Inversion

As stated at the outset, more recent pictures, especially Vietnam War combat films, invert the American mythic landscape, turning our ideas and ideals about our country's wars upside down. For example, *Platoon* (1986) inverts the individualist-to-team player conversion. Charlie Sheen's character arrives in Vietnam a fire-breathing true believer, a team player. But, little by little, he loses his John Wayne-ish illusions and realizes that his objective in Vietnam is not to win a war, but simply to survive. Sheen learns that this war has no meaning, no goals, no way to win. Winning is going back to the world outside of a body bag.

Inverting the selfish-to-selfless conversion, *Kelly's Heroes* (1970) was a very popular Vietnam-era film that is set in World War II. But it clearly deals with the moral bankruptcy of the military and a squad of men determined not to remain cannon fodder any longer. An excellent example of inverting the selfish-to-selfless conversion, Kelly's dog-tired infantry squad is sick of war and killing. They have fought at the point of the allied advance since the invasion of Normandy. Now with the war winding down, they happen onto an opportunity, discovering that behind enemy lines is a cache of millions in Nazi gold. They take off after it. In the World War II version of a "big caper" picture, Kelly's men perform heroics not for God and country, but for purely selfish aims. Securing their objective, the group, which now includes a German tank commander who would rather be rich than fight, splits up the gold and deserts, heading for Switzerland.

A classic, award-winning example of inverting the uncommitted to committed conversion is found in *Born On The Fourth of July* (1989). In the beginning of the film, Tom Cruise, who has fashioned himself into a gung-ho marine in the image of John Wayne in *Sands Of Iwo Jima*, volunteers to serve in Vietnam. Cruise, portraying real-life Vietnam vet Ron Kovic, is seriously wounded and is left paralyzed from the mid-waist down. The rest of the picture documents how he learns to cope with his handicap, his post-stress syndrome, and the growing realization that the Vietnam war was wrong. By the end of the picture, Cruise/Kovic addresses the 1976 Democratic Convention, a spokesman for his brother vets and against American adventurism in third-world countries.

In *Hanover Street* (1979), Harrison Ford inverts the coward-to-hero conversion. A courageous, perhaps over-aggressive bomber pilot, Ford falls in love with Lesley-Anne Down. His love for her takes away his aggressive edge, makes him cautious, even timid in the cockpit. On one occasion, as he taxies his plane to takeoff position for a particularly hazardous mission, Ford aborts the plane because he claims that something is wrong with one of the engines. But the engines check out O.K., and Ford is suspected of cowardice. Later, like others we have encountered, Ford flies a dangerous mission which results in his personal redemption. But unlike others, Ford does not volunteer for the mission. His commander, irked at the needlessly aborted mission, "volunteers" Ford for the hazardous flight rather than subject him to disciplinary action. Until the film's denouement, when he heroically rescues Christopher Plummer, Ford remains a reluctant, protesting participant in this dangerous mission.

An example of inversion of the antimilitary to military conversion is found in *Apopcalypse Now* (1979). Martin Sheen begins the film as a troubled but obedient soldier, sent on a secret mission to assassinate a colonel (Marlon Brando) who had become insane and out of control, the mad king of an army of savages loose in Cambodia carrying out murder and mayhem on his whims. Along the way, Sheen witnesses American atrocities committed by Col. Kilgore (Robert Duvall) and his men that are equal to or worse than those committed by his intended victim. For example, Kilgore's airborne attack force shoots, blows up, or napalms virtually every man, woman and child in a V.C.-held village. Why? Because the hamlet is located near "the best surf in Southeast Asia." While the carnage is still going on, Kilgore strips down, grabs his surfboard, and heads for the beach. Slowly, Sheen sinks into a mental state in which he feels more in common with his victim than with those who sent him. Director Francis Ford Coppola originally intended for Sheen to assassinate Brando, but then assume Brando's persona and take his place. Instead, he reluctantly kills Brando, leaving Sheen's future vague and uncertain.

An example in inverting the antiwar to prowar conversion is Craig Wasson's character in the Vietnam film, *Go Tell The Spartans* (1978). Wasson begins the film as a staunch supporter of America's advisory role in Vietnam (the time period of the film is pre-Tonkin Gulf). He fancies that he'll help win Vietnamese hearts and minds with smiles, American goodness, and Hershey bars. But Vietnam reality teaches him otherwise. Those he wishes to help turn out to be the enemy, and the Vietnamese troops he helps advise are as savage as the Japanese were pictured in World War II movies. Finally, the lone survivor of a V.C. massacre of Americans and South Vietnamese militia, Wasson staggers off into the sunset with a new, terse statement about the Vietnam War: "Insanity," he says, "Insanity."

Conclusion

The examples described in this chapter are only a sample of the thousands of repetitions and variations of the conversion convention found in American war films. From World War I until Vietnam, Hollywood made it clear to its audiences that citizens were required to sacrifice their ideas, ideals, and even their very lives without reservation for the good of the country called America. Providing the public with models who experience many of the concerns Americans might have about going to war or becoming committed to a war, the film industry dramatized their conflicts and glorified their resolutions.

In recent years, the Vietnam War did not permit Hollywood to exploit the old values—actually, very few films about this war were made during America's active involvement in the conflict. Only afterwards, when disillusionment about the war meant guaranteed box office, did the motion picture industry allow the inversions of the convention we continue to witness today.

Does this inversion mean the end of the line for this time-honored convention? Will slackers, selfish men, and cowards ever again have the opportunity to redeem themselves for the sake of dramatic resolution and audience edification? Count on it. Along with death and taxes, there are few realities human beings can rely on more than the likelihood of future conflicts. Even encounters such as the invasion of Grenada permit filmmakers to exploit the old values, as we witnessed in *Heartbreak Ridge* (1986). So, the next time America awakens the dogs of war (or perhaps before), Hollywood will be ready: Producers will dust off this old convention, cast the latest teen heartthrob in the lead, and once again demonstrate to American audiences how redemption can be earned through character conversion.

Filmography

1940	*The Fighting 69th*	Dir. William Keighley
1941	*International Squadron*	Dir. Lothar Mendes
1941	*Sergeant York*	Dir. Howard Hawks
1941	*A Yank in the RAF*	Dir. Henry King
1942	*Captains of The Clouds*	Dir. Michael Curtiz
1942	*Casablanca*	Dir. Michael Curtiz
1942	*Eagle Squadron*	Dir. Arthur Lubin
1942	*The Flying Tigers*	Dir. David Miller
1942	*Wake Island*	Dir. John Farrow
1943	*Air Force*	Dir. Howard Hawks
1943	*Bataan*	Dir. Tay Garnett
1943	*Bombardier!*	Dir. Richard Wallace
1943	*China*	Dir. John Farrow
1943	*China Girl*	Dir. Henry Hathaway
1943	*Corvette K-225*	Dir. Richard Rosson
1943	*Crash Dive*	Dir. Archie Mayo
1943	*Cry Havoc*	Dir. Richard Thorpe
1943	*The Edge of Darkness*	Dir. Lewis Milestone
1943	*Guadalcanal Diary*	Dir. Lewis Seiler
1943	*Hitler: Dead or Alive*	Dir. Nick Grinde

1943	*The Immortal Sergeant*	Dir. John Stahl
1943	*Sahara*	Dir. Zoltan Korda
1943	*Tarzan Triumphs*	Dir. William Thiele
1943	*This Land is Mine*	Dir. John Stahl
1944	*The Fighting Seabees*	Dir. Edward Ludwig
1944	*Lifeboat*	Dir. Alfred Hitchcock
1944	*The Purple Heart*	Dir. Lewis Milestone
1945	*Back to Bataan*	Dir. Edward Dmytryk
1945	*Objective Burma*	Dir. Raoul Walsh
1945	*They Were Expendable*	Dir. John Ford
1948	*Fighter Squadron*	Dir. Raoul Walsh
1949	*Battleground*	Dir. William Wellman
1949	*Sands of Iwo Jima*	Dir. Allan Dwan
1949	*Twelve O'Clock High*	Dir. Leon Shamroy
1951	*Flying Lethernecks*	Dir. Nicholas Ray
1959	*Pork Chop Hill*	Dir. Lewis Milestone
1961	*The Guns of Navarone*	Dir. J. Lee Thompson
1965	*The Heroes of Telemark*	Dir. Anthony Mann
1967	*Beach Red*	Dir. Cornel Wilde
1968	*The Green Berets*	Dir. John Wayne
1971	*Raid on Rommel*	Dir. Henry Hathaway
1978	*Go Tell The Spartans*	Dir. Ted Post
1979	*Apocalypse Now*	Dir. Francis Ford Coppola
1982	*An Officer and a Gentleman*	Dir. Taylor Hackford
1986	*Hanover Street*	Dir. Peter Hyams
1986	*Heartbreak Ridge*	Dir. Clint Eastwood
1986	*Platoon*	Dir. Oliver Stone
1987	*Hamburger Hill*	Dir. John Irvin
1989	*Born on The Fourth of July*	Dir. Oliver Stone

"Triumph of the Underdog" in Baseball Films

Linda K. Fuller

Even though the "Rocky" movie series is currently most identified with the "triumph of the underdog" plot convention, this sports-related theme predates itself in a combination of two of America's favorite pastimes: baseball and films. Universally, we all can relate to the battle of overcoming odds, and it is within our natures to be bolstered and buoyed by those who master them.

This article aims to discuss the triumph of the underdog in a variety of baseball film constructions, demonstrating what a pervasive theme it has been in motion picture history. First, lest you think the term "baseball movie" is an oxymoron, that topic needs some discussion. Film critic Andrew Sarris, in the early part of this decade, declared the sports film genre to be defunct: "Sports are now. Movies are then. Sports are news. Movies are fables. Despite the hectoring homilies of sports commentators, what is important in sports is not the moral, but the outcome. Someone wins; someone loses" (1980, p.50). More recently, novelist and critic Wilfred Sheed (1989) answered his own question, "Why Can't the Movies Play Ball?" by blaming the medium for not transposing the true subtlety of the game onto the big screen. Baseball writer Roger Angell notes, "Baseball movies make baseball fans feel good for the wrong reasons...we smile unpleasantly in the dark, smug in the knowledge that our sport and its practitioners are beyond imitation" (1989, p.41). And most recently, Kelly Garrett has written: "The general rule is that baseball movies are mostly about movies and only ineptly about baseball. So over the years they've tended to feed off each other, developing a litany of obligatory clichés: newspapers with huge headlines that twirl at you, the weasels from the press, the ubiquitous play-by-play man whose commentary keeps you up on the sub-plots, marching music over every shot of pre-game warm-ups, and lots of slides into third base" (1990, p.35).

Yet, the latter part of the 1980s has brought the North American public a spate of baseball books and baseball films (Fuller, 1990), and it can be argued that our continuing relationship with two of our favorite spectator/ entertainment activities is growing stronger than ever. Two great democratic institutions, baseball and films are uniquely all-American (Cohen, 1974; Guttman, 1978; Bergan, 1982; Boswell, 1982; Durso, 1986; Halberstam, 1989; Giamatti, 1989). They allow us to play out childhood fantasies, teach us to distinguish between the heroes and the losers, and, reciprocally, reflect some of our most basic cares and concerns.

A persistent theme in sports films, along with the fall (and sometimes resurrection) of the mighty and the "sporting event as pretext" (Zucker and Babich, 1987) has been the "triumph of the underdog." Webster's dictionary defines "underdog" as "a person or group that is losing, as in a contest or struggle; one that is handicapped or underprivileged, as in the struggle of life."

Hollywood is distinctly suited to juxtaposing underdogs in a range of plot conventions that are clearly demonstrated in baseball films. The "triumph of the underdog" theme in baseball movies is traced here via dramatic, comedic, biographical, and stereotypical portrayals.

"Triumph of the Underdog" via Dramatic Portrayal

Baseball is mostly lowlights, but baseball movies must suggest otherwise, often by edited, closeup snatches of bats meeting balls, gloves gobbling up grounders, spiked feet toeing a base, and so on, or by the opposite distortion—the super-slow-motion shot of the batter waiting and tensing as the ball spins in from the mound with all stitches showing, and then, after a flurry of intercut batter movements and grimaces, operatically soars up and away and, most of the time, into the bleachers. (Angell, 1989, p.41)

The baseball film genre is clearly wrenching and enticing in dramatic presentations, not the least in its portrayal of the triumph of the underdog. As early as 1915 came the Silent Era melodramatics of *Right Off the Bat*, in which major leaguer Mike Donlin rescues the damsel in distress, escapes being kidnapped by an evil gambler, and wins the Big Game in the nick of time. 1917s *Pinch Hitter* (remade in 1923) also was an early underdog prototype, focusing on a shy boy at a small college who becomes the butt of pranks and jokes, taken onto the baseball team by the coach as mascot; by chance, one time when the team runs out of players the kid hits the game-winning homer and becomes the campus hero. *Trifling With Honor* (1923) features ex-con "The Gas-Pipe Kid" who, despite blackmailers who threaten to reveal his past, becomes a baseball star. 1926 brought *The New Klondike* (the underdog in both baseball and business overcomes the odds) and *Out of the West* (a baseball western that triumphs over both physical and moral barriers), followed in 1927 with *Bush Leager* (the hero suffers from stage fright, but knocks in the winning homer) and 1928s *Warming Up*, about a small-town guy who goes big time by winning both the World Series and the girlfriend of the team's star. The moral theme re-appears in *It Happened in Flatbush* (1942), a classic wartime film. *Roogie's Bump* (1954) has the underdog helped by a baseball star ghost, a not infrequent plot device in baseball films.

Always good box office draws, there are a number of movies for and/ or about children including the baseball plot of the triumphing underdog: 1949s *The Kid From Cleveland*, in which a straying teenager who loves baseball is persuaded by Bill Veecks's Indians team to go straight. *The Kid From Left Field* (1953) features Dan Dailey as a has-been ball park peanut vendor who passes on shrewd coaching tips to the team through his nine-year-old batboy son, who eventually is asked to become its manager—then admits who's been responsible all along for the good advice.

Max Dugan Returns (1983), featuring an all-star cast including Marsha Mason, Jason Robards, Donald Sutherland, and Matthew Broderick, is about a wealthy grandfather who wants to help his grandson get beyond his perennial baseball team clutch; needless to say, the kid dramatically smacks a homer in the Big Game.

Bernard Malamud's *The Natural* (1984) deserves special mention here as a baseball film dramatization. Angell (1989, p.49) describes the magical-mystical story as weaving together "the legends of baseball and the thick, misty tangle of Arthurian fable—chivalry and the single combat, blood and betrayal and loss." Robert Redford stars as Roy Hobbs, a talented but naive farmboy who learns the hard way what can happen to superheros from the sticks. For film critic Roger Ebert (1987), "the message is: baseball is purely and simply a matter of divine intervention."

Besides baseball biographies, which will be mentioned later, other baseball dramas focus on individual growth. Of recent note are: *Bang the Drum Slowly* (1973), about a fictional catcher, a born loser, who is dying from Hodgkin's disease but who, nonetheless, has a tremendous influence on his fellow teammates; *Bull Durham* (1988), an aging baseball player whose life has been a failure, whose "only chance for immortality could come with the minor league home run record" (Mathieson, 1989, p.3) who pulls off the critical homer at the critical time; and *Field of Dreams* (1989), a Capraesque story about a struggling Iowa farmer who compromises it all after hearing a Voice that instructs him to build a ballfield in the middle of his corn field—an event that leads to an unravelling of a chain of wondrous events.

In both fiction and reality, there have been films dealing with the notion of *baseball players helping underdogs triumph*, such as 1921s *As the World Rolls On*, in which black boxing great Jack Johnson rescues a young man from a gang, teaches him to bat and play baseball, and eventually helps him win the bully's girl. Also, the aforementioned *Bang the Drum Slowly* (1973) doubles as a morality play about the Golden Rule and buddy-buddy teamsmanship.

"Triumph of the Underdog" via Comedic Portrayals

Probably the easiest way to recognize the underdog is through humor. Typically, these films show us a perennial loser who becomes the town or team hero through some kind of crazy circumstances. We're laughing the whole time in Buster Keaton's 1927 *College* (as Ronald, the school valedictorian who is a laughing stock when he tries out for the baseball team but who wins respect via a boating incident) and 1935s *One Run Elmer* (trying to win "the girl" via baseball prowess).

The comedian Joe E. Brown divided his loyalties between baseball and film, and even had a contract with Warner Brothers for support of his Joe E. Brown All-Stars, which included several pro-ball players. His 1932 *Firemen, Save My Child* portrays him as a dumb, peanut-chewing, hick fireman whose hobby is baseball, but who just happens to arrive at the ballpark in time to win the World Series. *It Happens Every Spring* (1949) stars Ray Milland as a college professor who is trying to invent a bug repellent for trees and inadvertently comes up with a wood repellent that propels him into becoming a pitching star for the St. Louis Cardinals. The movie's unique comic device of seeing a batter wildly swinging at a ball that greatly evades it was a later favorite by the Disney studios.

There is even a *cartoon* dealing with the triumph of the underdog motif: 1936s *Boulevardier From the Bronx*, a Merry Melodies animation with an all-bird cast of good guys beating the city slicker baseball team.

Zapped! (1982) recalls the comedic character of *It Happens Every Spring* when high-schooler scientific whiz kid Scott Baio, who's a flop for the baseball team, develops telekinetic powers that help him alter the path of baseballs.

The underdog(s) in plural form, as a team, is yet another familiar comedic plot convention in baseball films. 1956's *Great American Pastime* (community outcast Tom Ewell as a Little League coach to an inept crew leads them to eventual victory) was a precursor to the *Bad News Bears* series (1976, 1977, and 1978). The original screenplay to the box-office successes of the Bears featured Walter Matthau as the groaning manager of the hapless Little Leaguers: "It is made up of neighborhood misfits, rejects from other teams. The team includes a huge fat boy, forever munching chocolate bars, a couple of Mexicans who speak no English, a juvenile delinquent who does Hank Aaron impressions, a Jewish boy, a near-sighted pitcher and a 12-year-old retired pitcher named Amanda Whurlizer (Tatum O'Neal)." (Bergan, 1982, p.65). But the incredible twist to this story is that it goes for victory not in score but in character development. Following the success and the sequels, the overall theme was later imitated again in 1978's *Here Come the Tigers* and several other sports films, including even a Korean version.

Miracles help the underdog team in 1951's *Angels in the Outfield* when loud-mouthed, blasphemous Pittsburgh Pirates manager Guffy McGovern (Paul Douglas) mends his ways following the advice of a celestial messenger. *Major League* (1989), a baseball film comedy starring Tom Berenger, Charlie Sheen, and Corbin Bernsen, centered on a Cleveland Indians team of misfits that needed a miracle. Its new owner wanted to have it be the worst possible so that she could break a lease and move the team to Miami; headed for oblivion, the underdogs have nothing to lose, so they end up staging an exultant, victorious rally.

"Triumph of the Underdog" via Biographic Portrayals

Probably nothing more befits the art-imitating-life phenomenon for the "triumph of the underdog" theme in baseball films than true life stories about some of its players.

With the success of 1942's *Pride of the Yankees*, the Lou Gehrig Story in which the superstar is made human and, thus, someone with whom we could identify, the genre was born. Angell (1989, p.47) has a theory that, "A good many senior baseball people—coaches and manager and writers, and front-office people in particular" never got over this movie, that it became "an all-purpose valentine to filial duty, faithful marriage, uncomplaining loyalty to the boss, the rewards of athletic persistence, and the efficacy of good deeds for shut ins."

This popular thematic convention of revealing "truths" behind our national heroes lead to *The Babe Ruth Story* in 1948, focusing on William Bendix in a positive light as "The Sultan of Swat" in his unsurpassed climb from his days at a boys school and Baltimore bars to his last days dying of throat cancer.

The next year brought James Stewart, June Allyson, Frank Morgan, and Agnes Moorehead in Sam Wood's *The Stratton Story* (1949), the real-life story of White Sox pitcher Monty Stratton's dramatic comeback to baseball after his leg was amputated. The Academy-award winning story was overseen by Stratton himself acting as technical adviser.

Playing himself in *The Jackie Robinson Story* (1950), the first Black in the major leagues traces his odds of poverty and race into a turning point of jeers and cheers.

1952 brought another bio-pic in *Pride of St. Louis*, Dan Dailey playing Dizzy Dean's rise from his Ozark hillbilly days to being recognized for both his unique sportscasting and pitching abilities.

Ronald Reagan and Doris Day teamed up with Frank Lovejoy in 1952s *The Winning Team*, about Hall of Fame pitcher Grover Cleveland Alexander's life from being a Nebraskan telephone lineman to a rapid rise to stardom that becomes marred by epileptic seizures; Mrs. Grover Cleveland Alexander worked has Technical Advisor to the film, so this really becomes as much a story of her power as his struggle to overcome odds.

Another noteworthy baseball film biography is *Fear Strikes Out* (1957), featuring Anthony Perkins' performance of Red Sox outfielder Jimmy Piersall's nervous collapse due to pressures from his father, as played by Karl Malden. Baseball and psychiatry team up: "In effect, Piersall suffered from what has been called the Laius complex. Laius, the father of Oedipus, tried to kill his son at birth, but the boy grew up and killed his father instead....The fear of failure is so strong that the strain of the past years takes its toll." (Bergan, 1982, p.63). After the breakdown, Piersall manages to not only come back, but also have a reconciliation with his father.

"Triumph of the Underdog" vs. Stereotypic Portrayals

Representative of more universal societal concerns, the "triumph of the underdog" theme in baseball films is also evident in breaking ethnic and gender barriers.

The Jackie Robinson Story (1950) might surprise today's young baseball/movie fans to know that Blacks were barred from the game until 1947, when Jackie Robinson became the first player to cross the closed barriers of color. His underdog struggle against both overt and covert racism make for a poignant picture: "He finally silences the critics by his skills as a hitter, fielder and base runner. A non-smoker, non-drinker, Robinson was a man of extraordinary moral stamina who, by keeping his cool and playing the white man's game, opened up the sport for players like Willie Mays." (Bergan, 1982, p. 61).

Nearly a quarter-century later came *Bingo Long Travelling All-Stars and Motor Kings* (1976), starring Billy Dee Williams, James Earl Jones, and Richard Pryor as a team of Black barnstormers in 1939 who deal with prejudice by clowning around.

Women have typically appeared in baseball films, as in most sports films, as background supporters to their men and their teams. Stereotypical profiles of women range from Gwen Verdon's role as the Devil's temptress/handmaiden in aiding an underdog in *Damn Yankees* (1958) to Glenn Close's performance as Iris, the sweet, pure hometown girl in *The Natural*, "appearing in the stands with a heavenly halo of light around her head." (Angell, 1989, p.50).

Gender barriers of a sort were broken down with 1979's *Squeeze Play!*, the first feature-length film to deal with women's baseball in a half-century (*Girls Can Play* of 1937 was a low-budget, low-box office mystery/comedy); although it was billed as a "screwball sex comedy," it presents an interesting battle of the sexes. *Blue skies Again* (1983) is also worth mentioning, as it shows Robyn Barto as a women softball player trying to crack the big leagues.

Clearly, the plot convention theme of the "triumph of the underdog" in baseball films, seen in its many perspectives—dramatic, comedic, biographic, and breaking sexist and racist barriers—mirrors our continuing search for heroes via our national sport.

Works Cited

Angell, Roger. "No, but I saw the game," *New Yorker* (July 31, 1989), pp. 41-56.

Bergan, Ronald. *Sports in the Movies*. New York: Proteus Books, 1982.

Boswell, Thomas. *How Life Imitates The World Series*. Garden City, NY: Doubleday and Co., Inc., 1982.

Cohen, Marvin. *Baseball the Beautiful: Decoding the Diamond*. NY: Link Books, 1974.

Druso, Joseph. *Baseball and the American Dream*. St. Louis: The Sporting News, 1986.

Fuller, Linda K. "The Baseball Movie Genre: At Bat, or Struck Out?" *Play and Culture* 3 (February 1990): 64-74.

Garrett, Kelly. "Baseball Goes to the Movies," *Sport* (March, 1990): 35-37.

Giamatti, A. Bartlett. "The Story of Baseball: You Can Go Home Again." *New York Times* (April 2, 1989): S10.

Guttman, Allen. *From Ritual to Record: The Nature of Modern Sports*. New York: Columbia University Press, 1978.

Halberstam, David. *Summer of '49*. New York: William Morrow, 1989.

Mathiesen, James A., *"Bull Durham*: The Gospel According to Annie and Crash," paper presented at the Popular Culture Association annual meeting, St. Louis, MO (April, 1989).

Roger Ebert's Movie Home Companion. Kansas City, MO: Andrews, McMeel and Parker, 1987.

Sarris, Andrew, "Why Can't the Movies Play Ball?" *New York Times* (May 14, 1989), 2:1.

Zucker, Harvey Marc and Lawrence J. Babich. *Sports Films: A Complete Reference*. Jefferson, NC: McFarland & Company, Inc., Publishers, 1987.

Filmography

1915	*Right Off The Bat*	Donlin Productions
1917	*Pinch Hitter*	Dir. Victor L. Schlesinger
1921	*As The World Rolls On*	Camera: W.A. Anglauer.
1923	*Trifling With Honor*	Dir. Harry A. Pollard
1926	*The New Klondike*	Dir. Lewis Milestone
1927	*Out Of The West*	Dir. Robert DeLacy
1927	*Bush Leaguer*	Dir. Howard Bretherton
1927	*College*	Dir. James W. Horne
1928	*Warming Up*	Dir. Fred Newmeyer
1932	*Fireman, Save My Child*	Dir. Lloyd Bacon
1935	*One Run Elmer*	Dir. Charles Lamont
1936	*Boulevardier From The Bronx*	Supervisor. I. Freleng
1937	*Girls Can Play*	Dir. Lambert Hillyer
1942	*It Happended In Flatbush*	Dir. Ray McCarey
1942	*Pride of The Yankees*	Dir. Sam Wood
1947	*Babe Ruth Story*	Dir. Roy Del Ruth
1949	*It Happens Every Spring*	Dir. Lloyd Bacon
1949	*Kid From Cleveland*	Dir. Herbert Kline
1949	*The Stratton Story*	Dir. Sam Wood
1950	*The Jackie Robinson Story*	Dir. Alfred Green
1951	*Angels in The Outfield*	Dir. Clarence Brown
1952	*Pride of St. Louis*	Dir. Harmon Jones

1952	*The Winning Team*	Dir. Lewis Seller
1953	*Kid From Left Field*	Dir. Harmon Jones
1954	*Roogie's Bump*	Dir. Harold Young
1956	*Great American Pastime*	Dir. Herman Hoffman
1957	*Fear Strikes Out*	Dir. Robert Mulligan
1958	*Damn Yankees*	Dirs. George Abbott
		Stanley Donen
1973	*Band The Drum Slowly*	Dir. John Hancock
1976	*Bad News Bears*	Dir. Michael Ritchie
1976	*Bingo Long Travelling*	
	All-Stars and Motor Kings	Dir. John Badham
1977	*Bad News Bears Go To Japan*	Dir. John Berry
1978	*Bad News Bears*	
	In Breaking Training	Dir. Micheal Pressman
1978	*Here Come the Tigers*	Dir. Sean Cunningham
1979	*Squeeze Play!*	Dir. Sammuel Weil
1982	*Zapped!*	Dir. Robert J. Rosenthal
1983	*Max Dugan Returns*	Dir. Herbert Ross
1983	*Blue Skies Again*	Dir. Richard Michaels
1984	*The Natural*	Dir. Barry Levinson
1988	*Bull Durham*	Dir. Ron Shelton
1989	*Field of Dreams*	Dir. Phil Alden Robinson
1989	*Major League*	Dir. David S. Ward

Lively Spirits and Other Things
That Go "Bump" in the Movies:
The Supernatural Sit-Com and Plot
Conventions of the Ghost Comedy

Gary Hoppenstand

A recent television Diet Coke commercial has comedian Peter Cook playing a realtor and showing a house to a young, attractive couple. When asked about the place being haunted, Peter Cook dismisses the remark with a laugh. Suddenly, a ghost-like Madeline Kahn appears holding a can of Diet Coke. She forces the beverage to do supernatural tricks. She then floats up the stairs (past Peter Cook and his surprised clients) while yodeling an ethereal version of the diet soft drink jingle. As she attempts to disappear through a door with the can of Diet Coke in hand, she makes it but the can doesn't. Madeline Kahn opens the door, offers a surprised expression, utters "ooopps," grabs the can and shuts the door. The jingle concludes: "Just for the taste of it...Diet Coke." The above advertisement scenario has become part of American popular culture by virtue of its extensive play on television, but the commercial itself (a compact narrative teleplay that compresses a story into a brief time slot, as most effective commercials do) is one of the more recent illustrations of another popular culture tradition, a formula that can readily be found in television or the movies: the Supernatural Sit-Com.

At a casual glance, it would seem apparent that comedy and the supernatural tale do not mix well. One deals with a celebration of love, with marriage, with the wonderful fallibility of the human condition—and with people living life to the fullest. The other deals with evil, with destruction, with the inevitable mutability of the human condition—and with death. Yet, the Supernatural Sit-Com unites the disparate supernatural tale and comedy, in turn producing some of the most commercially successful films and television shows, including, for example, the three *Topper* movies from the late 1930s and early 1940s, *Ghostbusters* (1984) and its recent sequel *Ghostbusters II* (1989), *Beetlejuice* (1988), and the *Bewitched* television series from the 1960s. This essay will examine the plot conventions of the Ghost Comedy, which is one of the four formulaic divisions of the Supernatural Sit-Com, and consequently outline a possible cultural application of these conventions. But before specifically addressing the representative selections of the Ghost Comedy in American popular film, a definition of the Supernatural Sit-Com—and its four sub-formulas—is in order.

Romantic comedy, specifically the "screwball comedy," is a major component of what constitutes the Supernatural Sit-Com. In his book, *Romantic Comedy: From Lubitsch to Sturges* (1987), James Harvey characterizes the screwball comedy:

It [the romantic movie comedy] came to be widely known as 'screwball'—originally a publicist's term—around 1936, when Gregory La Cava's *My Man Godfrey*, with Carole Lombard's dizzy rampaging heroine, seemed to compel the description. But screwball comedy was a wider category than the term itself suggests: it named a style associated less with scattiness or derangement than with a paradoxical kind of liberation, with romantic exaltation of a very down-to-earth kind. (xi)

Wes D. Gehring, in his study *Screwball Comedy: A Genre of Madcap Romance* (1986), further suggests that the development of the screwball comedy can be seen in "the structural change of American humor in the 1920s and the 1930s" (37). He identifies five elements of the screwball comedy, including "abundant leisure time, childlike nature, urban life, apolitical outlook, and basic frustration (especially in relationships with women)" (Gehring 37). The Supernatural Sit-Com evolved in popular American literature and film during the 1920s and 1930s, and most of Gehring's five characteristics of the screwball comedy can also be found in the Supernatural Sit-Com.

Yet the situation comedy component of the Supernatural Sit-Com differs greatly from what's to be found in its screwball origins. Situation comedy thrives on aggressive, physical humor that can range in sophistication from the "pie in the face" gag to the sexually suggestive antics of the "bedroom romp." We find humor in another's misfortune, whether that misfortune is physical or emotional. The Supernatural Sit-Com offers an interesting twist to the execution (excuse the pun) or utilization of humor. In the screwball comedy, people struggle against social mores, conservative institutions or other people's limiting views of what constitutes proper social behavior. In the Supernatural Sit-Com, the conflict is between normalcy and aberration, between the mundane and the bizarre, between mortal man and supernatural force.

The Supernatural Sit-Com is unique among the various types of comedy in its reliance on typical horror formula motifs, like ghosts, vampires and demons. The supernatural tale can be defined as that story where humanity is pitted against the unknown in a great spiritual conflict—with the unknown representing supernatural creatures or events—and loses (Cawelti 47-49). However, in the Supernatural Sit-Com the unknown does not triumph over humanity. It instead educates humanity in the errors of its ways—showing that love can be found, that life is good—and the unknown thus molds itself to domestic conformity and romantic bliss. The supernatural contributes to the overall well-being of the story's characters rather than to their destruction. The Supernatural Sit-Com, then, is controlled by comedy. Horror is merely employed as a device for generating humorous situations.

John G. Cawelti in his study of popular formulas, *Adventure, Mystery, and Romance* (1976), offers a revealing insight from his own childhood that highlights the paradoxical function of the humorous horror story:

> I remember still the terror I experienced as a child when I saw the zombie lurch across the screen in Bob Hope's movie *The Ghost Breakers*. Ironically, this was a totally irrelevant response, since the portrayal was full of comic exaggeration, but I was too unfamiliar with this sort of formula to know that, and I was frightened for months. (48)

Of course what Cawelti is relating here is the young child's response to the primitive level cinematic scare of *The Ghost Breakers* (1940). In the Supernatural Sit-Com, the adult subordinates the SCARE to the situation comedy context. Horror is a much more instinctual emotion than humor, perhaps because it derives from our archetypal subconscious where being frightened of the dark and of the creatures that roam in the dark helped to insure our species' survival. Humor—even the crudest forms of humor, like slapstick—is a product of civilization having met the basic requirements of survival, of civilization providing a sense of security at a societal level. Security about life permits us to laugh *at* life. It's rather difficult to enjoy humor when one is being threatened with imminent extinction.

Cawelti's experience reminds me of the time I first saw the movie *Beetlejuice* at the theatre. A young child in the audience, who became frightened after witnessing Michael Keaton's snake monster transformation, cried and wailed throughout the remainder of the film. The older members of that audience understood the crucial relationship between the horrible special effects of Michael Keaton's snake monster and the overall comedy frame of the movie itself. Behind those beady snake-eyes and needle-sharp snake teeth there is the comedic Michael Keaton, portraying the horny, pot-bellied, goober-spitting, ghost clown, Betelgeuse. And if the ghost clown briefly terrifies us, we know that in the comedy story, everything will turn out right; the clown remains the clown. The horror that affects the child in all of us is thus diminished in the movie. Death is ridiculed, and life happily triumphs. Print, film, and television have handled this horror/comedy scenario in several different ways.

Indeed, the Supernatural Sit-Com can be divided into five areas, and they are 1) the Transformation Comedy, 2) the Monster Comedy, 3) the Mad Scientist/Wacky Gadget Comedy, 4) the Pseudo-Supernatural Comedy, and 5) the Ghost Comedy. The Transformation Comedy often has its characters involved in the typical "boy-meets-girl" story, with one crucial difference: one of the partners is someone who undergoes a supernatural physical (or moral) transformation. The romantic couple must then overcome this obstacle, with humorous results, to achieve mutual happiness. Transformation Comedies include such movies as *Splash* (1984), *Mannequin* (1987), and *Date With an Angel* (1987). Another type of Transformation Comedy pits a mortal protagonist against some type of supernatural force that subsequently enacts in the protagonist a beneficial spiritual transformation. *It's a Wonderful Life* (1946) is perhaps the best example of this type of story. The Monster Comedy pokes fun at the traditional monster archetypes that at one time were frightening images, creatures like the vampire and the werewolf. Monster movies such as *Dracula* (1931) and *Frankenstein* (1931) lost a great deal of their "spookiness" after World War II (what, after all, could compete with the real "horrors" of that event?), and thus became situation comedy material. Abbott and Costello were among the first to discover the entertainment value of the Monster Comedy in the late 1940s and early 1950s. *Young Frankenstein* (1974), *Love at First Bite* (1979), and *Teen Wolf* (1985) are recent examples of the Monster Comedy that effectively parody, in order, Frankenstein, Dracula, and the Wolf Man. The Mad Scientist/Wacky Gadget Comedy finds situational humor in the mad scientist character from the 1930s horror films, and in the wacky Edison-like inventor figure popularized by the dime novels. Movies like *Real Genius* (1985), *Weird Science* (1985), *My Science Project* (1985), and *Back to the Future* (1985) burlesque America's fascination with technology (as represented by the gadget or invention) and with the twentieth-century shaman of technology: the inventor/scientist. The Pseudo-Supernatural Comedy is a variant of the other Supernatural Sit-Coms where an event develops in the story that appears to be of a threatening, other-worldly nature, but which is instead something that has a rational explanation (e.g. crooks pretending to be ghosts in a haunted house in order to scare potential busybodies away from their hideout). The audience's realization that what appears to be supernatural is in actuality not supernatural at all contributes to the situational humor of the story. Several examples of the Pseudo-Supernatural Comedy are *Hold That Ghost* (1941), *The Ghost and Mr. Chicken* (1966), and *The 'burbs* (1989).

In the fifth type of Supernatural Sit-Com, the Ghost Comedy, one generally sees four standard plot conventions, 1) the pre-death situation, 2) the after-death recognition, 3) the supernatural antics of the ghosts and 4) the re-birth resolution. Ghost Comedies are movies like *Topper* (1937) and *Topper Takes a Trip* (1939)—the third film in the series, *Topper Returns* (1941), is not so much a comedy as it is a mystery thriller—*Kiss Me Goodbye* (1982), *School Spirit* (1985), *Beetlejuice* (1988), and *High Spirits* (1988). *Ghostbusters* (1984) and *Scrooged* (1988) are not good examples of the Ghost Comedy, despite the fact that they are comedies that have ghostly characters in them. These movies are more accurately Transformation Comedies. Though the above films range in quality from the big-budget, special-effects box office hit to the cheaply made sexploitation teen comedy, they all possess the four basic plot conventions of the Ghost Comedy. Disregarding the level of quality or sophistication that these Ghost Comedies possess, they nonetheless illustrate our collective attempts to diminish our fear of death, and in fact present a kind of secularized version of life-after-death. *Topper*, *Beetlejuice*, and *Kiss Me Goodbye* will be used to examine more closely how these four plot conventions operate.

The father of the Ghost Comedy (and of all four types of the Supernatural Sit-Com) is the humorist, Thorne Smith. Smith was the first person to mix the didactic elements of Charles Dickens' seasonal allegory, *A Christmas Carol*, with the supernatural situation comedy of Oscar Wilde's "The Canterville Ghost," thus creating in his time an Americanized variant of P. G. Wodehouse—a variant comfortable in dealing with *both* off beat humorous characters and sexual themes...Wodehouse was very much the Victorian in his treatment of sex—resplendent with hedonistic (and all too mortal) gods and goddesses, impish ghosts, passionate witches, drunken leprechauns, and befuddled ambulatory skeletons. Interestingly, Smith liked to think of himself as a realist (Young and Smith 22-29). The blurbs on several of his dustjacket covers advertised him as the inventor of a new American mythology. Smith himself said in an interview with his friend Roland Young that:

For years I've been bored with the arty attitude so many people take to American folklore. I've been bored with all this self-conscious stuff about Paul Bunyan, Scotch ballads slightly done over for cowboy use, precious books about Kentucky mountaineers. That isn't the true American folklore. The true folklore isn't planned as such. It just grows, like some of our comic strips or like the *Three Little Pigs* in the movies or Amos and Andy on the radio. It expresses in the most ridiculous way the deep-seated instincts of the people, their hidden desperations, their craving for laughter and a free sort of beauty. Also, their badly controlled impatience with convention and smug hypocrisy. (13-14)

In actuality, Thorne Smith's perception of an evolving, organic social satire focuses on a single aspect of American society: the sexual relationship between men and women. Smith made a successful career writing about the "war of the sexes." His Supernatural Sit-Com novels—humorous fantasies like *Topper* (1926), *The Stray Lamb* (1929), *The Night Life of the Gods* (1931), *Turnabout* (1931), and *Rain in the Doorway* (1933)—present circumstances where sexually charged comedy underpins a basic interpersonal conflict between men and women. This conflict can involve unmarried lovers, but it is more outrageously rendered—and more bitingly satirical—when it involves a bored (and boring) married couple. Smith's work is solidly part of the Roaring Twenties flapper era, when American sexuality was dusting off its Victorian outer garment and reveling in newly perceived liberation. Even for its time, Smith's fiction was racy stuff, full of lusty suggestiveness and sexually explicit situations. In Smith's novel, *Topper*,

Cosmo Topper's (with Roland Young as Topper in the movie) marriage to his wife is described most critically. Mrs. Topper (in the film played by Billie Burke) is narrow-minded, possessive, stupid, silly, and, worst of all, nagging. Cosmo Topper's adventures with the flapper-esque ghosts, George and Marion Kerby (in the movie portrayed by Cary Grant and Constance Bennett), offered Smith ample material to lampoon conventional notions of American marital relationships. The Hal Roach Studio's motion picture version of *Topper* takes a less harsh view of the stolid American marriage, but it nonetheless retains much of Smith's intended satire.

In terms of the first plot convention of the Ghost Comedy, the pre-death situation, this convention usually begins the film's story by showing the viewer a male/female relationship. In the movie, *Topper*, the viewer is presented with two marriages. Mr. and Mrs. Topper's relationship is staid and conservative, even boring; George and Marion Kerby's relationship is vibrant, exciting, decadent. Even though the Toppers have wealth and good social standing within the community, the dullness and predictability of their marriage conspires to destroy it. Specifically, Cosmo Topper rankles at the regimen his wife, Henrietta, imposes upon him. When he is a few seconds late for breakfast, Mrs. Topper scolds her husband. Mr. Topper rhetorically wonders where they would be if he wanted to "battle a trout or some oatmeal" for breakfast instead of what is automatically served him by the butler. Henrietta tells Cosmo: "Don't be silly. I've taken great pains to arrange your diet properly. You need sulfur. The eggs have sulfur." The line of communication between husband and wife here only proceeds in one direction. Cosmo Topper is a captive of his marriage, living a life of stultifying routine. He is ready for a change, a change that will enrich his life and save his conjugal union.

The Kerbys on the other hand, though also wealthy like the Toppers, lead a totally different existence. Where the Toppers are conservative, the Kerbys are wild, at the beginning of the film madly hopping from one nightclub to the next in endless search of pleasure. Where the Toppers are controlled by the clock, by routine, the Kerbys pay no attention to the social restraints of time. The Kerbys mock their upcoming appointment with the bank trustees (and with Cosmo Topper, as a symbol of the bank). What the Toppers value, like doing things the "proper" way, the Kerbys don't. The Kerbys race with life in the fast lane, literally. They play so hard, they burn themselves up. Their very lack of caution does them in. The Kerbys consume life too quickly, the Toppers not quickly enough, and thus the stage is set for a social transformation for both sets of couples.

In *Beetlejuice*, the pre-death plot convention follows much the same pattern as in *Topper*. There are again two married couples in the movie, Adam and Barbara Maitland (portrayed in the film by Alec Baldwin and Geena Davis) and Charles and Delia Deetz (Jeffrey Jones and Catherine O'Hara). One couple has the ideal romantic relationship. As the movie begins, the Maitlands are spending their vacation at home. They embrace frequently, kiss often and passionately. They are kind and gentle. When Adam removes a spider from his scale model town, he treats it kindly. They are constructive people, exchanging presents, such as wallpaper, that will improve their house. Young and deeply in love, their only problem is that they have no children. The Maitlands are also plain, uncomplicated folk. He wears a black and white checkered flannel shirt, she a cotton print dress. Their interests are simple, things like their house and Adam's model of the town which he keeps in the attic.

Charles and Delia Deetz are *very* different from the Maitlands. They are a society couple more concerned with their own self-centered, bizarre problems than with each other. Theirs is a passionless marriage, and though they have a daughter, Lydia (Winona Ryder), they show her no real love. Delia fancies herself a sculptor and an artist. She is neither. Her friend, Otho (Glenn Shadix), is a homosexual interior decorator who masks good taste with a desire for destructive, pseudo-originality. Lydia, because of the negative influence of her neurotic parents, is unusual, maladapted, suicidal. She wears black and sports a lace veil over her chalk white face. This weird family moves into the Maitland's house after the Maitland's death and attempts to adapt to the small town New England lifestyle. They fail at this, transporting their decadent ideas with them from the city (destroying the wholesomeness of the Maitland's environment), imposing those ideas where they don't fit. They resist becoming part of a rural simplicity that they simply don't understand. Charles and Delia are outwardly destructive. Lydia is self-destructive.

In the pre-death situation, confused communication signals are exchanged between romantic partners. A potentially serious problem exists, something that prevents the completion of a goal (like sexual intercourse). Sometimes, this problem is the protagonist's basic desire to indulge in promiscuity. Sometimes it's the absence of a romantic partner. In *Topper*, the Kerbys need to attain a goal. They have to perform a "good deed" in order to enter heaven, and thus discover an existence that is not self-centered. The Toppers lack the ability to live life to the fullest. They require a renewed sense of what's vital in life. They have lost the most important thing in their marriage, the give-and-take of love. In *Beetlejuice*, the Maitlands, already involved in a loving relationship, lack children. They need a family to complete what is already good. Charles and Delia Deetz lack the ability to think or care about other people, including their daughter. They have to be taught the lesson that *other* people are important as well, that other people count. These couples lack one thing or another that is crucial to their relationship, something that requires supernatural intervention to help mend.

The second plot convention of the Ghost Comedy, the after-death recognition, occupies a fairly brief moment in the story as it sequentially follows the pre-death situation. Usually one or more of the central characters die tragically, then have to prove to themselves (or to others) that they are now "changed," that they have transformed (or better yet, metamorphosed) into a new state-of-being. What makes the after-death recognition convention provocative from a Judeo/Christian point-of-view is the secularized vision of death. After our unlucky protagonists die, for the most part they are not whisked to the Pearly Gates to meet their Maker. The rare exception to this, of course, is the Transformation Romance starring Warren Beatty and Julie Christie, *Heaven Can Wait* (1978), which is a remake of the earlier film, *Here Comes Mr. Jordan* (1941). In *Heaven Can Wait*, the viewer actually sees the existence of angels and understands that the presence of Heaven is very real and very powerful. Yet even in *Heaven Can Wait*, the angels (wonderfully portrayed by Buck Henry and James Mason) are secularized. Lacking their wings, they dress in mundane suit and tie.

George and Marion Kerby become the ghosts in *Topper*, killed in a car crash caused in large part by their own recklessness. They drive too fast when they should be more aware of the road's dangers. But of course, this is emblematic of how they lived, fast and dangerous. The implication in the film, though not overtly stated, is that they get what they deserve. After their flashy sports car slams into a tree, the characters slowly pick themselves up from where their bodies rest. As they rise from the ground, they appear transparent. The viewer understands that these people are now ghosts, even before the characters themselves do, and the after-death recognition convention is established. The Kerbys sit on a log, soon noticing that they can see through each other. Realizing at this point that they have died, they deliberate about why they aren't in Heaven, eventually coming to the conclusion that they haven't done any "good deeds." They then decide to do a good deed (with Cosmo Topper becoming the recipient of this spiritual goodwill).

Adam and Barbara Maitland in *Beetlejuice* also die tragically in an auto accident, this time ironically done in by a cute dog and a venerable New England covered bridge, both icons of a rural heritage. They return to their house not knowing how they got there. Just before they arrive, a fire magically enkindles in the fireplace, allowing the viewer to speculate that things are perhaps not all that "sweet" in the home-sweet-home, that something startling and supernatural has occurred. Adam and Barbara enter their home, dripping wet and framed in the front doorway by ghostly white light. As they wonder how the fire got started, they place their hands near the flames for warmth. Barbara's hand ignites, but she feels no pain. Adam tries to exit the house, but as he leaves the door, he lands on an other-worldly landscape (Saturn, we later discover) populated by sandworm monsters. Just as he is about to be squashed by a sandworm, Barbara yanks him back through the portal (a literal entrance to another dimension). She tells him he's been gone for hours, though from his perspective it's only been a couple of minutes. She brings Adam to the mirror over the fireplace to prove a point. She demonstrates that neither of them have a reflection (thus, sure cinematic proof of death: note the endless list of vampire horror films where such a test is made). Barbara finally directs Adam's attention to a book lying on a table, *The Handbook for the Newly Deceased*, the final, conclusive evidence.

The after-death recognition in both *Topper* and *Beetlejuice* functions as a catalyst for positive change. The Kerbys and the Maitlands each needed something to improve their emotional well-being. The irony is that it took death to initiate change for the better. For a movie audience, the message here is compelling. Death is not the end of things, and in fact, after dying (which is not directly observed in either film, and consequently is a "painless" transition for the characters and the audience), things don't really change at all. After dying, the Kerbys are still together, still impish, still "wild and crazy" people. The Maitlands are also still together, having eternity laid before them in which to enjoy each other's company. In the Ghost Comedy, there is no Hell nor any visualized Heaven. People aren't punished in the afterlife for their sins—the Kerbys certainly *should* be punished, even if it's a little bit. In the Ghost Comedy, the afterlife we see is as attractive as what most organized religions offer us, and is much better than the "hell fire and brimstone" images supported by many Christian evangelists. Such a life-after-death change is socially comforting because there is little change. The horror story frightens us by zeroing in on our fear of the *unknown*. In the Ghost Comedy, there is no unknown; though some elements of mortal life are missing, there's just more of the same of what we have now.

The supernatural antics of the newly inducted ghost protagonists give us the third plot convention. At this point in the Ghost Comedy, the viewer is treated to various acts of situational humor. In *Topper*, Cosmo Topper becomes the "straight man" for George's and Marion's well-intended help. Roland Young's Topper is a classic foil for the ghostly couple. He is deadpan, somewhat slow intellectually, and is a symbol of 1920s and 1930s American moral conservatism that is just begging for ridicule. The ghosts tease and torment people around Topper, and we understand Topper's frustration with each new supernatural situation, laughing both at him and at ourselves, at the Topper in our nature. The ghosts initiate a fist-fight on a city street. Topper is saddled with the results of the fight. He has to face the courts and the legal ramifications, thus encountering the cold, unfeeling nature of social consequence. The ghosts also place him in morally compromising situations, such as in a hotel room with a woman who is not his wife and in a lady's underwear garment shop. Topper subsequently witnesses firsthand the silliness of a restrictive morality. This type of story *is* comedy, however, so of course Topper is never really hurt. He actually benefits from these madcap experiences. He learns to become less uptight. He begins to let his metaphoric hair down.

Adam and Barbara Maitland in *Beetlejuice* undergo more of a learning process than do the Kerbys as they hone their ability to perform supernatural antics. When Charles and Delia Deetz move into the Maitlands' home (forcing themselves upon the trapped Maitlands who can't leave the place) the Maitlands are compelled to act to try and remove the obnoxious presence of their new tenants. They attempt the typical Halloween fright strategies, such as pulling their faces off in the closet or standing in a room without their heads, but these antics don't seem to work: the Deetzes just can't see them, unlike their daughter, Lydia, who soon becomes good friends with the Maitlands. Adam and Barbara later function as Lydia's surrogate parents. The Maitlands learn to be more inventive with their scare tactics through necessity, playing a calypso song gag on Charles, Delia, and their guests during one of their dinner parties. The trick backfires. The transplanted urbanites, who are decadent and thrilled by the grotesque, think the supernatural trick is a gas and want more. At the end of their patience, the Maitlands enlist the aid of a "bio-exorcist," the ghost Betelgeuse (which is spelled in the vernacular, "Beetlejuice"). Betelgeuse then begins his work and terrifies Charles and Delia with some frightening effects.

The supernatural antics plot convention serves to reaffirm the *humanness* (and the humanity) of both ghost and mortal. Even the nasty Betelgeuse is not an evil creature. He merely is a practical joker who gets carried away with himself at times. The ghost couples in each film are attempting to improve their current situations: the Kerbys are trying to do their good deed for Topper and the Maitlands are trying to restore the rural harmony of their home. The respective ambitions here are amazingly banal, and because of their banality, they are easily understandable and easily appreciated by the movie viewer. The situational comedy that results from this plot convention at a social level diminishes our inflated notions of ourselves— and our place in the universe—by reminding us of our own fallibility. The ghosts, like their mortal counterparts, are fallible, as are *all* supernatural creatures in the Supernatural Sit-Com. Even with the gift of great power, with the ability to control others and the physical environment, the ghosts think and do little things. They want to do a good deed or they want to make a happy home. By implication, it's the little things that count in our appreciation of life.

The final plot convention of the Ghost Comedy, the re-birth resolution, usually concludes the story with the characters' needs being met, with the ghost and mortal protagonists getting what they really desire to obtain true happiness. In *Topper*, the Kerbys enact their good deed for Cosmo by giving him a taste of the wild life and by soothing the wounds of his marriage with Mrs. Topper (though the wounds aren't yet completely healed; that requires one more film, *Topper Takes a Trip*, to do the job). The Kerbys and the Toppers all benefit from their mad, tempestuous encounter with one another. In *Beetlejuice*, the Maitlands smooth the Deetzes' rough social edges. As the movie ends, the Maitlands are busy restoring their house to its former simple beauty. Adam and Barbara have also gained a daughter in Lydia. Like normal parents, they ask Lydia how her grades are going and reward her for academic accomplishment. Lydia is healed as well. She no longer has a morbid fascination with death and dying. Lydia becomes a better adjusted, less alienated teenager by story's end. Each couple in *Beetlejuice* has profited by the supernatural contact with each other. The only unhappy character is Betelgeuse himself, who is condemned to sit in an afterlife waiting room with a shrunken head.

The re-birth resolution in the Ghost Comedy ultimately serves a similar end purpose as does religion. They both seek to give us comfort and security. Religion guarantees an afterlife which rewards those who are good. Religion also organizes our chaotic universe into a cognitive frame which we can understand. It gives us meaning in a world where meaning is sometimes difficult to find. The grand promise of religion is that its followers will be transformed, given access to a higher, holier state of being. The charismatic Christian notion of re-birth—as it concerns one's conversion into the particular faith—is apt. Such a conversion, it is argued by the evangelists, is not only good, it's crucial, bringing the believer an enlightened life. Evidence of the power of the charismatic Christian's message is strong. People sacrifice huge amounts of money and time for their promise of a transfigured afterlife. The re-birth resolution in the Ghost Comedy operates on the same social wavelength as does religion, though certainly less ostentatiously and with a great deal more subtlety. The promise and security are there though. Not only is everyone happy at the end of the Ghost Comedy, everyone is also better off. People have been transformed into a superior state-of-being. They have been re-born so to speak, given a newer and finer life, a happier life. And in death for the Kerbys and the Maitlands, there is a re-born life. The movie public responds favorably to the Ghost Comedy because it fulfills the basic requirement of the comedy. In the Shakespearean version of comedy, for example, a marriage at the end of the play reinforces an optimistic outlook in the minds of the playgoers. Marriage is symbolic of divine creation and procreation. Both *Topper* and *Beetlejuice* accomplish this emotional reinforcement. There's no marriage in either of these movies —a marriage between Lydia and Betelgeuse is acutally thwarted—but there *is* a strengthening of all existing marriages in each story, a renewal of future happiness and future sense of purpose.

A brief analysis of the film, *Kiss Me Goodbye* (1982), can help to further demonstrate the narrative relationship of the four plot conventions of the Ghost Comedy. In the pre-death situation of *Kiss Me Goodbye*, Kay Villano (played by Sally Field) returns after a three-year absence to her elegant New York brownstone house. She had previously lived at the address when she was married to the famous Jolly Villano (played by James Caan), a Broadway dancer. Jolly died tragically when he fell down the stairs at the house during a party. Distraught over the death of her husband, Kay has only recently decided to move back to the scene where she believed she was once involved in a happy relationship, only to subsequently confront her pent-up feelings about her late husband. She is also about to marry a museum Egyptologist, Rupert Baines (played by Jeff Bridges). Rupert is staid, an academic, someone who is quite opposite of the fun-loving Jolly. Their respective Christian names, Jolly and Rupert, should clue the viewer about their personalities. While Kay examines her townhouse, she tells her mother, Charlotte Banning (played by Claire Trevor), and her good friend the magazine editor, Emily (played by Dorothy Fielding), of her desire to move back to the house and of her reluctance to tell her fiancé of her decision. As is typical in the first plot convention of the Ghost Comedy, one of the protagonists (in this instance, Kay Villano) feels an emotional lack (Kay's regret over Jolly's untimely death), and thus experiences a moment in his or her life where self-destructive tendencies need to be curbed by a supernatural agent. This agent will facilitate a positive change in the protagonist's life.

In the after-death sequence, Kay Villano gradually becomes aware that her husband's presence haunts the brownstone. As she supervises the moving of furniture and the refurbishing of the house, she hears ghostly tapping noises, which is emblematic of Jolly's dancing, and thus of Jolly's spirit. At a climactic moment, Jolly makes his appearance, and informs Kay that he haunts the house because this is where he died. At first, as is typical in this particular plot convention, she disbelieves her senses and thinks she is going insane. But, she finally accepts the existence of Jolly's ghost, and this acceptance forces Kay to re-evaluate her feelings for Jolly and for Rupert. Jolly has a love of life. He is exciting, a free-spirit, someone who is always having a party. He's a flirt. He's childlike in his exuberance. Rupert, on the other hand, is comfortable, dependable. Where Jolly is childlike, Rupert is very much the adult. And where Jolly is a flirt, Rupert is rather a bore. Rupert can't dance (a point which is raised several times in the film), but he is quite capable of devoting his life to Kay. Jolly, we learn, cannot devote himself to any one woman. Furthermore, the viewer understands that Kay's sense of melancholy (and her subconscious reluctance to get involved in another marriage) is due to her husband's death. Even Kay's mother, Charlotte, expresses unhappiness because Rupert does not measure up to Jolly's style. Kay must try to face up to these feelings, these insecurities, so that she can let go of the past—representative of death—and embrace the future. Jolly's appearance abruptly forces the issue of Kay's self-evaluation, and initially she is presented a choice, either to live in the past (and live with death) or live for the future. This decision provides the basic dramatic conflict of *Kiss Me Goodbye*.

The film becomes playful with its characters, and with the audience, in the third plot convention of the Ghost Comedy, the supernatural antics sequence. A standard motif of this convention has the protagonist as the only person able to see the ghost, and this is humorously portrayed in the movie when Kay observes Jolly sitting in a chair that furniture movers are about to transport. She is unaware that other people cannot detect her dead husband's spirit, so she makes a fool of herself in front of the movers and her mother by inventing silly tales to explain why she doesn't want the chair removed. Nearly all the humor in *Kiss Me Goodbye* is verbal; it's not a special-effects film like *Topper* or *Beetlejuice*. For example, while at a diner, Rupert attempts to humor (and at the same time, belittle) Kay by pretending that he, too, can communicate with Jolly. He insists that a third place is set at the table and that the waitress serves a third meal for the ghost. The waitress and others in the diner are confused and befuddled with Rupert's seeming irrational actions, but the viewer laughs at Rupert because he/she knows what Rupert doesn't, that Jolly really *is* sitting at the table talking with Kay. But perhaps the most humorous sequence in the film occurs when Rupert is having sex in bed with Kay at the brownstone, and in walks Jolly. Kay then proceeds to both converse with Jolly and try to prove the ghost's existence to Rupert. Rupert is finally convinced of the ghost's presence later in the story when Jolly provides a bit of revealing information about one of Rupert's past amorous affairs. Rupert then tries to have one of his museum associates, an ex-priest named Kendall, exorcise Jolly's ghost. Rupert and the ex-priest arrive at the haunted brownstone at the same instance when Kay's and Rupert's wedding rehearsal is about to begin. There are several wonderfully funny moments at this point in the story when, for example, the ex-priest, thinking that Jolly's spirit is in Kay's dog (Claire's husband, locked in the attic while trying to repair the fuse box, is calling for help by saying: "Let me outta here" just at the moment when the ex-priest, Kendall, is within hearing), tries to perform the exorcism ceremony on the animal while chasing it about the house.

The supernatural antics of the ghost, then, nicely frame the re-birth resolution, the final plot convention. As the moment when Kay and Rupert are required to participate in the wedding rehearsal, Kay learns from Emily of Jolly's numerous past marital infidelities. She begins to reconsider her infatuation for Jolly, seeing him in a new light, a much less flattering light. Jolly is not perfect, Kay comes to understand. During his life, Jolly erred as most humans do, but after his death, Kay dismissed her suspicions and fashioned the memory of her husband in a fantasy-like image. When Jolly confirms Emily's statement, he remarks to Kay about his own fallibility. The viewer at this point understands that Jolly's quest on earth is to provide Kay with the knowledge that the dream she holds of her dead husband is simply that, a dream, and that to truly enjoy life once again she must break away from this troublesome fascination with the past. The supernatural protagonist's sacred mission to help the mortal protagonist is a recurrent theme in the Supernatural Comedy, as evidenced in the films, *Date with an Angel* and *It's a Wonderful Life*. Kay does dispense with Jolly's memory. She proclaims: "I want to get on with my life...There's no room in my life for you." And in her own manner she accomplishes what the ex-priest could not do: she exorcises the ghost from the house. After making this momentous decision to abandon Jolly, Kay hears Rupert telling the dog that he loves Kay (Rupert believes what Kendall has told him, that Jolly's spirit is in the animal). She realizes then that Rupert, despite his stuffiness and the fact that he can't dance, is sincere and good-hearted, that his love is real, not a fantasy. Kay and Rupert then determine to actually get married, and not merely participate in a rehearsal ceremony. They immediately tell the minister and the rehearsal guests of their decision. And despite one last minor diversion as Rupert trips down the same stairs where Jolly died, Rupert gets to his feet unhurt while Jolly blows a goodbye kiss to Kay. Both Kay and Rupert have become revitalized. Because of Jolly's kindly intrusion, Kay's hurtful memories have been mended and Rupert's conventional view of life has been given a resounding jolt, an emotional shake much like, no doubt, his physical tumble down the stairs, a shake forcing him to commit to passion.

Ultimately, moviegoers enjoy the Ghost Comedy, and the other three types of Supernatural Sit-Coms, because they are made aware that existence as we know it doesn't end after death. From Thorne Smith's literary invention of the Supernatural Sit-Com, as established in several of his popular novels published during the 1920s and 1930s, the seemingly unmixable blend of the supernatural and humor has worked out quite admirably over the years, not only in print and film, but in television as well. For example, from the television network replacement line-up this past spring of 1989, the half-hour comedy, *Newly Departed*, starring British comedian Eric Idle in a contemporary up date of *Topper*, drew some measure of positive critical response. The television comedy *Free Spirit* (a remake of the successful and long running *Bewitched* series) was part of the fall, 1989 network programming; and with the success in the summer of 1989 of *Ghostbusters II* at theaters nationally, and with the popularity of the animated *Slimer and the Real Ghostbusters* and *Beetlejuice* currently airing on Saturday morning television, the continued popularity of the Supernatural Sit-Com seems assured. No doubt for years to come lively spirits will haunt our popular culture.

Works Cited

Cawelti, John G. *Adventure, Mystery, and Romance*. Chicago: The University of Chicago Press, 1976.

Gehring, Wes D. *Screwball Comedy: A Genre of Madcap Romance.* New York: Greenwood Press, 1986.

Harvey, James. *Romantic Comedy in Hollywood: From Lubitsch to Sturges.* New York: Alfred A. Knopf, 1987.

Young, Roland, and Thorne Smith. *Thorne Smith: His Life and Times with a Note on His Books & a Complete Bibliography.* Garden City: Doubleday, 1934.

Selected Filmography

Transformation Comedy:

1940	*Turnabout*	Dir. Hal Roach
1941	*Here Comes Mr. Jordan*	Dir. Alexander Hall
1946	*It's a Wonderful Life*	Dir. Frank Capra
1948	*The Luck of the Irish*	Dir. Henry Koster
1964	*Goodbye Charlie*	Dir. Vincente Minnelli
1978	*Heaven Can Wait*	Dir. Warren Beatty
1984	*All of Me*	Dir. Carl Reiner
1984	*Ghostbusters*	Dir. Ivan Reitman
1984	*Splash*	Dir. Ron Howard
1987	*Date with an Angel*	Dir. Tom McLoughlin
1987	*Hello Again*	Dir. Frank Perry
1987	*Like Father, Like Son*	Dir. Rod Daniel
1987	*Mannequin*	Dir. Michael Gottlieb
1987	*My Demon Lover*	Dir. Charles Loventhal
1988	*Big*	Dir. Penny Marshall
1988	*My Stepmother Is an Alien*	Dir. Richard Benjamin
1988	*Scrooged*	Dir. Richard Donner
1989	*Ghostbusters II*	Dir. Ivan Reitman

Monster Comedy:

1942	*I Married a Witch*	Dir. René Clair
1948	*Abbott and Costello Meet Frankenstein*	Dir. Charles Barton
1951	*Abbott and Costello Meet the Invisible Man*	Dir. Charles Lamont
1953	*Abbott and Costello Meet Dr. Jekyll and Mr. Hyde*	Dir. Charles Lamont
1955	*Abbott and Costello Meet the Mummy*	Dir. Charles Lamont
1958	*Bell, Book and Candle*	Dir. Richard Quine
1966	*Munster, Go Home*	Dir. Earl Bellamy
1974	*Young Frankenstein*	Dir. Mel Brooks
1979	*Love at First Bite*	Dir. Stan Dragoti
1981	*The Munsters' Revenge*	Dir. Don Weis
1985	*Once Bitten*	Dir. Howard Storm
1985	*Teen Wolf*	Dir. Rod Daniel
1987	*The Monster Squad*	Dir. Fred Dekker
1987	*Teen Wolf Too*	Dir. Christopher Leitch
1987	*The Witches of Eastwick*	Dir. George Miller

| 1988 | *Elvira, Mistress of the Dark* | Dir. James Signorelli |
| 1989 | *Teen Witch* | Dir. Dorian Walker |

Mad Scientist/Wacky Gadget Comedy:

1941	*The Invisible Woman*	Dir. A. Edward Sutherland
1961	*The Absent Minded Professor*	Dir. Robert Stevenson
1963	*Son of Flubber*	Dir. Robert Stevenson
1985	*Back to the Future*	Dir. Robert Zemeckis
1985	*My Science Project*	Dir. Johnathan Beteul
1985	*Real Genius*	Dir. Martha Coolidge
1985	*Weird Science*	Dir. John Hughes
1986	*Short Circuit*	Dir. John Badham
1988	*Short Circuit 2*	Dir. Kenneth Johnson
1989	*Back to the Future II*	Dir. Robert Zemeckis
1989	*Bill & Ted's Excellent Adventure*	Dir. Stephen Herek

Pseudo-Supernatural Comedy:

1941	*Hold That Ghost*	Dir. Arthur Lubin
1943	*Ghosts on the Loose*	Dir. William Beaudine
1966	*The Ghost and Mr. Chicken*	Dir. Alan Rafkin
1985	*Transylvania 6-5000*	Dir. Rudy DeLuca
1989	*The 'burbs*	Dir. Joe Dante

Ghost Comedy:

1936	*The Ghost Goes West*	Dir. René Clair
1937	*Topper*	Dir. Norman Z. McLeod
1939	*Topper Takes a Trip*	Dir. Norman Z. McLeod
1946	*The Time of Their Lives*	Dir. Charles Barton
1982	*Kiss Me Goodbye*	Dir. Robert Mulligan
1985	*School Spirit*	Dir. Alan Holleb
1987	*Ghost Fever*	Dir. Alan Smithee
1988	*Beetlejuice*	Dir. Tim Burton
1988	*High Spirits*	Dir. Neil Jordan
1990	*Ghost Dad*	Dir. Sidney Poitier

Movie Images of Electoral Politics

John. H. Lenihan

Throughout the 1988 presidential race, political pundits reiterated the now-familiar lamentation that television has transformed campaign politics into a media event in which images override issues. Another source of campaign imagery, and one that predates television, is the motion picture. In election years, weekly newsreels provided soundbites of their own from campaign speeches. Audiences have also been treated from time to time with fictitious motion picture accounts of American electoral politics, and it is these that will be explored in this essay.

To the extent that Hollywood has always fashioned its formulaic entertainment (including the "problem film") to accommodate the concerns and attitudes of its prospective audiences, the motion picture constitutes an important historical source by which to document changing popular perceptions, including those related to American politics. Though receptive to the sentiment and vision of particular directors and/or screenwriters and constricted by a self-imposed code of censorship, the American film industry has been first and foremost a commercial enterprise whose success has depended largely on fashioning a formulaic product with which a broad audience can identify. As historical evidence, motion pictures can therefore reveal something of widely-held preconceptions about the nation's electoral politics.

Because of their potentially provocative nature, political themes have never been a continuous staple of the American film industry. And when films have dealt with electoral politics, they have seldom been very praiseworthy of politicians or the conduct of political campaigns by which the nation's leaders are selected. What has changed over time is the notion of who or what is at fault. From the Capra-esque "populist" melodramas that dominated the Depression era to the more despairing visions of political alienation and inertia in the 1960s and 1970s, film images of electoral politics have been overwhelmingly negative, but negative in different ways as filmmakers have adapted familiar plot conventions to fit America's changing political climate.

In keeping with the muckraking spirit of the early Progressive years, political corruption was a recurrent theme in the silent message films of the period, including some of the one-reelers of D.W. Griffith as well as his epic masterwork, *Birth of a Nation*. Problem films in general waned in the 1920s as Progressive reform gave way to Republican conservatism and the promise of unlimited prosperity for all. Then came the Crash and Depression and with it a sense in the early 1930s that America's politicians were at odds with the people they were supposed to represent.

One measure of public disenchantment with the political status quo was the vogue for political criticism in films of the early 1930s. In addition to the satirical jibes of the Marx Brothers in *Duck Soup* or the spate of gangster films that intimated a decaying legal order, no less than four political message films appeared in 1932 alone. Permeating *Washington Masquerade*, *Washington Merry-Go-Round*, *The Dark Horse*, and *The Phantom President* was the assumption that politics had become the province of corrupt machines and special interests.[1] Although three of these films conclude with a protagonist overcoming his defeatist attitude and exposing the corruption around him, such last-minute redemptive efforts do little to dispel the prevailing sense that political campaigns are charades of carefully orchestrated doubletalk.

Interestingly, the one film made prior to Roosevelt's election that features responsible leadership from an elected official does so in the context of a fantasy. In *Gabriel Over the White House* (released in early 1933), a Harding-like president is transformed by the intervention of the angel Gabriel into a wise, dynamic leader who defies his party and suspends Congressional powers in order to set right the nation's affairs—to include wiping out gangsters, establishing an army of the unemployed, and forcing other nations to repay America's loans made to them in World War I. Having saved the nation from its own political lethargy, the enlightened presidential dictator conveniently dies, leaving intact America's constitutional democracy. Both Walter Wanger, who produced the film, and William Randolph Hearst, whose Cosmopolitan Pictures provided the financing, were avid FDR supporters calling for strong executive action in a time of national crisis (Roffman and Purdy 71-2,74). As if to disavow the fascist implication of *Gabriel*, Wanger a year later produced *The President Vanishes* in which a more mild-mannered president employs rather unorthodox (though not dictatorial) measures to expose a fascist plot to take over the government.

Despite President Roosevelt's efforts to restore public confidence in government, political chicanery remained a viable topic in the films of Frank Capra and Preston Sturges' satirical portrait of electoral spoilsmen in *The Great McGinty* (1940). As the threat of fascism loomed over the international horizon in the latter half of the 1930s, several films associated political villainy with a dangerous power-seeker in addition to the usual array of greedy machine politicians. Such was the case of Frank Capra's *Mr. Smith Goes to Washington* (1939) and especially *Meet John Doe* (1941). William Randolph Hearst himself became the thinly-disguised target of Orson Welles' dissection of a power-hungry newspaper tycoon who makes an unsuccessful bid for political office in *Citizen Kane* (1941).

In contrast to Welles, who played havoc with narrative orthodoxy, Frank Capra employed familiar plot conventions (evident in such non-Capra films as *Washington Masquerade* and *Washington Merry-Go-Round*) to express what film historian Jeffrey Richards has called the "populist vision" of many depression films (222-53). From *American Madness* in 1932 to the Deeds-Smith-Doe trilogy at the end of the Depression, Capra invited audiences to cheer the efforts of a decent small-town citizen to represent the interests of "the little people" against the shysters, selfish elites, and/or political bosses who control the nation's economic/political institutions. In *Mr. Smith Goes to Washington* and *Meet John Doe,* Capra structured his populist scenario with plot conventions that would underlie in varying degrees subsequent political films: 1) Opening scenes that juxtapose the protagonist's wholesome friendliness with the cynical, money/power interests that control the political process; 2) seeking to represent the "people's" interests, the protagonist becomes disillusioned in the face of overpowering efforts to discredit him and/or victimize his constituency; 3) hope and the will to fight for what he believes is rekindled by the heroine and a smattering of other good souls who continue to believe in him; 4) a final confrontation against the political evildoer(s) which results in at least the promise of a genuinely representative government. Acknowledging that the people were susceptible to the manipulation of would-be dictators (played by Edward Arnold in both *Mr Smith* and *Meet John Doe*), Capra nevertheless held out the hope that human decency and individual courage—rooted in traditional community values—could somehow defeat the politically-entrenched exploiters.

Virtually the same scenario resurfaced in the postwar production of *The Farmer's Daughter* (1947). Katherina Holstrom, a Swedish-American lass played with her best Hollywood-Scandinavian accent by Loretta Young, is defined early in the film as a female Jefferson Smith whose rural-based honesty and neighborly values contrast with the cynical "politics-as-usual" complacency that permeates the nation's capital. Katherina's model of a good congressman is "old Schmidlap," whom she characterizes as "a good neighbor, good farmer, and a good man," as opposed to Congressman Johnson, who lacks "a good heart for the people." Persuaded to run for Congress, Katherine wins overwhelming public support with her appeals for a government that represents the wisdom and interests of the people rather than special interest groups and political machines. As was the case of Capra's John Doe, Katherina's efforts to voice the public will are cut short by the smear tactics of a fascist-backed opposition. She returns disillusioned to her father's farm, until persuaded to fight back by her father and the veteran congressman (Joseph Cotton) she loves. The latter functions as a plot device in much the same way as did Jean Arthur in *Mr. Smith* and Barbara Stanwyck in *Meet John Doe*; at first disdainful of Katherina's bid for office, Glen Morley (Cotton) is smitten by her refreshing candor and champions her candidacy. Together they expose her fascist opposition, and the film concludes with Glen carrying his new colleague (and wife) across the threshold of the Capitol. If *The Farmer's Daughter* never directly raises the issue of sexual equality, it does avoid the more conventional Hollywood ending (*Ada* [1961], *Kisses For My President* [1964]) wherein a politically capable heroine subordinates career to wifely aspirations.

Two other films appearing on the eve of the 1948 election were less sanguine in their treatments of campaign politics. The alternately silly and cynical *The Senator Was Indiscreet* (1948) tells of how an eccentric windbag Senator blackmails corrupt party leaders into supporting his nomination for the presidency. To save its own hide, the party is willing to back Senator Mel Axton (William Powell), as on galleys whose latest legislative contribution is a bill that would protect the health of postmen by requiring people to write on tissue paper. As a bemused newsman tells a worried political boss, "If you can sell the American public the idea one cigarette is different from another or that one toothpaste is better than another, you can sell them anything—even Mel Axton." Although this same newsman experiences a surge of conscience and exposes the party's shenanigans, the film's sarcastic bent recalls the kind of political disenchantment that informed films like *The Dark Horse* and *The Phantom President* at the end of the Hoover administration. Billed as a romantic Spencer Tracy-Katharine Hepburn comedy, Frank Capra's *State of the Union* (released in April, 1948) was in some ways the director's most somber political commentary to date. Capra's target this time out is the presidential nominating process in which power brokers and interest groups rather than the people decide who is to run for the nation's highest office. A ruthless newswoman (Angela Lansbury) hires a professional party manager to package tycoon Grant Matthews' (Tracy) bid for the Republican nomination in hopes of deadlocking the convention and thus knocking out other hopefuls (Eisenhower, Dewey, Vandenburg, and Stassen are mentioned by name in the film). Although Matthews, like other Capra heroes, is a genuine common-sense idealist eager to do what is right for his country, he succumbs to party pressure to pocket his ideas in return for winning over powerful interest groups (business, labor, the farm bloc) who control the nomination process. His party manager (Adolph Menjou) tells him to forget about what may be good for the people: "The people have darn little to say about the nominations. You're not nominated by the people, you're nominated by the politicians."

If Grant Matthews is more culpable than Jefferson Smith, John Doe, or Katherina Holstrom in placing expedience before principle, like them he is ultimately inspired to do the right thing by the person he loves. Wife Mary (Katharine Hepburn) serves plot-wise to prod Matthews into eventually renouncing the machine. He apologizes to a nationwide radio audience for selling them out and vows to attend both party conventions to confront the candidates with the people's concerns. In the context of the film's bleak depiction of party politics, however, Matthews' erstwhile promise seems a trifle Quixotic. Capra makes clear that the party will merely select another dupe for its nominee so that the entire cynical charade will continue on its course. In short, Capra leaves his audience with the disquieting vision of an electoral process that excludes anyone determined to put principle ahead of placating the powers-that-be.

Capra was fully aware that 1947-48 was not the best of times for engaging in political criticism. Deviation from acceptable norms of patriotic thought and behavior was becoming suspect, as evidenced by Truman's establishment of a loyalty program in the Federal government and by the House UnAmerican Activities Committee's (HUAC) investigation of subversion in Hollywood. Prior to the completion of *State of the Union*, Universal's *The Senator Was Indiscreet* had drawn severe criticism in press editorials as well as from the American Legion (Sayre 55). In later years Capra recalled that he "was certain *State of the Union* would create angry repercussions, sure the House UnAmerican Activities Committee would not muff the opportunity to subpoena us all into a congressional spectacular called 'Film Reds on Parade'" (Capra 397). Although one critic did charge that the film's "indictment of this country...would not seem out of place in *Izvestia*," *State of the Union* eluded the attention of HUAC and other media watchdogs and enjoyed a modest, if disappointing, success at the box office (Capra 428).

The repressive atmosphere of HUAC hearings and studio blacklisting discouraged further attacks on "the state of the union" by a film industry already plagued by declining audiences. In the few instances where a film did address the subject of a corrupt electoral process, the culprit was no longer the political insider but the populist-style crusader. Instead of idealizing a farmer's daughter or a Mr. Smith for trying to resurrect a faltering democracy, *All the King's Men* (1949) and *A Lion Is in the Streets* (1953) characterized such populist endeavors as fascist demagoguery that threatened a basically just political system. Whereas earlier films such as Capra's *Meet John Doe* and Welles' *Citizen Kane* had also raised the spectre of an ambitious power-seeker manipulating popular anxieties to advance his own ends, such villainy came from rich tycoons rather than from among the exploited lower classes. *All the King's Men* and *A Lion Is in the Streets*, in effect, stood the populist theme of the thirties and forties on its head.

The two films begin in conventional fashion by establishing their lead characters, Willie Stark (Broderick Crawford) and Hank Martin (James Cagney) respectively, as likeable grass-roots spokesmen for an aggrieved populace. The point of departure from the populist scenario comes when Stark/Martin opts for corrupt methods to defeat the entrenched opposition and in the process becomes a demagogic threat to the democracy he purports to be liberating. The conflict between populist hero and corrupt elites is thereby transformed into a conflict between populist demagogue and legitimate authority (a legislative coalition led by a liberal—albeit vulnerable—judge in *All the King's Men*, a governor and honest business owner in *A Lion Is in the Streets*). The political process, which had been salvaged through the redemptive efforts of a Mr. Smith or "farmer's daughter," is now restored by having the populist demagogue assassinated by a disillusioned victim of his treachery. Just as earlier political scenarios had employed a romantic interest or spouse to provide the protagonist with moral support and encouragement, the wives of Stark and Martin at first support their husbands' struggle against corruption and then register disapproval when the struggle itself becomes corrupt.

If on the surface these films were analogues for Huey Long's political machinations in the Depression South, they were nonetheless produced for a contemporary audience whose recent experience and concerns involved a world war against fascist totalitarianism and, subsequently, a cold war fraught with the political divisiveness of McCarthyism. Robert Rossen, who adapted Robert Penn Warren's *All the King's Men* to the screen, was himself a target of the McCarthite hysteria that had gripped Hollywood in the form of HUAC hearings and studio blacklisting. Just as *All the King's Men* and *A Lion is in the Streets* associated populist crusaders with reactionary demagoguery, liberal intellectuals of the fifties attributed the repressiveness of McCarthyism to populist status anxieties and anti-intellectual impulses in mass society, all of which allegedly threatened America's pluralist democracy whereby the national interest was best served through reasoned compromise among contending interest groups. Willie Stark and Hank Martin were timely symbols of "the will-to-power" that, according to Reinhold Niebuhr, threatened to corrupt secular panaceas for social justice.

In *The Last Hurrah* (1958), director John Ford delivered his own revision of the conventional populist motif—to which he had contributed during the depression with *Young Mr. Lincoln* (1939) and *The Grapes of Wrath* (1941). The machine politician who had once personified greed and exploitation becomes Ford's protagonist in *The Last Hurrah*. Spencer Tracy plays an aging Irish political boss who faces a losing battle in his bid for a fifth term as mayor of a New England town. Never averse to a bit of blackmail or other form of intimidation against his Protestant opponents, Tracy's Frank Skeffington is nonetheless committed to looking after his predominately Irish working class constituency. For all of his shady machinations, he has protected the interests of his people against the avarice of bankers and other Protestant patricians. Now he faces the power of television which the opposition uses to package its own candidate with contrived images of a decent family man battling the corrupt machine. Colorful parades and rallies along with the personal handshake, Ford bemoans, are being replaced by the televised merchandising of a candidate.

(A year earlier, the corruptive power of the media had been the central theme of Elia Kazan's *A Face in the Crowd*.)

Ford's melancholic farewell to old-fashioned politicking was itself an anachronism in a postwar era in which intellectuals and filmmakers alike touted the virtues of a pluralist broker state while condemning any form of political extremism. Hence the one positive film portrait of political life at this time, Dore Schary's *Sunrise at Campobello* (1960), was an unabashed tribute to the principle figurehead of the modern pluralist state, Franklin Roosevelt. Subsequent films of the early sixties highlighted the dangers of extremism to the body politic. Advertised as an exposé that would blow the lid off the Capitol dome, Otto Preminger's 1962 film adaptation of Alan Drury's best-selling novel, *Advise and Consent*, was actually a diatribe against anticommunist witchhunters and idealistic peaceniks whose Machiavellian excesses violate established procedures of rational decision-making in the U.S. Senate. At stake is the integrity and stability of the nation's highest legislative body, a diverse collection of elected members engaged in an ongoing process of give-and-take on issues where there is seldom total agreement. When the President's nominee for Secretary of State (played by Henry Fonda) becomes the subject of shrill rhetorical outbursts backed by underhanded methods to discredit not only the nominee but opposing fellow senators, the majority leader (played in stately fashion by Walter Pigeon) struggles mightily to retain a semblance of decorum and civility while at the same time he dutifully solicits votes to approve his president's choice. The issue raised by the film is not whether the decidedly liberal Fonda is worthy of the nomination, but whether lawmakers are capable of resolving differences in a reasonable manner and thus preventing the extremes of right or left from undermining the legislative process.

Director John Frankenheimer delivered two of Hollywood's more entertaining attacks on political extremism in *The Manchurian Candidate* (1962) and *Seven Days in May* (1964). Once again the political center is under siege: in the former film by a McCarthy-like senator (who turns out to be the front for a communist plot to take over the government), and in the latter film by a reactionary military commander who plots a coup against a liberal president he believes to be a dangerous appeaser. As was the case with *Advise and Consent*, the republic is saved not by a Capra-style populist outsider but by loyal representatives of the establishment.

Gore Vidal delivered his own salvo at extremist politics in his 1960 Broadway play, *The Best Man*, which he adapted for the screen in 1964. Released during an election year that saw liberal Lyndon Johnson pitted against conservative Barry Goldwater, *The Best Man* centered on a presidential nominating convention in which a moderately liberal candidate (Henry Fonda) fends off the underhanded smear tactics of his rightist opponent (Cliff Robertson). Director Franklin Schaffner effectively visualizes the hectic atmosphere of a party convention in which candidates wheel and deal for delegates. Issues and ideas matter less, Vidal suggests, than knowing how to play the tawdry game of politics. However, when faced with a threatened smear from the nasty rightist, the liberal candidate cannot bring himself to respond in kind (he's discovered that his ostensibly all-American opponent had once succumbed to a homosexual affair). He thus withdraws from the race, but not before delivering his delegates to a dark horse who will presumably win the nomination. Thus, principle combined with a final act of pragmatic maneuvering assures the triumph of centrist politics against political extremism from the right.

Except for *WUSA* (1970) in which radio discjockey Paul Newman exposes a right-wing plot to use the media to whip up patriotic bigotry and thereby take over the government, most films, beginning with Stanley Kubrick's *Dr. Strangelove* in 1964, began to echo the rising disenchantment in America with the liberal center. Kubrick did not spare hawkish rightists in his film, but unlike previous political thrillers he held the entire political establishment (led in the film by liberal president Merlin Muffley) to account for policies that would inevitably destroy the world.

By 1968 it was not so much the nuclear arms race but the war in Vietnam together with race riots and campus upheavals that seemed to undermine the credibility of postwar liberal pluralism. In Chicago the politics of reason inside the Democratic convention conflicted with the politics of protest and reaction outside as young dissidents collided with Mayor Daley's finest. At the scene was cinematographer Haskell Wexler shooting live footage of the riot for *Medium Cool,* a film he wrote, produced, and directed for release the following year. Particularly in one abrupt cut from convention delegates singing "Happy Days Are Here Again" to the bloody confrontation brewing in the the city streets, Wexler conveyed the impression of a political process totally out of touch with the reality of social discord. Despite its vivid recording of establishment brutality and critical portrayal of media exploitation, *Medium Cool* was no apologia for America's counterculture. The real victims, Wexler suggests, are the nation's poor—poignantly represented in the film by a West Virginia widow struggling to raise her son in the Chicago slums. In this context, the youthful adulations of Robert Kennedy come across in the film as superficial as the "Happy Days Are Here Again" sloganeering of the convention delegates. (Released a year earlier, *Wild in the Streets* [1968] had gone so far as to identify countercultural involvement in electoral politics with incipient fascism.)

The next presidential election in 1972 proved significant not only for Nixon's "dirty tricks" campaign but for a significant drop in voter turnout, which to congresswoman Shirley Chisolm "was a disturbing barometer of the air of apathy and resignation which permeates the nation's political atmosphere" (Carroll 90). "Politics is bullshit," shouts a young Hispanic at the start of *The Candidate* (1972), a cynical political comedy that starred Robert Redford as an idealistic liberal who is persuaded by political managers to challenge a conservative incumbent in the upcoming Senate race in California. Updated to incorporate current issues such as abortion and the environment, much of the plot recalls Capra's scenario of the principled outsider taking on the political hacks and special interests. And, like Tracy's Grant Matthews in *State of the Union*, Redford's Bill McCoy finds himself being packaged by his managers into just another politician spouting empty platitudes instead of addressing the issues. But there is no last minute redemption at the bidding of a Katharine Hepburn. Unlike Matthews, McCoy (much to his own surprise) wins the nomination. In the final scene, a terrified McCoy pleads with his manager, "What do we do now?" Before the latter can reply, a crowd of well-wishers ushers them out of their hotel room to join the victory celebration.

In October of 1988 Robert Redford did a bit of real-life politicking when he visited a toxic dump site in Illinois to criticize the Reagan-Bush environmental record. Reporters asked him about a recent story that Dan Quayle had been inspired by seeing *The Candidiate* to apply his Redford-like good looks toward pursuing a political career. "Then Quayle missed the point," Redford replied, adding that the character he played in the film "was more substantial than Quayle" and "was at least agonizing over the system. The problem was that he got caught by it." Upon further reflection about the fact that the film character had after all won based on his good looks and avoidance of issues, Redford conceded that "Maybe he [Quayle] did get the point" (*Houston Chronicle* 6D).

In the wake of the Watergate scandal, political elections figured prominently in several films that grimly portrayed an America in a state of moral end emotional malaise. Set on the eve of the 1968 election, *Shampoo* (1975) implies that Nixon's election was indicative of a narcissistic "me too" society devoid of any sense of commitment beyond that of making a profit or scoring in the bedroom. Nixon booster and rich Beverly hills financier Lester (Jack Warden) listens intensely to the latest stock market report on his car radio as he drives home to make final preparations for an election-eve dinner; as soon as the newscaster moves on to a report on South Vietnam's refusal to attend the Paris peace conference, Lester rapidly switches stations until he finds another stock market report. Toward the end of the film, Lester (together with George, the film's hairstylist protagonist played by Warren Beatty) watches a televised speech in which president-elect Nixon is promising "an open administration" that will bring America together again. Lester turns to George with the observation that the "market went down ten points last week—goddamn Lyndon Johnson." Turning off the set, Lester adds wearily, "Maybe the next one will be better. What's the difference? They're all a bunch of jerks." But so are Lester, George, and practically everyone else in the film, which is the point: the state of American politics is a reflection of a purposeless, self-indulgent society.

The narcissism associated with the corporate, boudoir culture of Beverly Hills is equally apparent in the country music world of Robert Altman's *Nashville* (1975). Star singer Haven Hamilton's stirring Bicentennial anthem ("We must be doin something right to last two hundred years") belies a show-biz world of avarice and apathy. It is appropriate that Hamilton and the country music establishment should lend its media visibility to boost the campaign of populist presidential hopeful Hal Philip Walker whose sloganeering about getting rid of the electoral college, lawyers, and the national anthem is as pointless as Hamilton's homespun patriotic lyrics.

A presidential political campaign is also the backdrop of Martin Scorsese's apocalyptic vision of urban violence, *Taxi Driver* (1976). Juxtaposed with taxi driver Travis Bickle's (Robert DeNiro) night world of urban depravity is the day world of vacuous campaign planning at the headquarters of Senator Charles Palentine. Two yuppy aides, played by Albert Brooks and Cybill Shepherd, fuss about ordering campaign buttons and deciding how best to sell their man to the public: "First pick the man, then the issue," says Shepherd. After she prattles on about Palentine being so "dynamic...intelligent, interesting, fresh, fascinating," and even sexy, Brooks counters: "Listen to what you're saying. You sound like you're selling mouthwash." "We are selling mouthwash," she assures him. Mouthwash turns out to be an apt description for the Senator as he spouts the same hollow rhetoric before television cameras or at rallies about the importance of addressing the needs of a people who have suffered from Vietnam, unemployment, poverty, and inflation. "Let the people rule," he repeats ad nauseam. The people, however, include the alienated Travis Bickle along with the muggers, pimps, and prostitutes who inhabit the dark damp streets of a dehumanized urban environment. Electoral politics, Scorsese suggests (as did Haskell Wexler in *Medium Cool*), is out of touch with reality, a reality which, in *Taxi Driver*, provokes Bickle's demented outburst of vigilante retaliation.

Thus, on the eve of Jimmy Carter's election to the presidency and the celebration of the nation's Bicentennial, Hollywood films were conveying an intensely despairing image of electoral politics, a politics devoid of rational discourse in America, afflicted with complacency, inertia, and utter purposelessness. Hollywood had never found much good to say about the political scene, but at least there had been some hope for improvement—either in the form of a neighborly idealistic citizenry or a stable pluralist state. By the mid-1970s, however, the portrayal of politicians and the electorate resembled what Warren Beatty remarked concerning the characters in *Shampoo*: "a lot of...myopic people going to hell in a handcart and not noticing" (Cagin and Dray 239).

While these highly negative films were undoubtedly a reaction in part to the sense of disillusionment over the Watergate cover-up, the one film in the mid-seventies that did embody some hope for a redress of political wrongs was *All the President's Men* (1976). Less despairing than other conspiracy films of the seventies such as *The Parallax view* (1974), *Three Days of the Condor* (1975), or *Twilight's Last Gleaming* (1977), Alan Pakula's adaptation of Robert Woodward and Carl Bernstein's best-selling account of unfolding the Watergate affair invited the audience to cheer an intrepid endeavor against political corruption, even though the two journalistic heroes (as portrayed by Robert Redford and Dustin Hoffman) were hardly the scions of small-town idealism characteristic of Depression-era films.

Jimmy Carter in 1976 struck a decidedly more Capra-esque posture as the honest rural outsider promising to replace insider deception and elitism with grass-roots morality. Promises of traditional integrity wore thin, however, as the new administration floundered amidst growing economic instability and renewed international tensions. Consistent with the decline of public confidence in the Carter presidency was the negative depiction of electoral politics in three films released in 1979-1980.

In its opening scenes of Black schoolchildren touring Washington's famous monuments while Alan Alda argues for passage of a works bill for the unemployed, it was as if Frank Capra was at the helm of *The Seduction of Joe Tynan* (1979). Here was the familiar plot of a decent individual struggling to balance personal integrity (with Barbara Harris as the wifely voice of conscience) with the political realities of bargaining with pressure groups and legislative colleagues. But Alda's Senator Tynan is no wide-eyed idealist who in the end chooses principle over expedience and ambition. His liberal advocacy of civil rights and poverty programs is less a matter of principle than a platform calculated to fulfill his own presidential aspirations. The price of success is high (alienating a loving wife who hates politics, betraying an elderly colleague), but Joe Tynan is willing to pay it—as is clear when he stands before a nominating convention at the film's conclusion.

By identifying liberalism with political opportunism in its leading character, *The Seduction of Joe Tynan* reflected America's growing disenchantment with its liberal establishment, as evidenced by the further decline in voter turnout and the "Reagan landslide" of 1980. *Being There*, also released in 1980, expressed similarly relevant misgivings about the bankruptcy of sound political leadership and ideas, in this case regarding the nation's economic stagnation. Even Buck Henry's otherwise vapid comedy, *First Family* (1980), captured something of the current negativist mood in an opening sequence that shows a televised interview of a senator who is gloating over the fact that his party rather than the president's controls Congress:

Interviewer: "Ah, but Senator, the Congress will have to face the fact that President Link was elected to office by a slim but definite majority."

Senator: "Ah yes, but that victory must be weighed against the fact that his opponents, the presidential and vice-presidential candidates of my party, were killed in that tragic automobile accident three days before the election."

Interviewer: "Yet it must be remembered that nearly thirty million Americans actually voted for the two corpses.

Several years into Reagan's first term of office, Buck Henry scripted a political comedy uniquely reminiscent of the idealistic populist scenarios of decades past. In *Protocol* (1984), Goldie Hawn is literally a "farmer's daughter" enmeshed in Washington political intrigue. Bewildered but proud to be called upon to serve her government, Goldie (called Sunny in the film) eventually discovers that she has been duped by high-level aides into exchanging sexual favors for a strategic air base in a Middle East country. Her shattered idealism is quickly restored by rereading the Declaration of Independence, whereupon she delivers an eloquent address before a congressional committee about the public's responsibility to hold accountable the actions of its representatives. Like Loretta Young's Katherina Holstrom three decades earlier, Goldie Hawn's Sunny Davis runs for Congress and wins —thanks also to the professional and romantic support of her husband (Chris Sarandon filling in for Joseph Cotten).

Viewed in the context of a presidency that invoked the spirit (if not the programs) of Franklin Roosevelt along with a return to traditional values, *Protocol*'s slavish adherence to plot conventions formalized in the Depression years could not have been timelier. Those conventions had undergone several permutations to accommodate shifts in America's political climate only to reemerge in a Capra-esque scenario befitting a nation whose current movie-star president was once described as "typically American as apple pie" (Vaughn 372).

Note

[1]Regarding these four films, see Roffman and Purdy 35-40, 55-57; White and Averson 48-50; Christensen 31-33. The broad overviews of social-political message films provided by Roffman/Purdy and Christensen are particularly useful complements to the narrower focus of this essay.

Works Cited

Cagin, Seth, and Philip Dray. *Hollywood Films of the Seventies.* New York; Harper, 1984.

Capra, Frank. *The Name Above the Title: An Autobiography.* New York: Macmillan, 1971.

Carroll, Peter. *It Seemed Like Nothing Happened: The Tragedy and Promise of America in the 1970s.* New York: Holt, 1982.

Christensen, Terry. *Reel Politics: American Political Movies from "Birth of a Nation" to "Platoon"*. New York: Basil Blackwell, 1987.

Houston Chronicle 17 October 1988: 6D.

Richards, Jeffrey. *Visions of Yesterday*. London: Routledge, 1973.

Roffman, Peter, and Jim Purdy. *The Hollywood Social Problem Film: Madness, Despair, and Politics from the Depression to the Fifties*. Bloomington: Indiana UP, 1981.

Sayre, Nora. *Running Time: Films of the Cold War*. New York: Dial, 1982.

Vaughn, Stephen. "Spies, National Security, and the Inertia Projector: The Secret Service Films of Ronald Reagan." *American Quarterly* 39 (Fall 1987).

White, David Manning, and Richard Averson. *The Celluloid Weapon*. Boston: Beacon, 1972.

Filmography

1932	*American Madness*	Dir. Frank Capra
1932	*The Dark Horse*	Dir. Alfred E. Green
1932	*The Phantom President*	Dir. Norman Taurog
1932	*Washington Masquerade*	Dir. Charles Brabin
1932	*The Washington Merry-Go-Round*	Dir. James Cruze
1933	*Gabriel Over the White House*	Dir. Gregory La Cava
1934	*The President Vanishes*	Dir. William Wellman
1939	*Mr. Smith Goes to Washington*	Dir. Frank Capra
1940	*The Great McGinty*	Dir. Preston Sturges
1941	*Citizen Kane*	Dir. Orson Welles
1941	*Meet John Doe*	Dir. Frank Capra
1947	*The Farmer's Daughter*	Dir. H. C. Potter
1948	*The Senator Was Indiscreet*	Dir. George Kaufman
1948	*State of the Union*	Dir. Frank Capra
1949	*All the King's Men*	Dir. Robert Rossen
1953	*A Lion Is In the Streets*	Dir. Raoul Walsh
1957	*A Face in the Crowd*	Dir. Elia Kazan
1958	*The Last Hurrah*	Dir. John Ford
1960	*Sunrise at Campobello*	Dir. Vincent J. Donohue
1961	*Ada*	Dir. Daniel Mann
1962	*Advise and Consent*	Dir. Otto Preminger
1962	*The Manchurian Candidate*	Dir. John Frankenheimer
1964	*The Best Man*	Dir. Franklin Schaffner
1964	*Dr. Strangelove Or: How I Learned To Stop Worrying and Love the Bomb*	Dir. Stanley Kubrick
1964	*Fail Safe*	Dir. Sidney Lumet
1964	*Kisses For My President*	Dir. Curtis Bernhardt
1964	*Seven Days in May*	Dir. John Frankenheimer
1968	*Medium Cool*	Dir. Haskell Wexler
1968	*Wild in the Streets*	Dir. Barry Shear
1970	*WUSA*	Dir. Stuart Rosenberg
1972	*The Candidate*	Dir. Michael Ritchie

1972	*The Man*	Dir. Joseph Sargent
1973	*Executive Action*	Dir. David Miller
1974	*The Parallax View*	Dir. Alan J. Pakula
1975	*Nashville*	Dir. Robert Altman
1975	*Shampoo*	Dir. Hal Ashby
1975	*Three Days of the Condor*	Dir. Sidney Pollack
1976	*All the President's Men*	Dir. Alan Pakula
1976	*Taxi Driver*	Dir. Martin Scorsese
1977	*Twilight's Last Gleaming*	Dir. Robert Aldrich
1979	*Being There*	Dir. Hal Ashby
1979	*The Seduction of Joe Tynan*	Dir. Jerry Schatzberg
1979	*Winter Kills*	Dir. William Richert
1980	*First Family*	Dir. Buck Henry
1981	*Blow Out*	Dir. Brian De Palma
1984	*Protocol*	Dir. Herbert Ross
1986	*Power*	Dir. Sidney Lumet

The Celebration of Family Plot:
Episodes and Affirmations

Paul Loukides

Of the changes which have affected American family life between 1945 and the present, perhaps none was so abrupt or far reaching in its consequences as the "baby boom" of the immediate post war years. As Johnny came marching home again, the demobilization of America's war effort was accompanied by an unprecedented rush into marriage, domesticity and parenthood. The astronomical growth in birthrate and the mushrooming of whole cookie cutter suburbs like Levitown reflected a population that was weary of the uncertainties of war and eager to enact the most traditional pattern of our culture: the making of a family.

In 1945 there were 2,735,000 children born in the U.S.; in 1946 there were 3,289,000 and in 1947, 3,700,000, nearly a million more than just two years earlier. From 1940 to 1945 the birth rate had risen from a Depression rate of 17.9 births per thousand population to 19.2 per thousand. Two years later, at the crest of the baby boom, the rate had jumped to 25.8 births per thousand. Between 1940 and 1945, the yearly number of marriages in the U.S. had risen only slightly, from 1,596,000 to 1,613,000, but by 1946 there were more than 2,291,000 marriages as the rate per thousand went from 12.2 per thousand to 16.4 per thousand in a single year.

Ironically, 1946 also produced a record number of divorces—610,000— a record which was to hold for more than twenty years as the survival rate for post war marriages proved higher than for marriages contracted in the war years. In spite of the momentary aberration of the divorce rate, traditional attitudes against divorce still seemed to hold; by 1949, there were fewer than 400,000 divorces in the U.S., a decrease of more than a third from the peak of 1946. On the homefront, it seemed marriage, children, and the traditional virtues of family life reasserted their claim to the center of American life as the war began to fade into memory.

Not surprisingly, films about family life, which had been a minor staple of the movie industry since the early days of silent movies, began to take a greater share of the popular market. A major shift of customer interest and demand mirrored the upward spirals of the marriage and birthrates. Of the top 20 films of 1946, 1947, 1949, and 1950 approximately fifteen

91

percent were films which centered on the strengths and rewards of family life—a percentage never repeated in the history of the movies. Such films as *The Best Years of Our Lives* (1947), *Our Vines Have Tender Grapes* (1945), *A Tree Grows in Brooklyn* (1945), *Cheaper by the Dozen* (1950), *Father of the Bride* (1950), *Margie* (1946), *Life with Father* (1947), *The Green Years* (1946), *The Yearling* (1947), *The Bachelor and the Bobbysoxer* (1947), *Dear Ruth* (1947), *Date with Judy*, (1948), *Sitting Pretty* (1948), *I Remember Mama*, (1948), *Little Women* (1949), *Adam's Rib* (1949), and *Pinky* (1949) captured a large share of America's movie dollars. Never before—and never again—would so many films about the virtues of the family come to dominate the marketplace.

That the increase in demand for films of family was the result of changes in customer demand—rather than simply reflective of changes in studio offerings as they phased out war movies—is shown by the fact that other traditionally popular film types did not increase their share of the market in like proportion. What a great many Americans wanted after the war was not more Westerns or romantic comedies or crime films but rather more movies—of a special kind—about families and family life. Equally revealing of the correlation between social behavior and movie preference is the simple fact that as the baby boom began to dwindle, the popularity of films centered on the problems and joys of family life began to wane in spite of continued substantial offerings by the studios.

It seems no accident of the movie marketplace that films which celebrated the family as a source of individual strength and growth reached their highwater mark in the years in which Americans, in unheard of numbers, made new commitments to family life. Nor does it seem accidental that 1947, the year in which the greatest number of family films reached the top 20, was also the crest of the "baby boom."

The "family centered" movies which became so popular in the immediate post war years were not, of course, simply films about family life. Rather, all of the most popular films about families took as their basic plot device the testing and affirmation of the bonds of family life. In what can be called the "celebration of family plot," the destructive possibilities of family life so well known to psychology and literature and so vividly portrayed in movies like *Long Day's Journey into Night* and *Who's Afraid of Virginia Woolf* are, if not entirely absent, then easily vanquished by love. The family structure in the "celebration" film is a vehicle of nurture and reward for each of its members; family love conquers all, and no individual is ever outside the supportive framework of the family.

Within the "celebration of family" films, the most important human relationships are those between persons related by blood ties or by marriage, and an individual's interactions with the world outside the family are important (or not) primarily in respect to how they affect family relationships. In these films, the center of an individual's life is a family group whose members mutually owe and own the obligations due love and kinship. In the "celebration of family" film the most traditional patterns and values of family life are put to a series of tests and not found wanting.

This motif of testing and affirmation is central to the "celebration of family" film, and it is the similarity of both the plots and thematic motifs which link films of very different moods and structure. The formula of testing and reaffirmation central to the celebration of family plot is carried through the comedy of such films as *Life with Father* and the melodrama of movies like *A Tree Grows in Brooklyn*. It is present in the relatively tight melodramatic plotting of films like *The Yearling* and very loose episodic structure of films like *Cheaper by the Dozen*.

Because of the range of film types which carry the plot motif of testing and reaffirmation of family virtue, they have never—to my knowledge—been looked at as a distinct group of films. However, a close look at some of the more successful "celebration of family" films can help to reveal how, despite differences of mood, locales, and character types, the formulaic testing and reaffirmation ("celebration") of family lies at the center of a large number of films of the immediate post war period and confirms our sense that the post war baby boom had its counterpart in movie preferences.

One of the most critically acclaimed films of the post war years, and the most popular film of 1947, was *The Best Years of Our Lives*, a movie which recounts the story of three men returning to civilian life after the war. Each of the three, played by Fredrich March, Dana Andrews and Harold Russell, returns to very different circumstances. Their three separate stories are shown through a series of interwoven episodes and serve as a cross section of the problems which a whole generation of veterans faced in re-entering civilian life. March, who had been an infantry sergeant, returns to the late years of an affluent middle-class marriage (to Myrna Loy) and a $12,000 a year job in the loan department of the bank. Andrews, who had been a decorated Air Force officer, returns to a lower-class bride who has turned tramp, a civilian world where he is no longer an officer and a gentleman, and the prospect of a $37.50 per week job at the Midway Drug Store. Russell, an ex-Navy seaman who had lost both his hands, returns to face the love and pity of his lower middle-class family, a girl-next-door fiancée, and an uncertain future.

For each of them the world, or their view of the world, has been changed by the war. March has a drinking problem, problems with his family life, and problems at the bank. Andrews must face the fact that his medals, citations, and skills as a bombardier count for nothing in the civilian world he helped to defend. Russell must face a life without hands. Much of the film is devoted to small vignettes of experiences shared by millions of returning veterans; hitching rides in military transport, the return to home cooking, unemployment, homegrown bigotry, poor credit, unfaithful wives and the trials of readjustment are all part of the texture of the film. Yet for all the *Back Home* dimensions of the movie, the fundamental center of the action is the dream of marriage, home, and peace which each of the characters share.

Home and family, whatever the circumstances, are the assumed source of strength and security in *The Best Years of Our Lives*. Andrews, whose wartime bride cannot abide his dream of working class domesticity, finds comfort with his impoverished but supportive father and with Marsh's daughter (Teresa Wright), who is eager to provide Andrews with the home and family which his wife conveniently renounces. For Russell, his home and friends are a warm center to which he can retire to heal his psychic scars. The family (mom, pop, young sister) may, in the clumsiness of their love inflict the pain of pity, but it is clear that the loving care of the family is without malice. March, for all his urbanity and relative wealth, must put away the hard drinking infantry sergeant he has become and rebuild his home life.

For each of the three, the final trial which must be faced is a trial of love and family. At the end of the film, March must still control his drinking, maintain his integrity at the bank by continuing to fight for what he believes, and re-establish his relationship with his wife. Andrews must prove himself at a new career by his own efforts and must work toward his dream of home, wife and kids. Russell must discover if he and his new wife will have the love and courage they will need to make a whole life in spite of his handicap. For none of the three is the future assured, yet for each of them there is the prospect of a good life and happy home.

The motif of testing and reaffirmation of the ideal of family is worked in three different ways within the film; each of the separate sub-plots serves to reconfirm the value of family in the life of the individual. It is not money, or power, or career, which ultimately matters to the three men; marriage, children and family are more important. In the view of the family proposed in *The Best years of Our Lives*, the health and growth of an adult individual is best fostered in the environment of home and family.

The formulaic reaffirmation of the value of the family to emotional health and growth as shown in *The Best Years of Our Lives* is equally clear in the many popular films which center on children in the family. In such films as *The Yearling, A Three Grows in Brooklyn, Our Vines Have Tender Grapes,* and *The Green Years*, the central focus is on children and the problems of reconciling the individual needs of the child with the needs of the family.

In *The Yearling*, for example, the boy's love of the foundling fawn must be balanced against the consequences of that love to the health of the family. From the moment the fawn enters the boy's world, the father (played by Gregory Peck) knows that the demands of the growing animal will conflict with the well-being of the family, yet, out of his love for the boy, he allows him to keep the orphaned animal. As the plot unfolds, the boy's relationship with his father changes in response to the changes occasioned by the growing fawn, a mindless, natural creature which has no loyalties except to its own needs. When the fawn first destroys the family's crop, the boy is not yet ready to forgo his pet for the good of the family. Peck, the wise father, knows he risks losing the boy's love if he demands too much of him, and he again yields to the boy. When the family crop is again destroyed, the boy begins to learn his own responsibility to the health of the family. At the climax of the film, it is the boy himself who must destroy the yearling to save his father who, snake bitten, needs fresh internal organs to "draw" the venom from his wound. The yearling, who repaid the boy's love and loyalty with mindless, innocent destruction, dies for the sake of the family. The boy has put his childhood behind him and grown under the careful nurturing of his family. He has undergone a rite of passage and emerged a man. The family has been tested by an animal, by flooding rain, by illness and by disharmony, but in the end love and kinship are reaffirmed.

In *A Tree Grows in Brooklyn*, it is the girl, Francie, played by Peggy Ann Garner, who grows through her interactions with the family. The "princess" of her loving, ineffectual father (James Dunn), Francie is caught between his childish romantic dreams ("Someday, princess...") and the stern realities of poverty as presented by her mother (Dorothy McGuire). Her mother, who works as a scrub woman to support the family, fears that Francie will never forsake her father's childish dreams and learn to live in the world. As loving as her husband can be, mother knows he is still a seldom employed singing waiter given to drink, blarney, and impractical dreams of a better future when a fairytale "impressario" will discover his talents. For Francie, father, with his visible love and his musical tongue, is the favored parent; it is he who uses a harmless ruse to get her enrolled in a better school when mother said the idea was impractical, and it is he who sets her mind free to dream of better days.

Mediating between the rival claims of mother and father are Grandmother, the matriarch of the family, Aunt Cissy (Joan Blondell) who endlessly pursues men, and an assortment of neighbors and acquaintances. Grandmother, in her only sustained speech, delivers a panegyric on the virtues of education. Aunt Cissy helps Francie maintain her faith in her father and reminds her sister that a loving heart has virtue. A local bartender offers the family money; an old woman leaves them her piano. Without her knowing it, Francie and her brother are surrounded by a network of adults who work to sustain and enrich their lives as best they can. If, like mother, they are sometimes too hard, or if, like father, they are sometimes impractical, there is still always love.

The greatest crisis of the film comes when mother discovers that she is pregnant and will soon be unable to support the family. Husband and wife argue about what is to be done and he leaves the house, seemingly to drown his sorrows. With the family in dire straits, mother enacts her plan for the boy to take an after-school job and for Francie to quit her beloved school at the end of the term and take a full-time job. Faced with the loss of her father (who has, unbeknownst to all, gone off in search of work not drink) and the loss of her hopes for further education, Francie retreats into a bitter silence that is broken only when her mother comes to need her. When labor starts, her mother sends the boy to get Grandma and Aunt Cissy; Francie must face the prospect of helping her mother give birth. In the pain of labor, mother comes to show the loving heart beneath her stern exterior and Francie returns that love.

The final resolution of the film comes on the day of Francie's graduation from school. Her dead father has left money to send her flowers for that special day; the good Irish cop on the beat (Lloyd Nolan) has asked mother if he might someday hope to be a father to the family; Aunt Cissy has finally found a man who can control her and make her be a good wife; and, in a poignant, awkward moment, Francie is asked out on her first date. Birth, death, and poverty have tried the family, changed Francie from a child to a young woman, shown mother the importance of a loving heart, confirmed our faith in love and kinship, and not left a dry eye in the house.

In *The Green Years* and *Our Vines Have Tender Grapes*, the emphasis is yet again on the importance of love to the growth of the young. In *The Green Years*, an orphaned boy is sent to live with his stern grandmother, his penny pinching uncle and his tale telling, slightly alcoholic, but affectionate great grandfather. Through a series of loosely related incidents taking some two-thirds of the film (the visit of the boy's cousin, a schoolyard fight, boxing lessons, a tour through the town, the start of puppy love, etc.) the affection between the boy and his great grandfather is shown to grow, and the pettiness of grandmother and uncle are confirmed. In the last third of the film, a certain continuity of plot develops as the boy, over the opposition of his uncle, and with the aid of his great grandfather, tries to win a scholarship to the university, his only way to realize his dream of becoming a doctor. He is a brilliant student and studies hard, but fatigue and fateful Hollywood soaking in the rain take their toll; he gets pneumonia, misses the last part of the exam, and comes in second. Good try, but no cigar. Life, for the moment, has him trapped. He dons his worker's cap and reports for work, his future dim. But, again family love conquers adversity; great grandfather dies, full of years and good whiskey and leaves the boy enough insurance money so that he can go to the the university. Even in a family as poor and dour as the boy's, there is a strand of family virtue that overcomes whatever failings the family may have and nurtures the young in their green years.

In *Our Vines Have Tender Grapes*, the theme of nurturing is begun at the title and carried through a series of very loosely related incidents, each of which helps to reveal some facet of family virtue. What little structure there is to the movie is provided by the arrival, early in the film, of a new young school teacher to the farming community of Fuller Junction. She's from the city (Milwaukee) and does not understand the rewards of a life spent close to the land and the family. By the end of the film she is, of course, convinced; she will marry Nels and stay on in Fuller Junction. A barn burning, a death in childbirth, a Christmas program, the near drowning of two children, the generosity of friends and neighbors to those in need, and the kindly wisdom of father (Edward G. Robinson) have all pulled at her heartstrings. Family and community matter; at the end of the film there is "no more lonesome feeling," it is Spring and "We're all growing." The family, as exemplified by Robinson and his tribe, has been tested and not found wanting. The children have survived and grown; they have learned about generosity and selfishness, birth and death, anger and love, pain and joy in ways which have increased their humanity. The harvest of the family vines, we can be sure, will be a choice crop that can continue the heritage of careful nurturing.

It does not take any great cynicism to notice the indulgence in sentiment of films like *A Tree Grows in Brooklyn*, *Our Vines* or *The Green Years*. The loosely tied episodes which try the family are clearly used as occasions for the affirmation of love and sentiment. Less immediately noticeable is that in these films (and others like *The Yearling* and *I Remember Mama*) many of the trials of the family tend to have some economic root. Poverty, or some Hollywood approximation of being poor, provides many of the occasions for the testing of family strength. Thematically, the message seems to be that more money would make the lives of these families better, but the lack of money can never harm true family feeling.

This focus on sentimental poverty, while common, does not dominate the film of family trials. In the majority of celebration of family films, the center is a middle-class or even affluent family and, as one would expect, the episodic structure of such films is not economically centered. Without the plot device of economic stress, such films as *Cheaper by the Dozen*, *Life with Father*, *Margie*, *Date with Judy*, *Father of the Bride* and others, focus instead on the resolution of everyday tensions and commonplace crises.

Perhaps because these films do not have even the suggestion of a life and death struggle with poverty or frontier life to give them a center, the highly episodic structure with which they test and affirm family feeling is even more pronounced. Like an entire TV season with The Brady Bunch or My Three Sons, these celebration of family films combine a series of major and minor crises into two hours of positive resolutions affirming the value of family.

To reduce a dozen or more films to their formulas, in families with post-pubescent girls, there is typically a comedy of courtship built around Father's sense that no young man is good enough for his daughter. In families with preadolescent boys, there are boyish hi-jinks to deal with, and for every family there is either some officious public servant to contend with, a major or minor illness, a problem over pets, a vacation, a moment of jealousy, a birth and/or a death and some middle-class comedy of overspending. While the combinations may differ (*Cheaper by the Dozen* has a pet incident, a whooping cough sequence, a beach vacation, the courtship of the oldest daughter, a boyish prank, a recalcitrant school principal to set right, a birth [to make a dozen], a visit from a planned parenthood advocate, and a death [Father] to show how the family endures.), the structure and the recognizable, indeed commonplace, incidents of these films make it clear that something special is happening within these movies. Rather than developing a sustained action such as we ordinarily find in narrative films, each incident in the episodic chain simply attempts to reflect familiar incidents of American family life.

As such films make clear, the celebration of family movie is not simply a film about what happens to a particular or unique family, it is rather a distinctive form which uses a sequence of crises to test and affirm traditional attitudes toward family life. The celebration of family movie is, in a sense, a therapeutic dream of the family in which the very real tensions and traumas of ordinary family life are always resolved by love and good intentions. In not a single celebration film is any member of the family permanently injured by another of the clan; in the celebration of family film parents do not traumatize their children, nor children betray their parents' dreams. The episodic plotting of the celebration of family film is built on the premise that the strength of the family is great enough to overcome both external threat and internal disharmony. Reducible to a series of clichés (blood is thicker than water, home is where the heart is, etc.), the celebration of family film gives its audience a sequence of concrete instances for the testing and reaffirmation of a fundamental belief in the virtues of family life.

That the celebration of family film would find its greatest market during a period also marked by a rise in marriage and birth rates is no surprise for those willing to see how great a role the resolution of widely shared tensions plays in determining movie preferences. A World War close on the heels of a profound economic depression had put America and the American family to the test. Husbands, fathers and sons had been, by turns, unemployed, drafted, wounded, and killed; wives, mothers and sweethearts had struggled to make ends meet, had manned the factories, faced shortages, and lived in fear of black edged telegrams. For years the safety and comfort of traditional homelife had been disrupted or postponed. Throughout the war years Americans waited, and made songs like "White Christmas" and "Don't Sit Under the Apple Tree," with their strong sense of yearning for the old ways, among the most popular tunes of the times. Then, suddenly, it was over and as a nation we could put aside our fears and start families again while celebrating their virtues at the movies.

As we might expect, the popularity of the celebration of family film declined as the birthrate and marriage rate leveled off and some semblance of normalcy returned to family life. Still produced in ample numbers, such films as *Father's Little Dividend, For Heaven's Sake, Elopement, Room for One More, We're Not Married, Marrying Kind, Weekend with Father,* and *Small Town Girl,* some of which seem today at least as good—and often better—than earlier celebration films, did not do as well at the box office as their earlier, better timed conterparts. The days in which Americans would sit in moviehouses and laugh and cry at episodes of the familiar crises of ordinary family life were coming to an end. Some of that audience would doubtless form the audience for years of Ozzie and Harriet, Leave it to Beaver, and Life with Father on the tube. Others perhaps, would simply reject the simple formula wherein every crisis strengthens and reaffirms the value of family and no wound ever leaves a scar. As the baby boom declined in the 1950's, films like *East of Eden, Rebel Without a Cause* and *Blackboard Jungle* would again reaffirm the darker potentials of the American family.

"It's (Christmas) Morning in America:"
Christmas Conventions of American Films in the 1980s

Greg Metcalf

While there is nothing new about Christmas movies being made in America, there was a veritable explosion of Christmas movies in the 1980s. In those ten years at least thirty-eight films were made in America which used Christmas as a setting for at least part of their story. The films include romances, romantic comedies, action comedies, action adventures, thrillers, horror films, and a few others. They vary from independent low-budget productions to multi-million dollar major studio releases. Nonetheless, from all this variety, many similarities emerge. These similarities point to standardized conventions of Christmas as it appears in American film. Those conventions are the subject of this essay.

A Christmas Carol

While it may seem a strange place to start a discussion of Christmas in American films of the 1980s, I'd like to begin with a mid-nineteenth century British novella. This is because even a cursory examination of Charles Dickens' *A Christmas Carol* reveals most of the conventions that will be found in the 1980s Christmas film. In fact, one might argue that Dickens' popular Christmas story, which has been repeatedly adapted, republished, restaged and refilmed since its publication in 1843, should be credited with establishing many of the cinematic Christmas conventions. The story has been filmed at least five times, with a television movie version, a couple of cartoon versions and countless adaptations to seasonal episodes of television series. Besides its mere pervasiveness, the story also solves one of the potential problems for American Christmas movies by defining a set of non-offensive—and non-religious—Christmas values.

A Christmas Carol gives its reader the positive conventions of Christmas in the form of nostalgia, family bonding, reintegration of the outsider into a community or social consensus, and the theme of "peace on earth, good will toward men." But the story also presents the darker side of the Christmas coin: alienation and isolation in the midst of celebration, the threat of death and punishment, lost love, separation from family and, finally, the interests of business or the powerful—or more generally, greed—being prized over

100

Christmas good will. It is the story of an adult, not a child, and *A Christmas Carol*'s holiday is a decidedly secular one, Tiny Tim's "God Bless Us Everyone," not withstanding. The story also gives us the pathway for transcending the negatives of Christmas. After his Christmas Eve "night journey," the arrival of Christmas morning allows Scrooge to escape his alienation in a final conversion to good will that is represented by Scrooge rejoining his family, buying presents and—in the movie versions—turning his back on class distinctions as he joins his clerk's family for a turkey dinner.

Only one film in the 1980s directly adapts *A Christmas Carol*, but almost all of the presentations of Christmas in the decade's films—including those that parody of attack the conventions—find their precedents in the conventions found in Dickens' story. For example, the roots of the "disrupted office party" convention can be seen in Scrooge's alienated visit to the Christmas party of his days as an apprentice. Even the convention of a generalized nationalism can be seen as an outgrowth of the original story's resolution in social consensus. This nebulous form of Americanism—sometimes including a racial dimension—becomes part of the secular religion that is substituted for the holiday's specifically Christian beliefs.

The essay which follows is not intended to be comprehensive. Instead I hope to delineate some of the more common cinematic uses of the Christmas conventions by focusing on American films of the 1980s. Most of these films manipulate several conventions of Christmas simultaneously. For example, I would argue that *Trading Places* works with such diverse conventions as those of business versus Christmas, the alienated individual, the disrupted office party, the incongruous Santa, the reintegration of alienated individuals into a (non-traditional) family that ignores class distinctions, and Christmas Eve as an emotional nadir with a Christmas morning reversal. Generally, this essay will stress the individual conventions rather than their combination in separate films.

- In pursuit of this end, the essay also examines movies which use Christmas settings or which appear to take place during the Christmas season. This includes, for example, *Running Scared* in which the action takes place during the Christmas season although the only reference to the holiday is the Christmas-decorated lobby which provides the location for the final shoot-out.

Family and Alienation

Clearly the most dominant use of Christmas in the 1980s films is to heighten the isolation of an individual protagonist, underlining his separation from the pleasures of family or community. Most of the time the protagonist is eventually reintegrated into a romantic couple or some sort of family group. In fact, the reintegration often begins during the holiday season, but at Christmas itself the individual's alienation is generally at its peak. Examples of this convention would include *Sweet Heart's Dance*, *Dead Bang*, *Die Hard*, *Skin Deep*, *The Fabulous Baker Boys*, *Less Than Zero*, *When Harry Met Sally...*, *Suspect*, *D.O.A.*, *Funny Farm*, *Lethal Weapon*, *Trading Places*, *Scrooged*, and *The War of the Roses*.

The Christmas season is a time for loneliness, just as it was for Scrooge. The archetypical 1980s film image of Christmas may be that of Dan Aykroyd in the 1983 film *Trading Places*. We find Aykroyd's character standing on the curb in front of a locked up store on Christmas Eve, having humiliated himself and apparently blown his last chance at regaining his old life, Aykroyd is urinated on by a dog. He tries to shoot himself but the gun won't work. When Aykroyd throws the gun away it fires and breaks a window, setting off a burglar alarm. Finally, it begins to rain on him.

A less exaggerated form of this image was seen in the television series *Hill Street Blues* when Bruce Weitz, as Mick Belker, sits alone in his darkened apartment eating a TV dinner while watching *Mr. Magoo's Christmas Carol*. A similar scene occurs in the otherwise non-Christmas film, *Look Who's Talking*. Abe Vigoda—playing John Travolta's lonely, widowed grandfather—is seen alone in his room at a nursing home watching the ultimate Christmas community film, *It's A Wonderful Life*, on television.

In *A Christmas Carol*, Scrooge's insistence on Christmas being just another work day is shown to be the result of his having chosen business success over a wife and family. The conventional conflict between job and family—the consequences of Scrooge's choice—continues in Christmas films of the 1980s, at times updated to address the decade's over-achievers, but retaining a decidedly traditional view of gender roles. *The War of the Roses* provides two different Christmas scenes which stress this conflict. The first scene shows Michael Douglas as a young lawyer working on Christmas to advance his career, neglecting his wife and children in the process. The second scene shows the result of his decision; while carollers sing outside, Douglas tries to reunite his broken family through a disastrous attempt at a traditional Christmas which ends in literal and figurative flames. *Die Hard* and *Diner* both present a working woman whose Christmas season work challenges domestic harmony.

The convention of work-related isolation is frequently applied to separated husbands. The two Don Johnson vehicles—*Sweet Heart's Dance* and *Dead Bang*—present the husband separated from his wife and children over Christmas. In *Sweet Heart's Dance*, the couple is separated and Johnson is living in a trailer at his construction site. Johnson's separation from his children is intensified when his child shows up and finds a woman in his bedroom. In *Dead Bang*, Johnson plays a homicide detective who spends Christmas Eve with a strange woman, then telephones his ex-wife who will not allow him to speak to his children. His solution, like Scrooge's, is to turn to his work.

Isolation during the holidays is regularly repeated in 1980s films. In *Suspect,* Cher plays an unmarried lawyer who bemoans her social isolation, her lack of a child, and her lack of a boyfriend as she spends Christmas working as a public defender. *Skin Deep*'s John Ritter is an alcoholic writer-Lothario who really only wants to get his ex-wife back. Ritter's character becomes increasingly self-destructive over the Christmas season. Christmas in *D.O.A.* finds a college professor being divorced by the wife he loves. *Running Scared* has Billy Crystal playing a Chicago cop divorced from the wife he loves. *Less Than Zero* shows Andrew McCarthy and Jami Gertz torn apart by his having gone off to college. *When Harry Met Sally...* gives us lovers Billy Crystal and Meg Ryan estranged over Christmas, underscored by Sally having to drag her Christmas tree home by herself.

The social limitations of the single life at Christmas may best be seen in *The Fabulous Baker Boys.* Christmas Eve finds Jeff Bridge's Jack unable to get Michelle Pfeiffer's Susie Diamond to join him for coffee. Bridges' character has to threaten the life of a callous veterinary night clerk just to get the company of his dog. When he gets home, the abandoned little girl from upstairs is sitting in the dark in his apartment. Jack and she watch television and get drunk on 80 proof egg nog.

While Christmas is often a time of unrequited love in films of the 1980s, romantic relationships do occur. However, if a Yuletide romance is to succeed it takes time—generally until New Year's Eve—to work things out. Here we see a shift away from *A Christmas Carol*'s focus on Christmas morning. While some of the romances do culminate on or about Christmas day—*Die Hard, Running Scared, Suspect, The Package, Funny Farm*—New Year's "resolutions"—or at least consummations—appear to be an integral part of many 1980s Christmas movies. The convention as it appears in *When Harry Met Sally...*, *The Fabulous Baker Boys*, *Ghostbusters II*, and *Trading Places* seems to equate a new start with the new year. In the case of *Diner,* the resolution takes place at a post-Christmas wedding, combining the holiday with another conventional symbol of the new start.

Although romantic couples do not fare that well in these Christmas movies, the community does a little better. Just as Scrooge is finally brought back into his family and community, outsiders are continually reintegrated into society during the Christmas season. *Lethal Weapon* may offer the strongest example of this convention.

Lethal Weapon finds Mel Gibson playing a cop whose life has no meaning living in a trailer on a beach with his dog. Gibson's attachment to a canine companion, like Jeff Bridges' in *The Fabulous Baker Boys*, serves to accentuate Gibson's lack of human connection. When Gibson is not at the trailer, he is on the job, trying to get himself killed.

The movie opens with a young porn actress falling from a high-rise apartment building while the non-traditional rock Christmas Carol "Jingle Bell Rock" plays on the soundtrack. This juxtaposition is only the first of many challenges to the traditional view of Christmas. Mel Gibson's partner, Danny Glover, is a middle-class family man and an Army buddy of the dead actress's father. In the course of the film, the duo defeat a generic threat to the family (drugs), a philosophical threat to the family (the porn actress's father was responsible for her death), and a direct threat to the family (Glover's daughter is kidnapped by the drug dealers).

As he helps to eliminate these threats to the family, Gibson's suicidal cop is drawn back into the community. First, he is accepted by Glover. Next, he directs his rage outward toward threats to the community and to Glover's family. Finally, in the last scene of the film, he joins Glover's family for Christmas dinner. The alienated outsider is redeemed, becoming part of the family. To underscore the point, as Gibson joins—and completes—the Glover family, Glover screws in the last bulb of the ring of Christmas lights that encircle his home.

To add a specific social significance to *Lethal Weapon*'s family closure—actually a second one, since the movie ends with a bi-racial family group—Gibson's character is a maladjusted Viet Nam veteran being reintegrated into society. The Viet Nam vet is also welcomed home in *Suspect*, where Cher's mute, homeless defendant turns out to be a articulate Viet Nam vet, and in *The Package* where Gene Hackman and Dennis Franz play Viet Nam buddies who are reunited as they stop a Christmas assassination attempt. A 1980s societal interest in Viet Nam veterans is reflected in the application of the more general convention of reintegrating the outsider into a community.

In many Christmas films of this decade, reintegration takes place not in the established community but in a reconstructed one, generally a non-traditional family. Such resolutions take place in *Cookie, Trading Places, Dead Bang,* and *Less Than Zero.* In fact, "non-traditionality" has become a convention—if not a tradition—of Christmas movies in the 1980s. If the reintegration occurs within a traditional family, then other circumstances are skewed. For example, in *Funny Farm* Chevy Chase and Madolyn Smith play a couple who buy a New England farm expecting a traditionally idyllic rural town only to find that the townspeople are obnoxious and hateful. Chase and Smith come to hate the small town and their marriage collapses under the strain. To sell the farm and settle their divorce, Chase and Smith pay off the town to enact a Norman Rockwell-type Christmas for potential buyers. The act succeeds but, swept away by the illusion of a "traditional" New England Christmas, Chase and Smith once again fall in love with each other and the town and decide not to sell.

This model is helpful to keep in mind, for it illustrates the way in which the films of the 1980s—and perhaps their audiences, as well—simultaneously reject as illusionary, yet lovingly embrace, the Christmas conventions.

Nostalgia and the Nontraditional Christmas

While the nostalgic approach to Christmas can be readily traced to Dickens' story—with its Ghost of Christmas Past and invocations of traditional Christmas rituals—this convention is maintained in many Christmas films of the 1980s only to be twisted or stood upon its head. Just as Scrooge's Christmases past were far happier than his Christmas present, so 1980s films wax nostalgic for the Christmas traditions that are absent from the lives of most characters in these films. Unlike Scrooge, however, these characters frequently don't rejoin the traditional community. Often they can not, for it is not simply a matter of an individual who is alienated from society, but society itself which is alienated from its traditions. Nonetheless, even in the guise of nontraditionality, these films continue to return to the same conventions.

Funny Farm offers one of the few "traditional" Christmases of the 1980s, and it is a expensively staged deception. *A Christmas Story* approaches the nostalgic image of Christmas from a different angle, recollecting Jean Shepherd's childhood Christmas and the travails it entailed. Santa Claus is a fearsome individual, the child's parents oppose his desired Christmas rifle, and the family Christmas dinner takes place in a Chinese restaurant. While appealing, Christmas isn't as good as it used to be and it never was.

Most of the positive, non-critical images of Christmas in the 1980s occur in made-for-television movies and reruns of classic films. An exception may be found in *Prancer*, the 1989 release which tells the story of a girl who finds one of Santa's reindeer and nurses it back to health. Even this movie, for all its family, farms, sentiment and cuteness has a smart-ass brother who regularly defuses the sweetness with a cynical comment. What distinguishes this film is that his cynicism is shown to be wrong.

In fact, Hollywood Christmas is increasingly non-traditional, even in look. Rarely is Christmas white anymore. If it isn't rainy, it is a barren snowless Christmas. The snowless Christmas also underscores the lack of a holiday mood and heightens the disjunction between what Christmas is supposed to be and what it actually is for the protagonist. Woody Allen's character in the 1977 film *Annie Hall* commented on this absence of Christmas in California and a similar Christmas climate is used to great effect in the 1988 remake of *D.O.A.* In this film, Dennis Quaid plays a college English teacher who has been irreversibly poisoned. Quaid must deal with being divorced, the betrayal of his closest friend, the apparent suicide of a student who was his wife's lover, and being hunted as his wife's murderer; all while dying a painful death as he tries to understand why he was poisoned. This film takes place in the middle of a sweltering Christmas heat wave. *Skin Deep, Dead Bang, Less Than Zero, Deal of the Century,* and *Lethal Weapon* all use "California Christmases" to heighten the dislocation between traditional expectations of Christmas and their "realistic" version of the holiday.

In *Die Hard*, Bruce Willis, playing New York cop John McClain, has only just absorbed the Los Angeles Christmas weather when his driver turns on rap Christmas music, again stressing the lack of tradition. Non-traditionality continues to develop as McClain attends a Japanese corporation's Christmas party where he discovers that his estranged wife is working under her maiden name. Of course, foreign "terrorist"/thieves are also not traditional Christmas trappings and Willis' McClain eventually sets about making things right. He kills off the "terrorist"/thieves, saves the hostages and salvages his marriage. By the film's end, his wife has abandoned the trappings of an independent career woman and returns to calling herself Mrs. McClain.

If we continue to examine the elements of *Die Hard*'s non-traditional Christmas, we come to an undercurrent of ethnic nationalism in Christmas movies; the film asserts an American ethnic tradition in the absence of any other Christmas tradition. In *Die Hard*, Christmas is saved by an *American* cowboy-like hero wiping out *foreign* "terrorist"/thieves—the most easily stereotyped being Russian, Germanic and Japanese—and rescuing his wife from a Japanese firm. The pragmatic Japanese attitude toward Christmas is explained early in the films when a character tells the head of the corporation that he didn't know Japanese celebrated Christmas. The firm's leader responds that "We do since you defeated us."

Asian attitudes toward Christmas are questioned in other films as well. Bob Balaban's parole officer in *Dead Bang* asks whether the Chinese even celebrate Christmas. The ultimate failure of the traditional Christmas in *A Christmas Story* is that the Christmas dinner takes place in a Chinese restaurant. An old Chinese gentleman is the source of the creature that spawns the monsters of *Gremlins*, which almost destroy that small town Christmas. There are Asians among both the terrorists of *Die Hard* and the drug dealers of *Lethal Weapon*, who do their best to ruin Christmas for the heroes.

In the absence of a specifically religious meaning, Christmas appears to have become an American holiday. Foreigners, especially Asians, serve to define what is appropriate Christmas behavior by their deviance from those American traditions or Christmas traditions that still remain.

Dead Bang doesn't limit this "non-American" convention to Asians, though. the film also examines the darker implications of the traditional Christmas: the linkage of racism and nostalgia. Johnson's homicide detective goes to the upper Midwest tracking a white supremacist conspiracy. It is within the "traditional Christmas setting" of a snow-covered countryside of Christmas trees, churches and small town America that White Supremacy has its base. Johnson, with his dirty dozen of black deputies led by Tim Reid, battles his way into an underground network of tunnels to root out the evil heart of this idyllic Christmas setting.

Christmas nationalism, like Scrooge's night-time odyssey, is linked with a more general nostalgia for the way things used to be; Christmas represents the good old days. The discord between the way things are and the way they should be is emphasized in *Suspect*'s opening when a corrupt judge remembers that Abraham Lincoln used to hunt wild turkeys on his road and "you can still bag one there for Christmas dinner" before he kills himself with his turkey hunting gun. The film goes on to present a Christmas season trial in which another corrupt judge attempts to sacrifice an innocent man —and the integrity of the judicial system—to advance his career.

Each of these films, like Dickens' story, presents a "Christmas spirit" which is a generalized, non-religious statement of the societal consensus on relevant issues. Dickens' original story stressed the fact that Scrooge, though reformed and willing to help his clerk's family, stayed within his own class socially. In the second half of the twentieth century, American societal consensus on class had shifted and adaptations of *A Christmas Carol* stressed the reformed Scrooge's class-blindness. Likewise, when a societal consensus reflects anti-foreign, anti-racist, anti-Nazi, or anti-nuclear sentiments as being "American" values, those same sentiments become associated with Christmas.

We will return to the extremist threat to Christmas, but there are other Christmas conventions which are utilized, but critiqued, in 1980s films. *A Christmas Carol*'s underlying assumption that community results from enforced conformity is directly attacked, but it is combined with Dickens' linkage of Christmas and terrrifying death. The resulting Christmas horror films have included *Christmas Evil*, the Canadian *Don't Open Till Christmas*, *Gremlins*, *Silent Night, Deadly Night* and *Silent Night, Deadly Night II*.

The demand for Christmas conformity is criticized most blatantly in *Gremlins* and *Silent Night, Deadly Night* (AKA *Slayride*). These two films specifically address societal insistence that people must enjoy Christmas and its trappings, especially Santa Claus. *Gremlins* offers a version of Christmas in which little gremlins act out exaggerated human Christmas behavior and destroy much of the town in the process. In a non-sequitur monologue, Phoebe Cates' character explains that she hates Christmas because her father got stuck in a chimney and died trying to play Santa Claus.

The scary version of Santa Claus can be traced to Dickens' Ghost of Christmas Future who judges and deals in death. The terrifying Ghost of Christmas Future is the alter-ego of the Father Christmas-inspired Ghost of Christmas Present, who closely resembles our contemporary Santa Claus. *A Christmas Story* already presented the generally ignored scariness of Santa, but *Silent Night, Deadly Night* and its 1987 sequel develop this into full-fledged horror, drawing on the negative side of a Santa who judges who is naughty as well as who is nice. A deranged teenager, played by Robert Brian Wilson, sees his family killed by Santa Claus and blends that experience with his nun's insistence that sex is bad. Wilson's character dresses up as

Santa and kills sexually active teenagers, the nun who ruined Christmas for him by demanding conformity and gratitude, and drunken participants in a Christmas office party.

Business and Peace on Earth, Good Will Toward Men

The office of *Silent Night, Deadly Night*, with its drunkenness and unbridled libidos, is another convention of the 1980s Christmas movie. It is also part of the broader conventional portrayal of businessmen at Christmas. Just as Scrooge saw the office party he visited—and Christmas frivolity in general—in the terms of its effect on the bottom line, businessmen are portrayed as failing to understand the true spirit of Christmas. We have already seen the convention of the job-oriented individual who views Christmas as just another workday—emphasizing the alienated individual— but some of these films also present the businessman who cashes in on Christmas. The first victim of the homicidal Santa (as opposed to the deranged Santa) of *Silent Night, Deadly Night* is a store owner who only likes Christmas for the profits. Likewise, *Deal of the Century, Santa Claus: The Movie, Trading Places, Scrooged, Die Hard,* and *The Fabulous Baker Boys* show Christmas as a time when profits come before the holiday spirit.

Once again we can trace the Christmas office party back to Dickens' *A Christmas Carol*. While the parties are not as wholesome, the convention remains. In the 1980s, the Christmas office party has also appeared in *Die Hard, Cookie, D.O.A.* (as an Art opening), *Trading Places, The Package,* and, arguably, *Gremlins*. In its 1980s form, the party serves to reinforce social pressures on the individual and to heighten the contrast between what Christmas behavior should be and what it is. In each of these films, a character under the influence of seasonal chemicals violates decorum and embarrasses himself. In each setting, money and power are shown to be more important than human feelings or justice, a point made clear as the protagonist is often betrayed in this setting.

D.O.A.'s party is disrupted by the drunken protagonist who discovers that his wife was sleeping with his student. In *Trading Places* the office party is disrupted by a drunken, gun-waving Dan Aykroyd in a Santa Claus suit. Shortly after Aykroyd's exit, Eddie Murphy discovers that his employers are racists who have destroyed Aykroyd for their own entertainment and now plan to destroy him. A more extreme version of drunkenness is played out in *Silent Night, Deadly Night,* as "Santa" gets drunk and kills his sexually active drunken workmates. In *Die Hard* the drunk is replaced by a cocaine-user, who propositions the hero's wife, is then caught "inflagrante" with a secretary, and later is killed for his boorishness as he tries to treat the "terrorist"/thieves like just another business deal. Each of these films criticizes inappropriate Christmas behavior, harking back to traditional standards of appropriateness while also referring to cynical expectations of celebratory behavior.

Cookie presents a minor variation on the convention with a Mafia office party at which Mafioso Peter Falk discovers he has been betrayed by his partner and the partner's son crudely propositions Falk's illegitimate daughter. The daughter, played by Emily Lloyd, causes a scene by rejecting the powerful son's advances and is scolded by Falk for letting her enemy know how she feels.

We even find a variation on the office party in *The Package*, in the form of a celebratory meeting between the peace treaty negotiators. In this case the man who causes the scene is an American general who refuses to join the conspiracy against "the greatest Christmas present to the world." The betrayers of the plan—drunk, I suppose, on power—kill the patriotic General.

The office party becomes one more opportunity to reassert the Scrooge-based convention that people with money and power don't understand Christmas. The most extreme example is the greedy toy magnate played by John Lithgow in *Santa Claus: The Movie*. Lithgow's character wants to eliminate Santa Claus completely. *Deal of the Century* also plays on this potentially apocalyptic element in Christmas as it highlights the contrast of the Season of Peace by setting an arms show during the holidays. At one point, Chevy Chase's crazed boss tries to blow up the whole show and everyone in it, including himself, to prove the superiority of his product.

Peace on Earth, Good Will Toward Men

An interesting variation on this portrayal of crazed, powerful people trying to thwart peace and the will of common people at Christmas can be found in the film *The Package*, a film which also restates most of the other Christmas conventions. John Heard plays the Scrooge-like character, the leader of an attempt to block a major disarmament treaty. The treaty, which is specifically referred to as a "Christmas present to the world" in the "Season of Peace" is to be signed after a series of symbolic visits by the Russian and American leaders to sites around America. A group of military men from both countries decide to stop the treaty by having the Russian leader assassinated in Chicago.

Gene Hackman plays the loner sergeant—something of a Bob Cratchit with a gun—whom Heard falsely accuses of incompetence and then reassigns to a position that will make him the scapegoat for the assassination. Though American, the assassin has to be smuggled into America from Germany. Through much of the film, Hackman is apparently the only person who understands the true values of America and Christmas. The seasonal loneliness is underscored by the barren landscape around the home of another soldier's estranged wife who lives alone in a shabby house brightened only by a Christmas tree and decorations. The seasonal dissonance is underscored when she is strangled to death under a "Merry Christmas" banner in her kitchen.

Hackman is confined to sterile, cold quarters, alone, for the holiday season, but he escapes and defeats the assassin with the help of a loosely formed extended family which includes his estranged wife and a buddy from Viet Nam who is now a Chicago cop. In the course of saving Christmas, Hackman must stop the assassin and a conspiracy between Russians, White Supremicists and corrupt American intelligence officers. Hackman's estranged wife—who outranks him—abandons her job to help Hackman and returns to a traditionally subservient role, at one point even feeding and protecting the Viet Nam buddy's children.

The film is suffused with Christmas images, decorations and carols, and references linking "Christmas" and "Peace," although these all remain explicitly non-Christian. Just as the assassin has sneaked into America and hides within the military structure, he attempts the assassination hidden behind a Christmas display of an American home, perched on a box labeled "Santa's toys." Irony abounds.

Hackman's defeat of the assassin—and of Heard—becomes a victory for both the traditional Christmas values expressed in the phrase "Peace on Earth, Good will Toward Men," and the American democratic values which oppose the tyranny of a war-mongering military clique. At the film's end, Hackman and his estranged wife and his Viet Nam buddy are reunited. Having faced separation and the threat of death, the lovers, extended family and community are reunited. However, Heard's character will not be reintegrated into the community and, shortly after tossing a "Bah Humbug"-ish response to Hackman's criticism of his values, Heard is killed by his driver. For the moment, at least, Christmas and America are happy.

A Christmas Carol Once More

At the beginning of this essay, it was noted that only one 1980s film has directly adapted Dickens' story. That adaptation is the 1988 film *Scrooged*. Not surprisingly, the film clearly adheres to each of the conventions that this essay has delineated. Furthermore, the film illustrates both approaches taken to those conventions.

In *Scrooged*, Bill Murray plays a television executive who already knows the story of *A Christmas Carol*, making for a decidedly post-modern Christmas event. The film shifts between cynicism and sentiment, irony and sincerity, as Murray remains detached from the events even as the story leads us along increasingly sentimental paths. As the film progresses we are continually urged to laugh at the conventions in the story of Christmas redemption at the same time that we are urged to embrace them.

We are presented with two modern Cratchits—Murray's secretary, Alfre Woodard, who is unable to cure her mute and fatherless son, and Bobcat Goldthwaitt, who ends up comically stalking Murray with a shotgun after being fired for expressing concern about Murray's debasing of the Christmas message. We see Murray's sincere former girlfriend working to help the homeless, but we are also presented with such absurd humor as tiny antlers being stapled to the heads of mice and a young Murray getting meat as a Christmas present from his butcher father. The Ghost of Christmas Present, Carol Kane shows Murray's brother defending him to his justifiably critical family and friends, but we also see the wires that allow Kane's Ghost to "fly" and Kane knocks Murray around with a toaster.

As one might expect of a modern *Christmas Carol*, Murray's television executive undergoes his conversion on a live worldwide TV broadcast. Once Murray has gotten the mute fatherless child of his secretary to speak and Murray's old girlfriend returns to him, Murray—now more the actor than the character he plays—speaks directly to the theater audience and cajoles us into joining him in singing a Christmas carol as the titles scroll up. Even as he steps outside the story, though, Murray continues the film's approach to the conventions. On one hand we are asked to laugh at what is happening but on the other hand the audience is being asked to join in singing a traditional Christmas carol. (The pre-Christmas audience with which I saw the film in 1988 sang.). The combined chorus of audience members and film character reaffirms a nostalgic societal consensus and momentarily integrates the diverse individuals in the movie audience into a community.

For all its aesthetic or narrative flaws, this may be the film that best illustrates the approach to Christmas conventions taken in films of the 1980s. Like the characters in *Funny Farm*, the film ends up juggling respect for what it understands as the Christmas traditions embodied in Dickens *A Christmas Carol*, and cynicism about those traditions, and it ends up embracing them anyway. By working so closely to the original Dickens' story, *Scrooged* makes clear the ambivalence that underlies so many American Christmas films of the 1980s.

Filmography

1934	*Babes in Toyland*	Dir. Gus Meins
1935	*Scrooge*	Dir. Henry Edwards (British)
1938	*A Christmas Carol*	Dir. Edwin L. Marsh
1941	*The Man Who Came to Dinner*	Dir. William Keighley
1941	*Meet John Doe*	Dir. Frank Capra
1942	*Holiday Inn*	Dir. Mark Sandrich
1943	*Destination Tokyo*	Dir. Delmer Daves
1944	*Christmas Holiday*	Dir. Robert Siodmak
1944	*I'll Be Seeing You*	Dir. William Deiterle
1944	*Meet Me in St. Louis*	Dir. Vincente Minnelli
1944	*Since You Went Away*	Dir. John Cromwell
1945	*The Bells of St. Mary*	Dir. Leo McCarey
1945	*The Cheaters*	Dir. Joseph Kane

(AKA *The Castaway*)

1945	*Christmas in Connecticut*	Dir. Peter Godfrey
1946	*Black Narcissus*	Dir. Michael Powell (British)
1946	*It's a Wonderful Life*	Dir. Frank Capra
1947	*The Bishop's Wife*	Dir. Henry Koster
1947	*Christmas Eve*	Dir. Edwin L. Marin
1947	*Miracle on 34th Street*	Dir. George Seaton
1948	*Scott of the Antartic*	Dir. Charles Frend (British)
1948	*Tenth Avenue Angel*	Dir. Roy Rowland
1948	*Three Godfathers*	Dir. John Ford
1949	*Little Women*	Dir. Mervyn LeRoy
1951	*A Christmas Carol*	Dir. Brian Desmond-Hurst (British)
1951	*The Lemon Drop Kid*	Dir.. Sidney Lanfield
1951	*On Moonlight Bay*	Dir. Roy Del Ruth
1952	*Encore* ("Winter Cruise" segment)	Dirs. Pat Jackson Anthony Pelissier Harold French (British)
1953	*The Holly and the Ivy*	Dir. George More O'Ferrall (British)
1953	*Knights of the Round Table*	Dir. Richard Thorpe
1954	*The Glenn Miller Story*	Dir. Anthony Mann
1954	*White Christmas*	Dir. Michael Curtiz
1954	*Young at Heart*	Dir. Gordon Douglas
1955	*Conquest of Space*	Dir. Byron Haskin
1955	Walt Disney's *Lady and the Tramp*	Dir. Hamilton Luske
1957	*Desk Set*	Dir. Walter Lang
1959	*The Nun's Story*	Dir. Fred Zinnemann
1960	*The Apartment*	Dir. Billy Wilder
1963	*The Victors*	Dir. Carl Foreman
1964	*Robin and the Seven Hoods*	Dir. Gordon Douglas
1966	*The Christmas that Almost Wasn't*	Dir. Rossano Brazzi (Italian/US)
1967	*Fitzwilly*	Dir. Delbart Mann
1968	*The Christmas Kid*	Dir. Sidney Pink (Spanish)
1968	*The Lion in Winter*	Dir. Anthony Harver (British)
1969	*The Christmas Tree*	Dir. Terence Young
1970	*Scrooge*	Dir. Ronald Neame (British)
1972	*The Godfather*	Dir. Francis Coppola
1975	*Black Christmas* (AKA *Silent Night, Evil Night* AKA *Stranger in the House*)	Dir. Bob Clark Canadian
1977	*Annie Hall*	Dir. Woody Allen
1978	*The Silent Partner*	Dir. Daryl Duke

1979	*More American Graffiti*	(Canadian) Dir. B.W.L. Norton
1980	*Christmas Evil* (AKA *Terror in Toyland* AKA *You Better Watch Out*)	Dir. Lewis Jackson
1980	*Christmas Mountain*	Dir. Pierre Moro
1982	*Annie*	Dir. John Huston
1982	*Diner*	Dir. Barry Levinson
1983	*A Christmas Story*	Dir. Bob Clark
1983	*Deal of the Century*	Dir. William Friedkin
1983	*Merry Christmas, Mr. Lawrence*	Dir. Nagisa Oshima (British/Japanese)
1983	*The Survivors*	Dir. Michael Ritchie
1983	*Trading Places*	Dir. John Landis
1984	*Don't Open Till Christmas*	Dir. Edmund Perdon
1984	*Ernest Saves Christmas*	Dir. John Cherry
1984	*Falling in Love*	Dir. Ulu Grosbard
1984	*Gremlins*	Dir. Joe Dante
1984	*Silent Night, Deadly Night* (AKA *Slayride*)	Dir. Charles E. Sellier
1987	*Less Than Zero*	Dir. Marek Kanievska
1987	*Lethal Weapon*	Dir. Richard Donner
1987	*Silent Night, Deadly Night II*	Dir. Lee Harry
1987	*Suspect*	Dir. Peter Yates
1988	*Bellman and True*	Dir. Richard Loncraine (British)
1988	*Die Hard*	Dir. John McTiernan
1988	*D.O.A.*	Dir. Rocky Morton
1988	*Funny Farm*	Dir. George Roy Hill
1988	*Heart of Midnight*	Dir. Matthew Chapman
1988	*Sweet Heart's Dance*	Dir. Robert Greenwald
1989	*Cookie*	Dir. Susan Seidelman
1989	*Dead Bang*	Dir. John Frankenheimer
1989	*The Fabulous Baker Boys*	Dir. Steve Kloves
1989	*Family Business*	Dir. Sidney Lumet
1989	*Ghostbusters II*	Dir. Ivan Reitman
1989	*Look Who's Talking*	Dir. Amy Heckerling
1989	*National Lampoon's Christmas Vacation*	Dir. Jeremiah Chechik
1989	*The Package*	Dir. Andrew Davis
1989	*Prancer*	Dir. John Hancock
1989	*Scrooged*	Dir. Richard Donner
1989	*Skin Deep*	Dir. Blake Edwards
1989	*Steel Magnolias*	Dir. Herbert Ross
1989	*Stella*	Dir. John Erman
1989	*The War of the Roses*	Dir. Danny DeVito
1989	*When Harry Met Sally...*	Dir. Rob Reiner

California Dreaming:
Dream Sequences in Hollywood
Musicals, Melodramas and Horror Movies

Brooks Robards

What the hell *are* dreams?
Mysteries...Incredible body hokus pokus.
The truth is, we still don't know what they
are or what they come from.
                            Nightmare on Elm Street (1984)

As the oxymoron "Dream Factory" suggests, Hollywood has an affinity for dreams. Yet in many ways the cinematic use of dreams has been a subject more suited to the esoterica of the aesthetitians or avant garde filmmakers than to the plot conventions of popular American movies. Critics ranging from Hugo Mauerhofer and Suzanne Langer to Siegfried Kracauer and Christian Metz have made exhaustive (and exhausting) explorations of the analogy between film and dream. Bruce Kawin has even developed a complex theory of dream and film in the psychoanalytic critical tradition called mindscreen. *Dreamworks*, an interdisciplinary journal, reported tirelessly on the movie-dream connection from 1980 until 1988.

Long before the medium became a subject for scholarly study, however, movies used dream sequences as plot devices. In fact, dream sequences begin to appear almost as soon as movies have plots, and no genre or era of popular film is without its visits from the sandman.

Since their earliest representation, dream sequences have evolved in increasingly sophisticated ways, from the briefest verbal reference to cases where a dream envelops the entire movie. During the silent era, dreams remain relatively superficial plot devices, more literary in structure than cinematic. The basic conventions for dreaming are quickly established in the early silent years, however, and continue to vie for popularity with more complex investigations of the relationship between film and dreaming in the most contemporary movies.

The earliest documented dream sequence appears in Edwin Porter's *The Life of An American Fireman* (1903). The hero is shown asleep in his chair at the fire station. His dream, in which a mother is putting her child in bed, foretells their rescue. It is visualized for the audience in a circular inset—

called a "dream balloon"—superimposed on the upper right corner of the frame. At the time, this was movie convention for representation of the character's thoughts, whether dreamt or not. Porter advanced the development of film plotting significantly by dissolving from this "dream ballon" to a full frame of the fireman's dream. Similar, essentially "mechanical" means for the introduction of dream sequences prevailed, however, into the late fifties and are still popular.

The Life of an American Fireman, with its dream-warning, illustrates the first of four primary functions served by movie dream sequences. Prophetic dreams advance the plot by foretelling the outcome of events. Especially popular in the early days of the movie industry, they can have religious overtones, provide inspiration to the central characters, or suggest the proper course of action.

In 1906, Porter gave us a second prototype for the movie dream: nightmare. In *The Dream of a Rarebit Fiend*, an early example of Méliès-style trick photography, the hero overeats and suffers in his dreams as a result. Unlike most movie nightmares, his dreams are comical. A variety of causes both physical and psychological, including drugs, blows to the head, psychic trauma and anxiety, lead to movie nightmares and—ultimately—an entire movie genre in the horror film.

A third common category of movie dreams is wish fulfillment. In this case, the central character realizes his/her desires through the temporary release of a dream. Reality, as represented in the rest of the film, remains distinct and unchallenged. One early example of this type of dream sequence is Chaplin's classic comedy, *The Gold Rush* (1924), in which the Tramp dreams of the dance hall girl he has invited to Christmas dinner. As in many movies containing wish fulfillment dreams, the poignancy of the story comes from the contrast between dream and reality.

A fourth and final category of dream sequence is one in which the character's dream transports the movie entirely into the realm of fantasy. Dreaming here clearly becomes a vehicle for expanding the movie in directions which may have little to do with the rest of the narrative. Fantasy dream sequences accommodate the distortions, experiments and breaks in the conventional film world that are perhaps most easily illustrated by flashbacks, slow motion and sound distortions.

One of the earliest examples of dream as pure fantasy comes in Buster Keaton's *Sherlock Junior* (1924). Keaton, playing a movie house projectionist, falls asleep on the job and dreams himself into the movie he is projecting. What follows could, arguably, be described as an exploration of all the dream categories already mentioned. Buster's yearning for his sweetheart is what propels him into the more romantic environs of the movie's movie, "Heart and Pearls," but his inability to manage once inside the screen could be described as a nightmare. When he tries to sit on a park bench in one scene, he tumbles in quick succession onto a busy street, a mountain, a jungle, the desert, a rock in the ocean, a snowbank. At the end of the movie, Buster's dream becomes prophetic in the most literal sense, when the screen shows him how to win back his girl.

The result is sheer fantasy—an exploration of the medium that goes well beyond the ordinary conventions of plot and a brilliant expansion of movie time and space. Technically speaking, the double image of Keaton stepping out of himself and into his dream represents a quantum leap from the "dream balloon" in *The Life of an American Fireman.*

The *American Film Institute Catalogue of Motion Pictures Produced in the United States* has documented well over 150 films from the silent era that use dream sequences. In most, the dreaming process is used to advance melodramas of thwarted love or infidelity—such as the 1916 Theda Bara vehicle *The Serpent,* in which the heroine is raped but wreaks her revenge by marrying the rapist's son; parables of the evils of drink—as in *The Devil at his Elbow* (1916); or fantasies of trips to exotic lands or eras—as in *Wild Women* (1916), a comedy western where Harry Carey gets drunk and dreams he's shanghaied to Hawaii.

In its simplest forms, the dream allows for complications or reversals of the narrative structure to give a new twist to an old or risqué story. In one elaborate, proto-feminist example, *Man-Woman-Marriage* (1921), the heroine marries an attorney. When he falls victim to corruption, she runs for office against him. After he goes to prison on bribery charges, he is redeemed by her visits. At each crisis point, she dreams herself into a different era—the Stone Age, the age of chivalry; and into a different role—Amazon, Christian converting pagan Romans.

D. W. Griffith's *The Avenging Conscience; Thou Shalt Not Kill* (1914) offers another typical pattern. It combines Edgar Allen Poe's "The Tell-Tale Heart" and "Annabel Lee" to tell the story of a bachelor who becomes jealous when the nephew he has raised wants to marry. He is murdered by the nephew, who hangs himself, after which his sweetheart jumps to her death. The movie ends when the hero awakens from what has been a nightmare, reconciles with his uncle and marries his sweetheart.

Many of the original movie versions of other classic stories containing dreams appear during this twenty-year period: Joseph and his Coat of Many Colors, Alice in Wonderland, Joan of Arc, Scrooge, Little Red Riding Hood, Kathleen Mavoureen, The Blue Bird, A Connecticut Yankee in King Arthur's Court, Dr. Jekyll and Mr. Hyde, Dante's Inferno, Cinderella, The Wizard of Oz. They record both the fascination of early filmmakers with dreams as a literal device for advancing the plot and their recognition of the inherent affinities between film and dream. The more cinematic affinities remained unexplored for the most part, however, in the early days of the movies.

The fact that half as many of the films made in the twenties use dreams as a plot device as those in the teens suggests that the early popularity of dream sequences as a narrative device was gradually exhausted. If never again as popular as in those first decades of American movies, such dream sequences nevertheless remain perennial plot devices. They may serve as a means of creating humor, as in *Father of the Bride* (1950), where Spencer Tracy has an anxiety dream the night before his daughter's wedding. They may extricate the central character from hot water, as in *Risky Business* (1983), where Tom Cruise's escapades with a prostitute turn out to be "nothing more than a dream." They may signal the transport into fairy tale, as in *The Princess Bride* (1988), in which as his father reads to him, a young boy falls asleep and dreams the story. Or, they may function as a framing device for a realistic narrative, as in *Casualties of War* (1989), where Michael J. Fox initiates the story by falling asleep in a subway, his flashback dream stimulated by the young Oriental student he sees several seats away. No matter how updated, such uses of dreaming as a plot device remain superficial and primarily literary in structure like their predecessors.

While popular movies using dream sequences are notably few in the thirties—particularly in the early thirties—two important trends find their roots in this decade. The connection of dreams with song and dance in the musical genre and with psychological delvings in the melodrama, detective-suspense and horror genres heralds the evolution of movie dreams beyond simple narrative expedience. Beginning in the thirties, the movie dream developed a more purely cinematic structure as a plot device. The ultimately unwieldy and essentially literary mechanics of the transitions into dream states dissolve in the musical to the point where a character no longer has to put his head on a pillow and close his eyes for the audience to know that he has entered a dream state. Depending on the generic context, a look or a word may be enough to signify the transition.

With a screenplay by George S. Kaufman and Robert Sherwood and choreography by Busby Berkeley, *Roman Scandals* (1933) probably provides the earliest example of the use of dream in the musical genre. One of the biggest hits of the thirties, *Roman Scandals* uses the already well-worn plot device of transporting star Eddie Cantor back to ancient Rome in a dream.

Carefree (1938), one of the last of the Fred Astaire-Ginger Rogers pairings, is a more important movie in terms of the evolution of Hollywood dreams. A light-hearted send-up of Freudian psychoanalysis, which became popular in the thirties, the movie casts Astaire as a psychoanalyst who sets out to cure Rogers of her reluctance to wed fiancé Ralph Bellamy. Dreams enter in a literal, almost mechanical way that harks back to *The Dream of a Rarebit Fiend.*

Doctor Astaire orders a stomach-churning combination of foods to stimulate patient Rogers to produce dreams for analysis. The set for the dream sequence—flowers, tropical trees and water—is patently artificial. The dream frames are dry-iced, insisting on the fantastical nature of the dream, in which Rogers dances with Astaire in slow motion. While integration of the dream into the movie is psychologically superficial, its use as a device for the introduction of music and dance is a plot technique that quickly became a mainstay of the musical genre.

In the strictest sense, Dorothy's dream in *The Wizard of Oz* (1939) is used merely as a means to frame the narrative. But the dramatic shift from black and white to color in the land of Oz is the most successful of any movie attempt to make the transition from real to dream world since *Sherlock Junior*. It also captures the emotional power inherent in color and its potential for exploration of the surreal. Like music and dance, color in the movies can operate as pure expression—hence the appropriateness of the connection to dreaming in *The Wizard of Oz*.

As in *Sherlock Junior*, dreaming becomes a way of exploring the medium itself in *The Wizard of Oz*. Altman sees the dream device in the musical as part of the genre's opposition of art and reality and suggests that "the dream and the film both enjoy a freedom from the normal physical laws of time, space, and causality" (62). The combination of dream and color becomes a particularly generative one for the movies in the musical. After *The Wizard of Oz*, only one other major movie musical with a dream sequence appears in black and white.

Vincente Minelli's all-black *Cabin in the Sky* (1943) has been described as similar in structure to *The Wizard of Oz*. However, it uses a far more complicated—and less inherently cinematic—structure of dreams within dreams to allegorize the struggle between good and evil in hero Eddie "Rochester" Anderson.

Anderson's Little Joe is an inveterate gambler and womanizer who sneaks outside during church services for one last throw of the "calamity cubes." He ends up getting shot and spending the rest of the film unconscious in bed while devils and angels fight for his soul. Ethel Waters plays Little Joe's devout wife Petunia, whose prayers manage to tip the scales toward redemption. *Cabin in the Sky* was Minnelli's first feature film, and he seemed to bring from Broadway, where he had also directed the theatrical version of this musical, more literary notions of structure.

Mitchell Leisen's *Lady in the Dark* (1944) further demonstrates the importance of the combination of dream and color in the musical. Ginger Rogers stars again, this time as a fashion editor with psychological problems. Many of the Kurt Weill songs from the original play by Moss Hart were eliminated. In their place were three elaborately produced "dry ice" dream sequences: one in blue; one in shades of white, gold and rose; and one in multicolors. Elaborately designed costumes by Edith Head—in contrast to the work-a-day clothes in the rest of the movie—help signal the dream state. Such attempts to convey the dream state at less literal levels become increasingly important in later musicals.

Two important dream sequences are incorporated into *Anchors Aweigh*, the 1945 musical starring Frank Sinatra and Gene Kelly as sailors on leave. The first is not a conventional nocturnal dream, but placed in juxtaposition with the movie's second, more conventional dream and in context with similar sequences in other musicals, its function is clear. In both cases, the dream state signifies by its very form the expressive freedom appropriate to music and dance.

In the first sequence, sailor Kelly's dream state is implied by his inability to express his love to his sweetheart Kathryn Grayson in ordinary ways. The traditional narrative machinery used to signal a shift into a dream state is dispensed with, leaving only changes in lighting and camera, along with a highly stylized mise-en-scene, to cue the audience. Grayson appears on a balcony dressed as a Spanish senorita, watching while Kelly performs a fandango. A cut to a new scene is all it takes to signify the end of the dream sequence. Plot connections are somewhat tenuous: the setting is a movie lot; Jose Iturbi is featured as an actor as well as a conductor; Grayson has a job performing at a Chicano restaurant. The dream functions primarily to furnish Kelly with an excuse to break into dance.

Integration of the dream into the rest of the story anticipates and may have provided the prototype for the more famous Kelly dream-ballets in *An American in Paris* (1951) and *Singin' in the Rain* (1952), as well as similar dream sequences in *Oklahoma!* (1955), with Gordon MacRae and Shirley Jones, and the Fred Astaire vehicle *Daddy Long Legs* (1955). In each case, the more literal transition markers are erased, but the message remains clear to the audience that a dream state has been entered. A similar pattern of integration occurs with dream sequences in Hitchcockian melodramas, and the horror genre occasionally plays hide and seek with dream sequences.

The second, more conventional sequence in *Anchors Aweigh* is equally as innovative as the first, but at a different level. Grayson's nephew, played by a juvenile Dean Stockwell, falls asleep and dreams of Kelly singing and dancing in a mythical cartoon kingdom where these entertainments are outlawed. Kelly ends up persuading the king—MGM's star cartoon character Jerry the Mouse —to dance with him.

It is important to emphasize that this excursion into cinematic fantasy takes place within the context of a dream. In the musical, dream sequences explore states of pure fantasy. In the case of *Anchors Aweigh*, the exploration takes place on both the narrative level—in the first dream, and the structural level—in the second dream. The third highest moneymaker of the year, *Anchors Aweigh* received an Academy Award nomination for best picture.

Three hybrid comedies deserve mention in passing because of their proximity to the musical genre and their use of daydreams. The relative lack of popularity of *The Secret Life of Walter Mitty* (1947), starring Danny Kaye, could be due to the absence of song and dance, logical extensions to milquetoast Mitty's exotic daydreams. The best-remembered part of the movie, Kay's Anatole-of-Paris routine, implies the missing elements.

Preston Sturges' 1948 comedy, *Unfaithfully Yours*—it was remade in 1984 with Dudley Moore—flirts even more directly with the musical genre. Rex Harrison is cast as an orchestra director who suspects his wife, Linda Darnell, of cheating. Using a conventional movie device for signifying a dream state, the camera enters Harrison's eye as he plays three separate pieces during a classical concert. In each case, he imagines how he will win his revenge, while reality is always a comic disaster. Sturges rejects the standard resolution from silent movies, where the cuckholded husband wakes up and finds it was all a dream, letting a bogus infidelity unravel of its own accord.

Yet another hybrid musical is *Artists and Models* (1955), starring Dean Martin and Jerry Lewis in one of their last collaborations. Comic book addict Lewis's dreams are invaded by nightmarish fantasies about Bat Lady, played by Shirley MacLaine. The combination of comedy, song and dance, and Freudian style dream analysis makes for an ambitious but undercooked stew.

By the time the musical reached its peak in movies like *Singin' in the Rain*, the dream sequence was fully integrated into the structure of the musical. The transformation of "The Dueling Cavalier" into "The Dancing Cavalier" is accomplished by means of a dream event mentioned in passing by Kelly's Don. A modern hero will be transported back in time to the French Revolution after a sand bag hits him on the head, a dream transition device that, appropriately enough, harks back to the silents. Kelly's "dream dance" with Cyd Charisse is accomplished by a dissolve.

Two more recent musicals also use dreams. In keeping with the Chagall-inspired title of the movie, the dream sequence in *Fiddler of the Roof* (1971) was shot to reflect the artist's famous painting. On the narrative plane, the dream is a fake one, a device used by Tevye to persuade his superstitious wife Golda that he may break his agreement with a wealthy butcher and let his daughter Zeitel follow her heart. Reversing the relationship between black and white and color set up by *The Wizard of Oz*, the dream sequence is shot monochromatically with actors in white-face, a stylized, theatrical set, and a character who flies. The dream state is cued by the absence of color and the fact that the actors are wearing night gowns.

Bob Fosse's *All That Jazz* (1979) borrows from Fellini to create his dream sequences. His conversations with a mysterious woman in white, played by Jessica Lange, mimic *8 1/2* and are coded as dreams only through the use of soft focus and lighting. The finale falls more directly in the dream-dance tradition established by *Carefree*. The heart disease that kills the choreographer, played by Roy Scheider, becomes the theme for the final number. Scheider's "dream of death" can be taken as a metaphor for the fate of the musical as a genre—and in retrospect, a haunting foreshadow of the impact AIDS would have on the performing arts in the eighties.

As generative as dream sequences in musicals have been for the medium, present-day movie dreams are probably most often thought of as a form of psychological investigation. As such, they turn up either in the emotional inquiries of the melodrama, as part of the process of ratiocination in the detective-suspense genre or in the excesses of the horror film.

One of Frank Capra's least popular but self-proclaimed favorite movies, *The Bitter Tea of General Yen* (1933), coincides with the growth in popularity of Freudianism in the thirties and anticipates the psychological trend in Hollywood's use of dreams. The movie's dream sequence adds psychological depth by revealing heroine Barbara Stanwyck's true feelings about the Shanghai war-lord who abducts her. One of the few films by the master of comedy and sentimental drama to lose money, *The Bitter Tea of General Yen* was attacked by Protestants because of its anti-missionary stance and was banned in the British Empire.

A W. Somerset Maugham novel provided the material for another thirties psychological melodrama in *Of Human Bondage* (1934). Bette Davis's role as Mildred, the waitress with whom a club-footed medical student becomes obsessed, helped establish her stardom. The dreams of Leslie Howard's Phillip become the wish fulfillment for his doomed romance with Davis's Mildred and the measure of the irony of his sexual desires.

A number of forties melodramas demonstrate some of the difficulties of incorporating dream sequences into film structure. Edward G. Robinson stars as a staid college psychology professor who becomes embroiled in a complicated murder in Fritz Lang's *The Woman at the Window* (1944). After sending his wife and children off to Maine on vacation, he meets a young woman, played by Joan Bennett, who has posed for the painting he is admiring. While visiting her apartment, he kills her attacker in self-defense and then attempts to cover up the murder.

In a surprise ending that harks back to the silents, the entire incident is revealed to have been nothing but a dream. *Variety* called the movie "a top liner in its particular field" but complained about its unsporting finish (10/11/44).

Robert Siodmak used the same device in *The Strange Affair of Uncle Harry* (1945) and was roasted even more severely. Bosley Crowther's complaint that "this business—compelled by the Hays Office—of having murderers dream their crimes is becoming extremely aggravating" points out the industry-related motivation behind use of dream sequences as a plot convenience (2077).

The temptation to use dream sequences as an escape from over-elaborate narrative structure has sometimes vied with the appeal of dream sequences as a means of psychological exploration. Joan Crawford plays a woman on the verge of more than a nervous break-down in *Possessed* (1947). As Louise Howell, Crawford becomes convinced that she's murdered her husband's first wife. Her treatment by narco-hypnosis induces dream states complete with hallucinations and hollow voices, but psychiatric delving and melodrama never quite mesh.

When the approach becomes less clinical and more concerned with ratiocination in the crime genre, the use of dream sequences is more successful. The hero of *Fear in the Night* (1947) awakens from a nightmare in which he has killed a man and attempts to dispose of the body. Despite the discovery of incriminating evidence in his pocket, he learns that he has been hypnotized, and with the help of his brother-in-law detective uncovers the true killer.

William Dieterle's *Portrait of Jenny* (1948) is an ambitious attempt in a genre outside the musical to take dreaming beyond the superficialties of plot construction and incorporate it more directly into film structure at a technological level. The story, about an artist's obsession with the ghost-like subject of his paintings, Jennie, played by Jennifer Jones, was adapted from a Robert Nathan novella and won an Academy Award for special effects.

Anticipating the introduction of Cinerama in the fifties, along with the advanced audio systems and colorization of the 80s, *Portrait of Jennie* features a finale with a green-tinted hurricane during which the screen doubles in size and additional speakers flood the audience with the roar of the elements. The flamboyant David O. Selznick gimmickry, including a final shot in technicolor of artist Joseph Cotton's finished portrait, was not enough to render the movie more than a curiosity.

Probably the most famous example of attempts to capture the dream state in celluloid come through a collaboration of artist and early avant garde filmmaker Salvador Dali with Alfred Hitchcock in *Spellbound* (1945). Hitchcock used dreams in four of his thriller-melodramas, and their use in films of psychological investigation probably reaches its zenith in his work.

Hitchcockian dreams take their most literary form in *Rebecca* (1940), where heroine Joan Fontaine launches the narrative in voiceover by saying "I dreamt I was back at Manderley." The rest of the film proceeds in flashback. In *Spellbound*, dreaming is integrated more explicitly into the narrative but nevertheless remains a set piece inserted into the fabric of the film.

Dreams, explains psychiatrist Ingrid Bergman, "tell you what you are trying to hide. But they tell it to you all mixed up—like pieces of a puzzle that don't fit." Amnesiac Gregory Peck then has a nightmare, designed by Dali, in which objects—eyes, playing cards, scissors, a distorted wheel, clouds—are dissociated from any conventional context and reassembled into a surreal dreamscape.

Bergman proceeds to interpret the dream in order to solve the mystery of who Peck really is. While remaining discrete, the dream sequence in *Spellbound*—as in *Fear in the Night*—is successfully integrated into the film's structure and functions as part of the genre's conventions. It can also be read as a formal exposition of the relationship between film and the objects it images, reminding us of the artifice involved in the reconstructive process of moviemaking.

Hitchcock's fascination with psychological aberration and his treatment of dreams reach new levels of sophistication first in *Rear Window* (1954) and then *Vertigo* (1958). Film historian Gerald Mast calls *Rear Window* "perhaps Hitchcock's most explicit examination of the moviegoer's forbidden fantasies, a film in which photography itself becomes a metaphor for voyeurism..." (271). If photography becomes a metaphor for voyeurism, film becomes a metaphor for dreams in *Rear Window*.

Initially, the dreams of photographer L. B. Jeffries, played by James Stewart, are implied rather than made explicit. As he recovers at home from an accident, Jeffries is shown drifting in and out of sleep. The audience cannot be sure if Jeffries' observations of his neighbors from his rear window which set the plot in motion are real or part of a dream state. At one point when he is wakened by his finacée Lisa, the connection between sleep and dream as erotic wish fulfillment becomes obvious. By the end of the movie, Jeffries is asleep again, this time with a smile on his face, while on the soundtrack a baritone sings "If I'm dreaming, I hope I'll never awake." The suggestion is that dreams are a primarily pleasurable form of wish fulfillment.

The mood is much darker in *Vertigo*, which begins with hero Scotty, played again by James Stewart, in the throes of a nightmare. While in rooftop pursuit of a suspect, Scotty slips, hangs on the edge and watches, horrified, as the police officer friend who is trying to rescue him plunges to the street below. The dream sequence begins where Gregory Peck's nightmare in *Spellbound* left off. It serves to explain the source of Scotty's vertigo.

It also presents the hero's dilemma at a more profound level. In *Rear Window* parallels between the frictions in Jeffries' neighbors' romantic lives and his own merely imply that dreams might be chosen as an escape from reality. In *Vertigo* Scotty becomes the captive of his dreams; he chooses them over reality. The narrative can be read as Scotty's reconstruction of his life as dream. The dream fetish which becomes Scotty's obsession is, of course, a woman—Madeleine. Hitchcock refers explicitly to these connections, telling Donald Spoto "I really made the film in order to get through to this subtle quality of man's dreamlike nature" (432). Madeleine, played by Kim Novak, dies twice in the film. The doubling of the action reinforces both the inevitable loss of the fetish, with its resulting anguish and relief, and the inextricably dual nature of film as dream and reality.

After Hitchcock, the development of dream sequences as a plot device takes place primarily in the horror movie, with occasional excursions into the melodrama and suspense genres. The movie version of William Inge's play *Come Back, Little Sheba* (1952) won an Oscar for Shirley Booth. As Lola, the disillusioned wife of alcoholic Doc, played by Burt Lancaster, she dreams of her husband competing at the Olympics and finds her pet dog Sheba dead. The dream capsulizes her hopes and sense of loss in the conventional Freudian terms developed by Hitchcock.

Dreams have a more explicitly cinematic function in John Sturges' version of the Hemingway novel *The Old Man and the Sea* (1958). The movie is confined primarily to fisherman Spencer Tracy's solitary struggle with a marlin. Tracy's dreams of his youth spent on the coast of Africa allow the director to open up the film visually.

By the sixties, it became difficult to use dream sequences as a Hollywood plot device outside of the horror genre. Between Hitchcock and the metaphysical explorations of such European directors as Fellini, who released *8 1/2* in 1963, and Bergman, who released *Persona* in 1966, perhaps Hollywood's enthusiasm for dream sequences cooled. Certainly their use in the spy spoof *Gambit* (1966), starring Michael Caine, and *Farewell My Lovely* (1975), the British remake of *Murder, My Sweet* (1944) starring an aging Robert Mitchum, suggests the kind of exhaustion of forms analyzed by John Cawelti (192).

Oscar-winning *Ordinary People* (1980) uses dreams to capture the disturbed psychological state of Timothy Hutton, once again in a conventional Freudian context, one which Robin Wood suggests has misogynist overtones (173). The use of dream at the end of *The Elephant Man* (1980) when John Merrick is, in effect, united with his mother in the heavens, is similarly an extension of the Freudian model developed by Hitchcock.

Two exceptions to the neglect of dream sequences outside the horror genre are *Manchurian Candidate* (1962) and *Deliverance* (1972). Despite their intellectual pretensions, both employ dream sequences in a manner that is closer to the horror film's access to frightening and/or forbidden information than it is to examination of the human psyche from a psychoanalytic viewpoint.

In *Manchurian Candidate*, which experienced a revival of paranoic popularity at the end of the eighties, a number of the members of an Army squad stationed in Korea have disturbing dreams that ultimately reveal the fact that they have been brain-washed and one of their members programmed to murder the President. In *Deliverance*, the horrifying weekend that four Atlanta businessmen spend on a canoe trip comes back to haunt Jon Voight in a nightmare image of a hand reaching out from beyond that will be used again in *Carrie* (1976).

The horror movie is a logical extension of Hitchcock's pairing of dream with the pathology of aberrant impulses. The beginnings of this tendency can be seen in *Nightmare*, the 1956 remake of *Fear in the Night*. This time Kevin McCarthy, better known for his performance in *The Invasion of the Body Snatchers* that year, is a New Orleans musician caught in a murder plot involving hypnosis and dreams. The remake was far less successful than its model, perhaps because it was a generic misfit.

While retaining some of the characteristics of earlier crime melodramas, William Castle's *The Night Walker* (1964) situates itself more firmly in the horror genre. Barbara Stanwyck plays the widow of a blind electronics engineer who accuses her of infidelity before disappearing in a lab explosion. Strange things happen in Stanwyck's recurring dreams.

Roman Polansky's 1968 horror classic, *Rosemary's Baby*, weds a gothic realism with supernatural happenings that conveniently occur while Mia Farrow's Rosemary—and the audience—think she's dreaming. After neighbor Minnie, played with charming and eccentric authenticity by Ruth Gordon, feeds Rosemary a drugged mousse, Rosemary falls asleep and is impregnated by the devil. Her recall of the incident as a form of dream allows Polansky to manipulate the audience's sense of belief, using archetypal religious and psychoanalytic emblems and maintaining realism by suggesting that it all could have been just a dream.

Brian de Palma, the self-appointed heir to Hitchcock, reworked *Rear Window* in *Sisters* (1973) with the added horrific of Siamese twins. Dreams allow one sister, played by Margot Kidder, to enter her dead sister's memory. *Obsession* (1976) rehashes *Vertigo* with the help of Paul Schrader as screenwriter. Michael Courtland, played by Cliff Robertson, loses his wife and daughter when they are killed in a kidnapping. In fact, his daughter has survived. He falls in love with her and manages to marry her— at least in a dream. The incest theme coarsens the use of dream and the movie.

De Palma's *Carrie* (1976) and *Dressed to Kill* (1980) are less literal borrowings from Hitchcockian plots. Both address the issue of dreams as disturbed psychological states far more explicitly than the master of suspense does. Norman G. and Anaruth Gordon suggest that de Palma attempts to recreate a specific dream state, night terror, experienced primarily by young children. They describe night terror as a pathological state in which an individual becomes incapable of resolving conflict (139).

In *Carrie* it is Cissy Spacek's classmate Sue, played by May Irving, who has the nightmare. Her dream that Carrie's hand reaches up and grabs her as she places flowers on the site of the White's house comes at the end of the movie and suggests the permanent rupture of normality. *Dressed to Kill* is framed by nightmare sequences at the beginning and end. The first is a sexual fantasy that turns into a nightmare as Kate Miller, played by Angie Dickinson, showers while watching her husband shave. In the second, Liz, played by Nancy Allen, imagines her own murder—again in a shower— but this time wakes up and ends up in her lover Peter's arms. More explicitly sexual than in *Carrie*, the dream sequences in *Dressed to Kill* nevertheless convey the same message. Nightmare has replaced conventional reality.

Two eighties movies move away from horror toward science fiction. In keeping with the shift, their investigation of the dreaming process attempts to be more cerebral than De Palma's but is equally crude. Ken Russell's *Altered States* (1980) casts William Hurt as a Faustian psychologist eager to use the unconscious to help him revert to primitive states. Hurt employs flotation tanks and drugs as aids into dream states and finds himself physically transformed into a carnivorous Neanderthal. Even more fancifully science fiction, *Dreamscape* (1984) investigates a process known as dreamlinking, in which individuals project their consciousness into others' dreams.

John Landis' *An American Werewolf in London* (1981) takes the self-reflective stance of a post-modern sensibility. Nightmares are the hero's connection to his horrifying experience with a werewolf on the English moors. When David Kessler sees the apparition of his murdered friend Jack, he discounts it as just another bad dream, and he often belittles his own recurrent nightmares. Allusions to earlier horror movies, like *The Wolf Man* (1941), abound, and at one point David is assured, "If there'd been a monster loose we'd have seen it on the telly."

The implication of media in the creation of living nightmares is an important contribution to the evolution of dream sequences made by horror movies and culminates in *A Nightmare on Elm Street* (1984). Freddy Krueger has the capacity to enter and kill in the dreams of teenagers. The proliferation of Krueger paraphernalia and the alarm sounded by concerned parents attests to the popularity of this movie (Gordon A1). Its masking of sexual anxiety is obvious, but more significant in terms of the use of dream sequences is the implication of mass media in blurring the line between dream and reality.

Unlike the typical helpless horror heroine, Nancy, the teenager who is plagued by murderous nightmares in *A Nightmare on Elm Street*, vows not to let herself fall asleep and dream. When she nods off in class—while the teacher is reading *Julius Caesar*—Freddy invades her dream until she wakes up screaming and finds a burn mark on her hand, an indication that the dream could be real. Such blending of dream and reality continues until she vows to confront Krueger, enlisting the aid of her boyfriend, Glen.

Glen, however, with a portable TV set propped on his stomach and stereo headphones covering his ears, is unable to stay awake. Nancy has to face the dream demon alone. By the end of the film, the audience is encouraged to believe that it's impossible to distinguish between dreams and reality. The mass media have replaced reality with a dream world of their own making and the audience is trapped in a Wellesian house of mirrors that demands demolition.

At the end of the eighties, less pathological dream sequences occur in such movies as Woody Allen's *Another Woman* (1989) and Brian De Palma's *Casualties of War*, and the popularity of Freddy Krueger sequels declined. Maybe once Hollywood wakes up from its horror-movie-induced bad dreams —and the audience escapes from inside a nightmare not of its own making— movie dreams will turn sweeter again.

Works Cited

Altman, Rick. *The American Film Musical*. Bloomington: Indiana UP, 1987.

American Film Institute Catalogue of Motion Pictures Produced in the United States. 3 vols. to date. New York: R.R. Bowker, 1971-1988.

Cawelti, John. "*Chinatown* and the Generic Transformation in Recent American Films." *Film Genre Reader*. Ed. Barry Keith Grant. Austin: U of Texas P, 1986. 183-201.

Crowther, Bosley. "Uncle Harry." *The New York Times Film Reviews: 1939-1948*. New York: Arno, 1970. 2077.

Gordon, Suzanne. "Hooked on Horror." *Boston Globe* 15 Oct. 1989: A1+.

Kawin, Bruce F. *Mindscreen: Bergman, Godard, and First-Person Film*. Princeton: Princeton UP, 1978.

Kracauer, Seigfried. *Theory of Film: The Redemption of Reality*. New York: Oxford UP, 1960.

Langer, Suzanne. "A Note on the Film." McCann, 199-204.

Mast, Gerald. *A Short History of the Movies*. 3rd ed. Indianapolis: Bobbs-Merrill Educational, 1981.

Mauerhofer, Hugo. "The Psychology of Film Experience." McCann, 229-235.

McCann, Richard Dyer, ed. *Film: A Montage of Theories*. New York: Dutton, 1966.

Metz, Christian. *The Imaginary Signifier*. Trans. Celia Britton et al. Bloomington: Indiana UP, 1982.

Spoto, Donald. *The Dark Side of Genius: The Life of Alfred Hitchcock*. New York: Ballantine, 1983.

"The Woman at the Window." *Variety Film Reviews: 1907-1980*. Vol. 5. New York: Garland, 1983. 11 Oct. 1944.

Wood, Robin. *Hollywood from Vietnam to Reagan*. New York: Columbia UP, 1986.

Filmography

1903	*The Life of an American Fireman*	Dir. Edwin Porter
1906	*The Dream of a Rarebit Fiend*	Dir. Edwin Porter
1914	*The Avenging Conscience: Thou Shalt Not Kill*	Dir. D.W. Griffith
1915	*The Magic Skin*	Dir. Thomas Edison
1916	*The Serpent*	Dir. Raoul Walsh
1918	*The Blue Bird*	Dir. Maurice Tourneur
1918	*Wild Women*	Dir. Jack Ford
1921	*Man-Woman-Marriage*	Dir. Allen Holnbar
1922	*Dusk to Dawn*	Dir. King Vidor
1923	*The Shriek of Araby*	Dir. F. Richard Jones
1924	*The Gold Rush*	Dir. Charles Chaplin
1924	*Sherlock Junior*	Dir. Buster Keaton
1925	*Three Weeks in Paris*	Dir. Roy Del Ruth
1927	*Monte Blue*	Dir. Roy Del Ruth
1933	*Roman Scandals*	Dir. Frank Tuttle
1933	*The Bitter Tea of General Yen*	Dir. Frank Capra
1934	*Of Human Bondage*	Dir. John Cromwell
1935	*Dante's Inferno*	Dir. Harry Lachman

1938	Carefree	Dir. Mark Sandrich
1938	The Wizard of Oz	Dir. Victor Fleming
1939	Gone With the Wind	Dir. Victor Fleming
1940	Rebecca	Dir. Alfred Hitchcock
1943	Cabin in the Sky	Dir. Vincente Minnelli
1944	The Woman at the Window	Dir. Fritz Lang
1944	Lady in the Dark	Dir. Mitchell Leisen
1944	Murder, My Sweet	Dir. Edward Dmytryk
1945	The Horn Blows at Midnight	Dir. Raoul Walsh
1945	Anchors Aweigh	Dir. George Sidney
1945	Spellbound	Dir. Alfred Hitchcock
1945	The Strange Affair of Uncle Harry	Dir. Robert Siodmak
1945	Yolanda and the Thief	Dir. Vincente Minnelli
1947	Possessed	Dir. Curtis Bernhardt
1947	The Secret Life of Walter Mitty	Dir. Norman Z. McLeod
1948	Fear in the Night	Dir. Maxwell Shane
1948	The Pirate	Dir. Vincente Minnelli
1948	Portrait of Jennie	Dir. William Dieterle
1948	Unfaithfully Yours	Dir. Preston Sturges
1949	A Connecticut Yankee in King Arthur's Court	Dir. Tay Garnett
1950	Father of the Bride	Dir. Vincente Minnelli
1951	An American in Paris	Dir. Vincente Minnelli
1952	Come Back, Little Sheba	Dir. Daniel Mann
1952	Singin' in the Rain	Dir. Gene Kelly & Stanley Donen
1953	The 5000 Fingers of Dr. T	Dir. Roy Rowland
1954	Rear Window	Dir. Alfred Hitchcock
1955	Oklahoma!	Dir. Fred Zinnemann
1955	Daddy Long Legs	Dir. Jean Negulesco
1955	Artists and Models	Dir. Frank Tashlin
1956	Nightmare	Dir. Maxwell Shane
1958	The Old Man and the Sea	Dir. John Sturges
1958	Vertigo	Dir. Alfred Hitchcock
1962	The Manchurian Candidate	Dir. John Frankenheimer
1964	The Night Walker	Dir. William Castle
1966	Gambit	Dir. Ronald Neame
1968	Rosemary's Baby	Dir. Roman Polansky
1972	Deliverance	Dir. John Boorman
1973	Sisters	Dir. Brian De Palma
1975	Farewell, My Lovely	Dir. Dick Richards
1976	Obsession	Dir. Brian De Palma
1976	Buffalo Bill and the Indians	Dir. Robert Altman
1976	Carrie	Dir. Brian De Palma
1979	All That Jazz	Dir. Bob Fosse

1980	*Ordinary People*	Dir. Robert Redford
1980	*Dressed to Kill*	Dir. Brian De Palma
1980	*Altered States*	Dir. Ken Russell
1980	*The Elephant Man*	Dir. David Lynch
1981	*Fiddler on the Roof*	Dir. Norman Jewison
1981	*Pennies from Heaven*	Dir. Herbert Ross
1981	*An American Werewolf in London*	Dir. John Landis
1983	*Risky Business*	Dir. Paul Brickman
1984	*A Nightmare on Elm Street*	Dir. Wes Craven
1986	*The Fly*	Dir. David Cronenburg
1988	*The Princess Bride*	Dir. Rob Reiner
1989	*Another Woman*	Dir. Woody Allen
1989	*Casualties of War*	Dir. Brian De Palma

Revelation, Humanity, and a Warning:
Four Motifs of 1950s Science Fiction Invasion Films

Garyn G. Roberts

"Something was wrong in this house."
Dr. Miles Bennell-*Invasion of the Body Snatchers* (1956)

Wisconsin senator Joseph McCarthy and fear of communism, atomic power and invaders from outer space in the fifties, late night and weekend local television programming in the seventies and eighties, fear of a fatal sexually transmitted disease, and racism in the eighties. What do they all have in common? It can be argued that they have direct reference to and reflection of a science fiction movie formula of the fifties: the Science Fiction Invasion Film.

This formula initially achieved definition and articulation in 1951 in *The Thing From Another World,* and culminated in 1956's *Invasion of the Body Snatchers.* It is comprised of four specific plot conventions, and has found rebirth in the eighties and nineties, for it reflects much contemporary social paranoia—paranoia which is remarkably similar in nature to popular apprehensions of the fifties. Between *The Thing From Another World* and *Invasion of the Body Snatchers,* other science fiction films centered their story lines around these four plot conventions. After 1956 and *Invasion,* more film emerged and utilized the same formula. The focus here is upon these two motion pictures, two others which appeared between them and adhered closely to the formula—*Invaders From Mars* (1953) and *It Came From Outer Space* (1953), a film which refined and revolutionized the formula during this same time period—*The Day the Earth Stood Still* (1951), and the four identified component motifs.

The first plot convention of the Science Fiction Invasion Film is the discovery of the previously intangible, unnameable invader at the end of the story. The second is closely related to the first. In plot convention number two, the previously intangible, mysterious invader at the time of discovery takes physical form (often assuming human physiognomy). The third plot convention is tied to the first two—the discovery of the invader leads to a pessimistic, cautionary, moralistic ending for the film. Plot convention number four pervades the entire story line of each of these movies. This is the negative portrayal of humanity in general.

Howard Hawks' *The Thing From Another World* was a landmark film of the Science Fiction Invasion formula of the fifties. It was the first motion picture to define these four motifs. The first plot convention—in which the intangible, unnameable invader is discovered at the end of the story— is the device in *The Thing* which pulls the audience through the story at a rapid pace. We are intensely interested in seeing the movie creators' conception of the invader, and to see if this conception will parallel our own. At the beginning of the film, military sources discover a spaceship beneath the recently refrozen ice of the North Pole. The investigators (military personnel and scientists) destroy the find by accident, but are able to salvage a block of ice harboring one of the creatures from the craft. Hence, relatively early in the story the invader is discovered, but under the cloak of ice (and an ensuing escape from the ice) is not revealed in totality until the movie's finale. The actors and the audience do not confront or see the monster until that climactic, epic moment when the "human carrot" is electrocuted and burned to death. However, the ice begins to melt before the invader's initial escape. With this clearing and melting, we are tantalized by the revelation. After the monster escapes, it does repeatedly attack the military base, but we only get fleeting glimpses of it during any and all of these occasions. The anticipation of revelation is the compelling dramatic force behind the film.

This same anticipation is also essential to the success of the story line of *Invaders From Mars*, and once again the military (that socially prescribed institution designed for the enforcement of justice and preservation of society) and scientists are important elements in the total tale. The anticipation of the revelation in this film is heightened when soldiers are periodically sucked down into the sandy abyss which houses the Martians. But, unlike that of *The Thing*, the final revelation in *Invaders* consists of two component stages. First, the theory advanced that the alien life form in the buried spaceship is comprised largely of "mutants"—creatures designed by the Martians to do their bidding—is proven reality when David and the alluring Dr. Blake are enveloped by the sand and meet the mutants face to face near the film's end. Second, after this initial unveiling of the mutants, David, Dr. Blake and the audience meet life and intelligence in their ultimate state— the being in the glass globe. As with *The Thing, It Came From Outer Space*, and *Invasion of the Body Snatchers*, fear is born and nurtured in the unknown. Had the mutants and the being in the globe been revealed any sooner in the story line, the film would not have been much more than a conventional, campy monster movie. In fact in *Invaders*, the story is essentially over when the invaders are revealed. After this, the tale is reduced to a simple race against time as the humans scurry to be free of the bomb blast set for the underground arena of horror. There is absolutely no doubt that David and his friends will beat the clock with seconds to spare. Even the most conventional of old movie serials spiced up this theme.

John encounters the invaders at the Excelsior mine shaft near the close of *It Came From Outer Space*. Shortly thereafter, a confrontation at this same site between a mob of angry townspeople and the invaders completes the revelation. (John is the mediator between the two factions.) The invaders, we find out, have been forced to land on earth because of a problem with their spaceship. These creatures reveal themselves to John, and explain that they believe themselves so horrific in physical appearance to humans that they do not want any meeting; their goal is to effect repairs and quietly slip away. Of course, a smooth departure would kill the story line, and a confrontation necessarily occurs. The audience is once again fascinated by the upcoming revelation of the monster, and is pulled through the movie by this anticipation. When the invaders reveal themselves to an incredulous John, the excitement is further heightened. At the movie's end, we get the opportunity to compare the movie creator's vision of the alien creatures with that of our own. The revelation is disappointing, but the anticipation of the same has carried us to the film's finale.

The discovery of the true nature of the invader unfolds steadily in *Invasion of the Body Snatchers*. The most convincing, and subsequently terrifying of the 1950s Science Fiction Invasion Films, *Invasion* showcases a story line and ending which, more than those of any other fifties sci-fi thriller, leaves doubt as to the entire parameters of the invader. *Invasion* is the most frightening of such films because of the unanswered questions that remain after Miles (Kevin McCarthy) is interrogated by psychiatrists and after the invaders leave the confines of Santa Mira. The invaders are never totally revealed; thus, the unknown begets the most intense of fears and anxieties. The story line is constructed on fear and anticipation, and it utilizes these to induce riveting suspense. Right from the beginning, we suspect something is not right in this "sleepy" (no pun intended—the monsters use sleep as their vehicle of invasion) little community. Little Jimmy Grimaldi runs in front of Miles' car, "Uncle Ira isn't Uncle Ira," huge seed pods appear in Miles' greenhouse and begin a hideous metamorphosis, Jack is "converted" and returns, and finally Becky (Miles' love since childhood) falls prey to the invaders, never again to love. But, who or what is perpetrating this evil, and why?

The second motif of the Science Fiction Invasion Film is the invader, now revealed, assuming physical form—usually with selective human physiognomy. When the invader is fully revealed near the end of *The Thing From Another World*, we see that this creature in may ways resembles man. The being has a head, two arms, two legs, and "must be eight feet tall." But, by this point, Dr. Carrington has surmised that the creature has no animal tissue, and no arteries or nerves. The monster is likened to a vegetable and "super carrot," and bullets have no effect on its form. Like the transformed seed pods of *Invasion of the Body Snatchers*, the creature is sexless, and it experiences no emotion, no pain. These characteristics, or lack of characteristics, have both positive and negative connotations, but unlike Dr. Carrington, other members of the military outpost in *The Thing* and the audience, are generally unsympathetic with such a being. Whether the human qualities of the Thing are important or not is perhaps unclear. Given that this was the first of the 1950s Science Fiction Invasion Films, it seems likely that Howard Hawks and company were reluctant to make the monster too inventional and hence less believable. Perhaps the producers did not have much faith in the audience's ability to imagine. Nonetheless, the invader in *The Thing* is conventionally human in many ways.

The being in the glass globe in *Invaders From Mars* creates two forms of mutants. Near the end of the film, we see the lumbering, wide-eyed, green giants that mindlessly do their master's bidding. Both the being and the mutants have physical human qualities. But more importantly, the primary invaders in this movie are "synthetic humans"—actual human beings transformed into invaders throughout the film. The first of such converts is George McClean, David's scientist father. The fear generated in this movie is not only derived from the unknown, but stems from the known. The horror is born in the control of the human brain and behavior. Synthetic people have been compromised of love and compassion. Hence, David is terrified when his father, whom he has always loved and admired so much, and whom has always been a known constant, falls prey to this control. George McClean is human, yet he is not. As bad as being human may get, we treasure being human, and we become afraid of the prospect of anything else. Hence, the compromised creature in the guise of George is frightening to his son David, and to us, for we see events through David's eyes.

John climbs down the hillside to investigate the newly arrived invader from outer space. Later, George and Frank, line repairmen, encounter the invader on the road. As the invader reveals itself more and more in *It Came From Outer Space*, we see that the intruder in part resembles a human eye, or at least that is part of the monster we see. The physical form of this invader is significant in that it commonly appears in fifties science fiction films. The probing, scrutinizing eye suggested a larger abomination of real life fifties paranoia—fear and suspicion of anything atomic, communist, or in some way foreign to American society of the time. Like *Invaders From Mars*, *It Came* provides two distinct forms of invader. The first is the being that is physically horrific in appearance to man. The second is the mutant utilized by this being. This mutant appears physically to be human, since the higher order invader has created the mutant from man. The invaders in *It Came* shanghai human bodies much the same way as the invaders in *Invasion of the Body Snatchers* take over bodies of Santa Mira townsfolk. In *It Came From Outer Space*, George and Frank are duplicated and converted expressly to do the invader's bidding.

Conversion is the consummate evil in *Invasion of the Body Snatchers.* The invaders, seed pods adrift from outer space, transform themselves into the exact physical likenesses of people in Santa Mira. It is purposefully unclear as to whether the seed pods duplicate the original human being and then destroy the original, or whether the invading pods ultimately take over the original human body. Several theories are advanced in the story, but evidence suggests the former. What is important is that the original human being is compromised in the worst possible way. The invader in human physiognomy is incapable and intolerant of love. States Miles about his invaded Becky, "I'd been afraid a lot of times in my life, but I never knew the real meaning of fear until I kissed Becky." The suggestion is that without love all is lost. But, in *The Thing From Another World,* the invader is at least in part plant life. This dialectic between plant and animal life illustrates both positive and negative aspects of being human: love and mortality do indeed have their drawbacks.

Discovery of the invader and its human qualities sets the stage for the third motif of the 1950s Science Fiction Invasion Film. This plot convention involves the discovery of the invader leading to a pessimistic, cautionary ending. The potential conquering army represented by James Arness in the title role of *The Thing From Another World* quite obviously will use humans as food—the Thing consumes the blood of sled dogs and humans by the story's end. Dr. Carrington's risk of mass production of the organism inherent in the invader is thus monumentally foolish. The naivety of the scientist is very dangerous, and must be circumvented at any cost. This, of course, directly comments on those involved in nuclear science—a field of study greatly mistrusted and misunderstood in the fifties. In *The Thing,* newscaster Ned Scott provides the overall pessimistic, cautionary ending when he broadcasts,

Alright fellas, here's your story. North Pole, November 3rd, Ned Scott reporting. One of the world's greatest battles was fought and won today by the human race. Here at the top of the world, a handful of American soldiers and civilians met the first invasion from another planet. A man by the name of Noah once saved our world with an ark of wood. A few men performed a similar service with an arc of electricity. The flying saucer which landed here and its pilot have been destroyed, but not without casualties among our own meager forces—And now before bringing you the details of the battle, I bring you a warning. Everyone of you listening to my voice, tell the world, tell this to everybody wherever they are. Watch the skies, everywhere. Keep looking, keep watching the skies.

The final warning established in *The Thing* for the Science Fiction Invasion Film reflects the paranoia of the era. A situation exists. In the movie, further invasion from armies of outer space vegetables seems quite likely. In postwar American society, attack and invasion from other world powers also seem a distinct possibility. In both cases, the form the invasion will take is unknown, and hence doubly frightening to consider. How many of these "super carrots" will invade the earth? What intelligences and abilities do these foreigners possess? If communism in the guise of the Soviets should infiltrate the U.S., what methods of dissemination will it employ? Will apocalyptic, as yet fully tested, nuclear warfare be the catalyst for such an invasion? Or, will the proliferation of the "red menace" be more subversive, coming into this country through traded products and ideas? When Ned Scott warns the world to "watch the skies," we do not know exactly for what to look. After all, none of us actually saw the spaceship in which the Thing arrived, did we? Even if we can identify the invaders, what do we do to destroy them? What happens when the Soviets launch a missile carrying the atomic bomb? Even if we know when and where, is there anything we can do to stop the invasion and resulting devastation? The fear is once again rooted in the unknown. The third plot convention of the Science Fiction Invasion Film then turns this story form into a morality play of sorts. In this formula thus far, we are presented with the revelation of a monster which is closely tied to ourselves, and we are warned of the possible dangers of such a creature. But, as we begin to see, the ending to this morality play is not a happy one. Moreover, it is a prophecy of impending doom.

Invaders From Mars hypothesizes that man has brought about, and will bring, much of his own destruction. In this story, rockets and atomic power have scared the Martians into responding to the dangerous humans with the threat of mutants. Remember, the being in the globe is intelligence and life in their ultimate states. The idea of the superior being (in terms of intelligence) thwarting the foolishness of humanity was, of course, not unique to *Invaders*. Two years prior to this film, *The Day the Earth Stood Still* (1951) focused an entire story line on this idea, and subsequently provided the Science Fiction Invasion Film with its most conscious, intense and profound object lesson. But, like *The Day*, *Invaders* provided a glimmer of hope. At the conclusion of *Invaders*, we discover that David McClean was only dreaming. Yet as David awakens from his night's sleep, we see a flying saucer landing outside his window, much as one did during his dream. The horror is not yet a reality, but as it approaches, maybe David and company will now know better how to deal with the invader. We hope so. The revelation of the story as a dream serves to warn us of what might be.

John, the mediator between the invaders and the townspeople of *It Came From Outer Space*, sums up the situation at the end of the story when he states, "It wasn't the right time for us to meet." The warning is implied very clearly. Humans need to broaden their acceptance and appreciation of other forms of life and lifestyles—whether they be outer space aliens or aliens from other cultures. The moral of the story in *It Came* is that humans often destroy things they do not understand. Naivety and foolishness can only lead to trouble. Hence, in this film, we are warned against such naivety and foolishness, and we are reminded of our extreme arrogance in our narrow-minded beliefs. The monsters in this movie are horrific in appearance only because we make them so. Maybe this is the case with many of our real life "monsters."

The ultimate crime of the seed pod invaders in *Invasion of the Body Snatchers* is that they rob humanity of its most precious commodity—love. Without love, claims the film, life is not worth living . When Becky is converted, all hope is lost for Miles. So by all means, we are to protect against such robbery and loss. The lesson of *Invasion* is very dark and threatening. Near the end of the story, Miles screams, "Look you fools, you're in danger!" and "You're next, you're next!" But, people are quick to dismiss him, or not listen at all. This is where the real horror is born. Naivety, foolishness, and complacency are the deadly sins of 1950s Science Fiction Invasion Films, and society of the time. Perhaps in terms of love lost, some of the invasion and conversion is already complete, and perhaps this is also part of the message of this film. In *Invasion*, there is a fate worse than death: it is the fate where all love is lost.

The fourth prominent plot convention of 1950s Science Fiction Invasion Films pervades each of these movies from start to finish. This is a negative portrayal of humanity. Included in this portrayal are such human characteristics as ineptness, naivety, foolishness, complacency, selfishness, narrow-mindedness—you get the picture. Motif number three, which provides the cautionary and pessimistic warning, is particularly effective because of motif number four. Ineptness plagues the military in *The Thing From Another World*. The military blows up the flying saucer lodged under the ice of the North Pole in an attempt to free the invading spaceship. Later, after one of the inhabitants of the flying saucer is pulled from the wreckage in a block of ice and relocated at the outpost (the Thing), one sentry covers the cake of ice with an electric blanket, so as to obscure its appearance. This, of course, melts the ice, and the invader escapes. States newscaster Ned Scott, "We're about to become famous....So few men can boast they lost a flying saucer and a man from Mars all in one day." Dr. Carrington provides the negative stereotype of the knowledge-hungry scientist. Looking for the monster with a geiger counter, one soldier discovers a room full of radioactive isotopes. These are the work of Dr. Carrington, who claims that "knowledge is more important than life." It is Dr. Carrington who discovers the physical make-up of the creature, and it is the good doctor who turns off the generator for the iron grid at the end of the film when the military men are trying to electrocute the "super carrot." Carrington's perspective is admirable to a point, but reaches insanity when he is willing to sacrifice all of humanity for research purposes. He is also naive when he feels he can communicate with the invader. When he attempts communication, the monster roughly knocks him out of the way. Upon the initial discovery of the flying saucer and the invader beneath the ice,

Captain Hendry of the military makes a telling statement, "Could be Russians, they're all over the [North] Pole like flies."

Disbelief and narrow-mindedness are the chief evils of the society in *Invaders From Mars*. Almost no one gives little David McClean any credence when he warns of the invading flying saucer. His father, the scientist, is the first to be skeptical, and his skepticism is doubly bad because he, of all people, should be open-minded enough to deal with such ideas. The desk sergeant and the Chief of Police at the Police station do not believe David either. This is particularly frightening to David and the audience because these fellows are supposed to be the guardians of American society as we know it. Little Kathy Wilson's mother does not believe David either, and her daughter starts their house on fire after being converted into a mutant. Only Dr. Blake and Dr. Kelston believe David's story. Thank goodness, for along with David these two scientists save the world, or at least that is how David's dream goes. The portrayal of humanity and society in this film in general is thus not a good one. We begin to wonder just how much and what of humanity is worth salvaging.

In *It Came From Another World*, John is the positive portrayal of what man can become, but as the hero he is misunderstood by people around him. The evil inherent in society as portrayed by this film is conformity. Society pays no attention to John because he does not conform to prescribed modes of thinking. Dr. Snell, as representative of society in the movie, describes Johnny as "individual and lonely...a man who thinks for himself." Obviously, these traits should be celebrated, not condemned. In *It Came* the military is once again portrayed as a group of bumbling buffoons. The movie shows men destroying things they do not understand—like the duplicated, converted Frank. The people evidence a strong mob mentality, letting baser emotions override intelligence and common sense.

In the fifties, there was both faith and doubt in the relatively new field of health care called psychiatry. In *Invasion of the Bodysnatchers*, Danny Kaufmann is the psychiatrist who is both Miles' friend and colleague. (Miles, as we remember, is a general practitioner who refers some of his patients to Kaufmann.) Danny is skeptical of Miles' theories, and ultimately becomes invaded and converted himself. As a leader of those who have been invaded, Kaufmann does not present a positive image of someone who is invested with the responsibility of protecting society and its mental health. It is important to remember, however, that any negative portrayal of humanity that emerges from *Invasion* stems from the doubt, disbelief, and naivety of the uninvaded people of Santa Mira. Once invaded and converted, the people are no longer "people." Yet, what kind of people so quickly forsake love and compassion?

It has been said of the "Hard-Boiled" detective story that the archetype of this formula of mystery fiction has already been written, and appeared during the early years of the story form—Dashiell Hammett's *The Maltese*

Falcon (1929). The same can be said of the Science Fiction Invasion Film. In 1951, the same year that *The Thing From Another World* appeared, the quintessential Science Fiction Invasion Film also appeared. Like *The Thing*, this film was based on a science fiction story which originally appeared in the pulp magazine *Astounding Stories*. *The Thing* appeared in the August, 1938 issue as "Who Goes There?" by John W. Campbell, Jr. *The Day the Earth Stood Still* appeared in 1940 as "Farewell to the Master" by Harry Bates. The film adaptation of the Bates story, starring Michael Rennie, proved the definitive work of the formula. Yet, too, *The Day the Earth Stood Still* proved the perfect counterpoint to all those Science Fiction Invasion Films that would follow. This film made the four identified plot conventions inventional and exciting.

Plot convention number one (in which the invader is discovered at the movie's end) assumes a little different form in *The Day*. In this motion picture, the discovery is of Klaatu's mission and message as well as of "Mr. Carpenter" as Klaatu. However, masked in a spacesuit, Klaatu introduces himself at the very beginning of the film. He blends into society so well throughout the story because he physically resembles man. Thus, in plot convention number two, *The Day* follows suit perfectly. Klaatu's last speech— a warning he has tried to give Earth and inhabitants since the beginning of the story—provides a very pessimistic, cautionary message as prescribed in plot convention number three. He states,

I am leaving soon, and you will forgive me if I speak bluntly. The universe grows smaller every day, and the threats of aggression by any group, anywhere, can no longer be tolerated. There must be security for all or no one is secure. Now this does not mean giving up any freedom except the freedom to act irresponsibly. Your ancestors knew this when they made laws to govern themselves and hired policemen to enforce them. Other planets have long accepted this principle....It is no concern of ours how you run your own planet. But if you threaten to extend your violence, this earth of yours will be reduced to a burned-out cinder. Your choice is simple. Join us and live in peace or pursue your present course and find obliteration. We shall be waiting for your answer. The decision rests with you.

The warning is clear, and should be obvious, yet because what we have seen in plot convention number four—a negative portrayal of humanity in general—is necessary. From the beginning of the movie, violence defines the people of the Earth. A soldier shoots Klaatu and breaks a gift with which the President might have studied life on other planets. Early in the film, Klaatu addresses Secretary to the President Harley, "I am impatient with stupidity. My people have learned to live without it." Replies Harley, "I am afraid my people haven't." In the guise as Carpenter, Klaatu discusses atomic power, suggesting positive uses for the force. Tom sells Carpenter out for money, the military ultimately kills Klaatu, and the violent transgressions continue. Klaatu's warning applies to the fictional characters of the film and real life society alike.

In the 1950s, we became very voyeuristic, carefully scrutinizing ourselves and our neighbors for the evils of communism and atomic power, and the vehicles which bring these evils into play. Joseph McCarthy led the witch hunt for the "red menace," and soon the seed pods in *Invasion of the Bodysnatchers* came to suggest something more than the horror of a science fiction film. The pods represented communism, as did the Thing, the Martians in *Invaders From Mars*, and the hideously ugly invaders of *It Came From Outer Space*. Prescribed agents of society—physicians, physiciatrists, the military, police, and more—intensified the horror by becoming the agents of such invaders. We distrusted things we knew little about; we distrusted and feared the unknown. Several fine books have been produced since the fifties which deal specifically with the social implications of the Science Fiction Invasion Film. Most of these provide their own definitions and parameters for discussion, but all seem to allude to the inner meanings and implications of such films. After all, popular film, like all popular culture, is a commercial enterprise in which profit is the bottom line. To generate profit, producers of popular film and culture need to generate sales. The consuming public buys that to which it relates. To say that all popular culture creates some kind of catharsis or profound religious experience for the consumer would, of course, be erroneous. But when that product provides reinforcement of large, constructed realities, the product has guaranteed itself a reasonable chance at considerable market share. The incorporation of real life paranoia into 1950s Science Fiction Invasion Films was done consciously. But, these films not only exploited and satirized such public sentiment; they, in some cases, provided a moral to the story.

In the 1980s and 1990s, cable television made and has made these films available at late night and on weekends. The videotape market has also exploited these old classics. Most are available for $20 or less, and most all can be rented for a dollar or two. During the 1960s and 70s, the 1950s Science Fiction Invasion Film found rebirth during the local broadcasting time of many television stations. The "Creature Feature" has been standard fare late nights and Saturday afternoons for more than two decades. Why do these films remain popular? Why are Kevin McCarthy and Michael Rennie cult heroes of a large magnitude? The answer to both questions is that the story lines of these movies are dated, but more importantly timely. As fictional forms, they tell us about nonfiction and "real life" of the 1950s. As stories with timeless messages, they also give us insight into our condition today. In the 1950s, we feared communism, atomic war, and related unknowns. In the early 1990s, we fear communism (though to a lesser extent), racism, and people who test HIV positive at the doctor's office. Today, we scream "racism" as we screamed "communism" a few decades back. We are rightly terrified of narcotics and the mysteries of the always fatal disease AIDS. The unknown, as much as ever, terrifies us more than anything else.

During the decades that have followed the "Cold War" years of the 1950s, a number of motion pictures have been produced which utilize parts of the Science Fiction Invasion Film Formula. Yet, none has totally captured the charm and urgency of the five films discussed in this essay. These films are dated and timely alike, and they have never been effectively duplicated. Remakes of *The Thing* and *Invasion of the Bodysnatchers* have met with moderate public response at best. The originals with their now seemingly simplistic special effects alone retain the charm. The celluloid invaders of the 1950s exploited social paranoia the best. Today, the real life invaders have not yet been conquered, and new ones have arisen. "Watch the skies, everywhere. Keep looking, keep watching the skies."

Filmography

The Thing (From Another World): Released April, 1951. Directed by Christian Nyby, often credited to Howard Hawks who was the producer. Winchester Pictures. Screenplay by Charles Lederer from the John W. Campbell novella "Who Goes There?" Black and White. 87 minutes.

The Day the Earth Stood Still: Released September, 1951. Directed by Robert Wise, produced by Julian Blaustein. Twentieth Century Fox. Screenplay by Edmund H. North from the short story "Farewell to the Master" by Harry Bates. Black and White. 92 minutes.

Invaders From Mars: Released May, 1953. Directed by William Cameron Menzies, produced by Edward L. Alperson. Twentieth Century Fox. Story and screenplay by Robert Blake. Color. 78 minutes.

It Came From Outer Space: Released June, 1953. Directed by Jack Arnold, produced by Clifford Stine. Universal. Screenplay by Harry Essex from the Ray Bradbury story. Black and White in 3-D. 81 minutes.

Invasion of the Body Snatchers: Released February, 1956. Directed by Don Siegel, produced by Walter Wanger. Walter Wanger Pictures. Screenplay by Daniel Mainwaring from the novel of the same title by Jack Finney. Black and White in SuperScope. 80 minutes.

1952, April	*The Man from Planet X*
1953, February	*The Magnetic Monsters*
1953, April	*Port Sinister*
1953, May	*Phantom from Space*
1953, June	*The Beast From 20,000 Fathoms*
1953, June	*The Neanderthal Man*
1953, June	*Robot Monster*
1953, June	*The Twonky*
1953, September	*Donovan's Brain*
1953, October	*War of the Worlds*
1953, December	*Invasion U.S.A.*
1954, January	*Killers from Space*
1954, February	*The Cosmic Man*
1954, March	*The Creature from the Black Lagoon*
1954, April	*The Rocket Man*

1954, May	*Monster from the Ocean Floor*
1954, June	*Gog*
1954, June	*Them!*
1954, September	*Tobor the Great*
1954, November	*The Snow Creature*
1954, November	*Target Earth*
1954, December	*Tarantula*
1955, May	*Revenge of the Creature*
1955, June	*This Island Earth*
1955, July	*Creature with the Atom Brain*
1955, July	*It Came From Beneath the Sea*
1956, January	*The Beast with a Million Eyes*
1956, January	*The Day the World Ended*
1956, January	*The Phantom from 10,000 Leagues*
1956, March	*The Atomic Man*
1956, March	*The Indestructible Man*
1956, April	*The Creature Walks Among Us*
1956, April	*Unidentified Flying Objects*
1956, June	*The Black Sheep*
1956, July	*Earth vs. the Flying Saucers*
1956, July	*It Conquered the World*
1957, March	*The Attack of the Crab Monsters*
1957, March	*The Man Who Turned to Stone*
1957, March	*Not of this Earth*
1957, April	*Kronos*
1957, April	*She Devil*
1957, May	*The Deadly Mantis*
1957, June	*The Giant Claw*
1957, June	*Invasion of the Saucer Men*
1957, June	*The Monster That Challenged the World*
1957, July	*The Cyclops*
1957, July	*Twenty Million Miles to Earth*
1957, July	*The 27th Day*
1957, July	*The Unearthly*
1957, August	*From Hell It Came*
1957, September	*The Amazing Colossal Man*
1957, September	*The Unknown Terror*
1957, October	*The Black Scorpion*
1957, October	*The Invisible Boy*
1957, November	*The Giant Gila Monster*
1957, December	*The Monolith Monster*
1957, December	*Teenage Monster*
1958, February	*The Astounding She Monster*
1958, March	*The Giant from the Unknown*
1958, March	*She Demons*
1958, April	*The Flame Barrier*
1958, May	*Attack of the Fifty Foot Woman*
1958, May	*Missile Monsters*
1958, May	*Zombies of the Stratosphere*
1958, June	*The Colossus of New York*

1958, June	*The Fly*
1958, June	*The Space Children*
1958, June	*Space Monster X-7*
1958, July	*Monster from Green Hell*
1958, July	*Plan 9 from Outer Space*
1958, August	*It! The Terror From Beyond Space*
1958, October	*The Blob*
1958, October	*Earth vs. the Spider*
1958, October	*I Married a Monster from Outer Space*
1958, October	*Monster on the Campus*
1958, October	*Terror from the Year 5000*
1958, October	*War of the Colossal Beast*
1958, November	*Night of the Blood Beast*
1958, December	*The Brain from Planet Arous*
1958, December	*The Crawling Eye*
1958, May	*Invisible Invaders*
1959, June	*The Man Who Could Cheat Death*
1959, June	*Monster of Piedras Blancas*
1959, June	*Teenagers from Outer Space*
1959, August	*The Alligator People*
1959, August	*The Return of the Fly*
1959, October	*Attack of the Giant Leeches*
1959, October	*The Tingler*
1959, October	*The Wasp Woman*
1959, November	*The 4-D Man*
1959, November	*The Killer Shrews*
1959, November	*Outer Space Visitor*
1959, December	*The Atomic Submarine*
1959, December	*The Hideous Sun Demon*

The Armadillos in Dracula's Foyer:
Conventions and Innovation in Horror Cinema

Clinton R. Sanders

Approaches to the Analysis of Film

Of all the popular mass media perhaps only television receives as much contemporary attention within the popular culture literature as does film. A variety of analytic approaches have been employed to examine films. A psychoanalytic perspective, typically focusing on what the analyst presumes to be sexual aspects of the presentation, is relatively popular (see Greenberg, 1975). This particular approach is especially common in discussions of horror film (eg., Evans, 1984; Twitchell, 1985: 65-104) given the sexual connotations of the typical woman-in-jeopardy plot elements and the dream-like imagery frequently employed.

Political analyses are also popular. Largely informed by feminist ideology (eg., Fisher and Landy, 1987; Kaplan, 1986) or neomarxist critical theory (eg., Modleski, 1986; Polan, 1987), these approaches focus on the political content of the filmic material and center on the idea that films are created by a paternalistic power-elite intent upon maintaining cultural hegemony.

The hermeneutic approach to film analysis is another common procedure. This strategy typically involves "reading" the film as a "text" and stresses an orientation in which the analyst's purpose is to ferret out the "true meaning" of the film—usually quite apart from the filmmaker's intentions. These discussions are often given a Levi-Straussean structuralist spin (eg., Wright, 1975; Dika, 1987) or, more currently, employ a postmodern, poststructuralist approach with all of the arcane verbiage and ungrounded supposition which characterize this orientation (see Barthes, 1980; cf., Gitlin, 1987).

Understandably, most social scientists concerned with film have focused their analyses primarily upon the interactions among various socio-historic factors and their impact on the style and content of filmic presentations. This approach also tends to move beyond the sociostructural context to discuss the functions of film for audience members embedded in a particular cultural and historical milieu. Huaco (1965), for example, has emphasized the relationship between film "styles" and the nature of the political and social climate which provided the "production context" (see also Jarvie, 1970; Derry, 1977).

Discussion of what films and the viewing experience do for audience members enjoys considerable popularity within the sociology of film literature. These discussions focus primarily on the medium as 1) a source of social and personal information, 2) a source of vicarious personal experience, and 3) a means of escaping from socially generated pressures. Following the sociological assumption that art styles and thematic content reflect and sustain a relevant contemporary world view, the approach to film-as-information-source emphasizes patterns in filmic presentations (eg., ethical messages, characterizations, portrayals of problems and resolutions) typically identified through the use of content analysis. Authors employing this perspective consistently conclude that a major function of film is the graphic portrayal of conventional normative precepts and the broadly shared perceptions of the nature of the self and the social environment (see Jarvie, 1970: 121-31).

Emphasis upon the cinema as a medium of mass entertainment gives rise to a focus on the escapist and cathartic functions of film. From this perspective films act primarily as sources of fantasy-based relief from both the pressures and boredom of contemporary life. For example:

The cinema offers compensation for lives which have lost a great deal of their substance. It is no less than a modern necessity, as yet unsung by any poet. The film makes us sad and it makes us gay. It urges us to reflect and delivers us from worries. It alleviates the burden of daily life and nourishes our impoverished imagination. (Mauerhofer, 1949: 105)

As seen in the above quote, the sociological analysis of film-as-escape is closely related to the view of film-as-vicarious-experience. From this perspective, the cinema experience provides the viewer with a situation and characters to which she or he can relate on a non-threatening fantasy level. As anthropologist Hortense Powdermaker (1950) observes in her classic discussion of the Hollywood film industry:

Like all drama and literature, movies extend the experiences of the audience vicariously, and translate problems which are common to mankind into specific and personal situations with which identification is easy. (quoted in Mendelsohn, 1966: 63; see also Fearing, 1947: 120)

These various social scientific perspectives on the function of film tend to be reasonably grounded in systematically collected data and are not mutually exclusive. A complete analysis of the film experience would do well to take them all into account. In the following, I am primarily concerned with examining the cinematic elements which generate audience experience and which are purposefully manipulated by the filmmaker so as to affect the viewer/consumer. The analytic framework I am employing is one which increasingly has come to be favored by sociologists interested in exploring the creation and utilization of contemporary cultural materials. The *production of culture perspective* focuses on the social organization of the cultural production process and the networks of interaction surrounding that activity. This organizational structure and the modes of interaction which it constrains shape, from this viewpoint, the stylistic features of the product itself and, in turn, the experience of the cultural consumer. Factors external to the production world which constrain production activities (eg., legal restriction) (see Peterson, 1982; Becker, 1982: 165-191; Sanders, 1989: 30-32), resources (especially money and personnel) available to producers (see Lyon, 1974), technological changes (see Kealy, 1982), creator backgrounds and orientations to their work (see Sanders, 1989: 62-108; Hirsch, 1972), and the demands and characteristics of the consumers/audience (see Turow, 1982; Rosenblum, 1978) are key factors shaping the style (form and content) of cultural materials (for general discussions of the production of culture perspective see Hirsch, 1974; Jensen, 1984; Peterson, 1976; Becker, 1974; Sanders, 1982).

I employ the general orientation provided by the production of culture perspective to present some of the key conventional elements in horror cinema—a central category of genre film. In the first quarter of 1989 science fiction, horror, and fantasy genre films accounted for almost 31 percent of all film box office revenue and horror films accounted for almost 7 percent of all films released (*Cinefantastique*, July 1989, p. 14). I focus much of the discussion by drawing examples from the classic horror films of the 1930s and the B-films of the 1940s and 50s. In that the conventions established in these early works provided the basis for presentational features of subsequent horror films, I also make reference to more contemporary examples of the genre. The major data upon which this presentation is based are drawn from the systematic qualitative content analysis of 316 films over a three year period (see Fields, 1988).

Film Genre and Convention

In order for those involved in the complex process of creating cultural products to coordinate the production process—from conceptualization through distribution—they must share a basic body of knowledge. In previous work (Sanders, 1982) I have referred to these shared understandings which are the foundation of the "collective action" (Becker, 1974) of cultural production as "production conventions." These coordinating mechanisms have arisen out of earlier agreements and interactions and determine, as Becker (1974: 771) puts it 1) "the materials to be used," 2) "the abstractions to be used to convey particular ideas or experiences," 3) "the form in which materials and abstractions will be combined," and 4) "the appropriate dimensions of the work." A variety of writers have focused on the collective action of cultural production and the production conventions around which it is organized (eg., Lyon, 1982; Kealy, 1982; Faulkner, 1983; Sanders, 1974).

The second type of convention relevant to popular cultural materials—and the type which is central to this present discussion—are features of the product itself which are known to and expected by creators and cultural consumers. These "product conventions" in popular culture consist of common plot themes, types of action, modes of typical representation, and other elements which provide consumers with the familiar context they employ to order their participation in the consumption experience.

The conventions utilized by filmmakers and anticipated by audience members are the essential elements of genre film. Conventions focus audience expectations and provide the grounding for "the experience of an ordered world" (Sobchack, 1977: 39). In essence, genre film consists of an institutionalized network of product conventions determining such things as standard features of plot, characterization, visual presentation, pacing, and sound-track elements (see Kaminsky, 1974; Schatz, 1981; cf., Cawelti, 1976).

The major reason popular cultural products in general, and genre film in particular, are highly conventionalized is due to the "commercial uncertainty" (Hirsch, 1972) inherent in cultural production. Creators and their administrative support personnel are uncertain as to those features which will ensure commercial success. Consequently, they reproduce materials displaying those elements which have proven in the past to be economically viable (see Schatz, 1981: 4-6; Kilday, 1989). This basically conservative tactic has, over time, some liabilities. Most obviously, formulaic features come to be overused, and viewers, listeners, and other consumers become bored by the mechanistic repetition of conventional elements.

A certain degree of innovation within established conventions and experimentation with new elements are essential features of popular cultural production. Innovation leads to the identification of new conventions, provides a means of recapturing an audience diminished by saturation, and allows key production personnel to see their work activities as entailing some level of creativity.

Ideally then, product conventions in genre film and other formulaic products act as an organizing core around which innovation takes place. Creative modification or rearrangement of conventional elements provides cultural consumers with a bit of novelty while maintaining the essential features which are the valued basis of the familiar experience. As Warshow (1971: 129-130) observes in his discussion of the gangster film genre:

For such a type to be successful means that its conventions have imposed themselves upon the general consciousness and become the accepted vehicle of a particular set of attitudes and a particular aesthetic effect. One goes to any individual example of the type with very definite expectations, and originality is to be welcomed only in the degree that it intensifies the expected experience without fundamentally altering it.

Product Conventions In Horror Cinema

Plot and Character Conventions

Plot conventions provide the basic framework around which the other conventional elements in genre film adhere. Characterization, visual features, sound elements, and other product conventions act to advance and support the plot and to increase the likelihood of audience involvement. The typical conventions of plot structure in horror cinema and other forms of genre film entail 1) the establishment of the characters and the basic dramatic conflict in which they are involved, 2) the animation of the conflicts through the activities of the characters, 3) the intensification of the conflicts, and 4) the resolution of the plot conflicts resulting once again in the establishment of equilibrium (Schatz, 1981: 30). The dominant plot conventions in horror film revolve around basic fears experienced commonly by members of western culture—fear of powerlessness and the unknown, fear of being dehumanized, and fear of loss of individuality and self control (White, 1977; see Kaminsky, 1977: 152-153 for a basic typology of plot conventions in horror and science fiction film).

Madness and Loss of Self

Throughout the history of horror cinema the loss of control over the self to mysterious and sinister forces has been a central plot convention. Among the most recurrent of these nightmares is dehumanization—loss of self either through demonic possession or madness (Moss, 1974:79). While evil action impelled by the assertion of the evil side of the human personality has long been a conventional theme (see *Dr. Jekyll and Mr. Hyde*, 1920, 1932, 1941; *The Other*, 1972), in the 1970s possession by demonic forces became one of the cinema's most marketable plots. Riding on the phenomenal success of the occult theme popularized by *Rosemary's Baby* (1968) and its various spin-offs (e.g., *Mephisto Waltz*, 1971; *It's Alive*, 1974), the cinematic presentation of possession became a popular cultural phenomenon with the release of Friedkin's record breaking film, *The Exorcist* (1974).

A key plot convention found in many of the possession films links demonic control with mental illness—both phenomena are implicated in the conventional concern with loss of individual control over the self. This relationship between mental illness and possession is most clearly portrayed in *The Exorcist* and in *The Diary of a Madman* (1963). The latter film is particularly illustrative of the "evil spirit theory" of insanity. The plot concerns the experience of a late 19th century French magistrate (played by Vincent Price) who is possessed by a "horrla," an invisible being from another dimension which delights in causing its human host to commit acts of excessive violence. Understandably concerned by the various manifestations of the horrla and the uncharacteristically violent acts in which he becomes involved, the magistrate seeks the advice and assistance of an "alienist" who, in characteristic psychiatric fashion, diagnoses the phenomenon as being caused by his patient's "overactive imagination" and prescribes recreational therapy (a vacation, involvement in a hobby and social activities) as the route to mental health. Predictably, these simplistic solutions prove ineffective and, after perpetrating further atrocities, the distraught magistrate resorts to self-immolation as the ultimate cure.

The Social Group

In addition to their focus on loss of individuality and self control, horror film plots typically involve the elemental conflict between rationality—usually entailing the use of scientific approaches—and faith—or some related ideational perspective (Hess, 1977). Most commonly, the solution to the central problem around which the plot revolves derives from the power of the social collectivity. Salvation comes from the collective efforts of the social group.

The major social unit which commonly confronts the terror/threat is "the team." Typically, the core team is composed of three major characters—an older, fatherly scientist who often sacrifices himself in the course of the battle, the youthful scientist/hero who combines knowledge and physical skill, and the young heroine who commonly fills the subordinate role of daughter/assistant to the older scientist even though she is often as technologically knowledgeable as are the other scientific members of the team (eg., *Them*, 1954; *The Deadly Mantis*, 1957; *Monster A-Go-Go*, 1965; *Monster on Campus*, 1958; *Attack of the Crab Monsters*, 1957; *Angry Red Planet*, 1959; *Beast from 20,000 Fathoms*, 1953; *Fiend Without a Face*, 1958; *Night of the Blood Beast*, 1958; *Space Monster*, 1965; *Planet of the Vampires*, 1965; *Leviathan*, 1989; *The Abyss*, 1989).

Since science is often the source of the monster as well as the route to salvation, the scientist typically is presented with some ambivalence within the genre (see Sontag, 1961: 209-225). This presentation ranges from the scientist whose unconventional ("mad") theories and researches have alienated him from the scientific establishment (eg., the Frankenstein films; the Dr. Jekyll and Mr. Hyde films; *Island of Lost Souls*, 1933; *House of Dracula*, 1945; *The Horror Chamber of Dr. Faustus*, 1959; *Re-animator*, 1985; *From Beyond*, 1986) through the dedicated knowledge-wielder who provides the information necessary to conquer the threat (see Peary, 1974:58; Charney, 1988).

Allied with the team's scientific personnel is the military/policeman protagonist who is alternately presented as a hero (because of his expertise) and as a fool (because of his single-minded reliance on conventional force). Like the older scientist, he frequently is killed in a valiant attempt to defeat the creature. His demise also has a plot function in that he usually complicates the love relationship of the hero and heroine (eg., *Them*, 1954; *The Eye Creatures*, 1968; *The Indestructible Man*, 1956).

The presentation of the public whose property and well-being are threatened by the monster is also highly conventionalized in the horror genre. Much of the team's activity is commonly devoted to keeping information about the existence or extent of the threat from the public or controlling panic once the threat is known. A massive panic reaction of the populace is typical in those films of the 1950s and 1960s that tend to deal with creatures which threaten the well-being of whole societies or the entire world. In the earlier films, however—in which the threat is not so grandiose—the efforts of the local citizenry are directed against the monster. In these instances the hostile action of the people commonly impels the creature to react destructively. Yet, when the antagonistic activity of the public is directed by legitimate authority (for example, the mayor, police chief, head of a powerful and respected local family), the efforts to protect the community are usually effective (see the majority of the Frankenstein films and *The Wolf Man*, 1941).

Monsters

As the central character element in horror cinema, monsters have traditionally been the major focus of the horror film literature. Rather than attempting to develop yet another descriptive typology of monsters (see Clarens, 1967; Edelson, 1973; Manchel, 1970; Aylesworth, 1972; Frank, 1974; Needleman and Weiner, 1976; Alloway, 1972; Wright, 1986), I will deal briefly with those conventional plot elements which create and motivate the creature.

It is rare for the cinemonster to be presented entirely unsympathetically within the horror genre. Monstrous (ie., deviant) behavior is commonly impelled by chance misfortune, insanity, external control, or stressful interaction with an ignorant and fearful populace. In short, the deviant is a product of factors beyond his/her/its control and deviant behavior is motivated either by the exploitative demands of the scientist/creator or the reaction of "normals" to the clearly visible deviance (deformity) of the creature. For example, even the bloodthirsty habits of vampires are impelled by an hereditary curse or the contagion of a vampire's bite. With the exception of the Mexican vampire films and some of the Hammer Studio films starring Christopher Lee, vampires commonly evidence sorrow over their peculiar affliction (see *Near Dark*, 1987 and *The Lost Boys*, 1987 for contemporary examples of this conventional display of remorse). Many monsters are created by scientists who are experimenting with technologies and powers which are "not meant for mortals." Chance misfortune often plays a large part in the creation of deformity or the motivation of monstrous behavior. Characters are bitten by various monsters (eg., the vampire films; *The Wolf Man*, 1941; *Werewolf of London*, 1935), mistakenly ingest dangerous transforming substances (eg., *Monster on Campus*, 1958), victimized by scientific accidents (eg., *The Amazing Colossal Man*, 1957; *War of the Colossal Beast*, 1958; *The Fly*, 1958 and 1986) or become the unwitting puppets of aliens bent on world conquest (eg., *War of the Satellites*, 1958; *Night of the Blood Beast*, 1958; *Invasion of the Body Snatchers*, 1956 and 1978; *Human Duplicators*, 1965). This latter type of film is particularly interesting in that the controllees are not easily identifiable as deviants. Generally, however, they can be distinguished from normals by their wooden movements, blank stares, and obvious lack of affect.

Conventional Visual Techniques

Since the major development of film as a medium to communicate terror by the German Expressionists, visual elements have been of central importance to the mood of horror film. The Expressionists initiated most of the central visual techniques (subjective camera, stark lighting and use of shadow, diagonal camera angles, set distortion) which have been conventionalized through extensive use by later filmmakers. Visual conventions carry and amplify the horror of the scene and/or act as a cue to the viewer that a horrifying scene is about to occur.

The subjective camera is a central technique designed to experimentally incorporate the audience member into the projected action (see Geduld and Gottesman, 1973: 168). The two major types of subjective shots conventionally employed in horror film are the monster-point-of-view (MPOV) and the victim-point-of-view (VPOV). The former is the most common; it allows a shot of the terrorized victim while delaying the revelation of the monster. This increases the anticipatory tension of the viewing experience. The MPOV shot also allows the viewer to experience the distorted perception of the creature. Prime examples of this distorted perception technique are found in the use of the fisheye lens in *The Oblong Box* (1969), *The Man with the X-Ray Eyes* (1963), *It Came from Outer Space* (1953) and the prismatic effect employed in *The Fly* (1958) and *The Return of the Fly* (1959). The MPOV technique also commonly involves the use of diagonal camera angles in conjunction with distortion. The "down shot" is used to convey a sense of the terrifying size (or occasionally, as in the horror doll films, the angle shot conveys the misleading smallness) of the monster (see *Tower of Terror*, 1971; *Night of The Blood Beast*, 1958; *X-The Unknown*, 1956; *Attack of the Crab Monsters*, 1957; *Tarantula*, 1955; *Earth vs. the Giant Spider*, 1958; *Trilogy of Terror* [made-for-TV], 1975).

The monster POV technique continues to be utilized by contemporary makers of horror film. The presentational convention enjoys special popularity among the makers of "slasher" or "splatter" movies such as the Friday the Thirteenth films, the Halloween series (McCarty, 1981), and the more recently established Nightmare on Elm Street cycle. Some critics (eg., Ebert, 1981) have decried the use of this convention in that it encourages the audience to identify with the killer rather than the (usually female) victim (see Starker, 1989: 89-105 for an historical discussion of critiques of and crusades against movie violence).

Distortion is used to boost the horror experience—to remove the scene from the realm of ordinary perception—as well as to convey the subjective view of the creature. This technique is especially common in the Poe films made by American International in the 1960s (eg., *The Pit and the Pendulum*, 1961; *Tales of Terror*, 1962; *House of Usher*, 1960). The victim POV technique is usually a type of revelation scene (discussed in detail below) in which a shot of the terrified victim is followed by a "low shot" of the creature which speeds the action of the film and heightens the importance of the subject. The VPOV sequence commonly ends with a blackout as the victim is summarily dispatched by the monster.

Revelations and Transformations

The major conventional scene found in essentially all monster films is the one in which the audience is allowed an unimpeded and (hopefully) terrifying view of the creature (Stephen King [1981] refers to this instant of revelation as "oogah-boogah"). The filmmaker's use of revelation plays an important part in determining the impact and effectiveness of the film as a whole. Should the creature be shown too much during the film, the viewer becomes accustomed to the deformity and the impact is considerably decreased. Should the initial revelation scene occur too early, the power of the viewing experience is lessened because there is not sufficient buildup of audience anticipation (see, for example, *X-The Unknown*, 1957 and *Phantom from 10,000 Leagues*, 1956). The impact of the film may be decreased as well if the filmmaker chooses to withhold full revelation until the final scenes. Audience expectation tends to dissipate and the late revelation rarely lives up to the promise of the long delay (see King, 1981). In short, manipulation of audience suspense leading to revelation is a major tool of the horror film creator. As Harrington (1952: 159) observes in his classic article on horror cinema:

(T)he power of the camera as an instrument to generate suspense in an audience lies not in its power to reveal, but in its power to suggest; that what takes place just off-screen in the audience's imagination, the terror of waiting for the final revelation, not the seeing of it, is the most powerful dramatic stimulus toward tension and fright.

Audience tension is manipulated in a variety of conventional ways. Rarely is the creature revealed prior to a variety of anticipation-building pre-revelation sequences. Standard pre-revelations may be divided into *pseudo-revelations* and *partial revelations*. The former consist of those scenes which have the earmarks of the central disclosure (eg., monstrous rustlings, appropriate setting, anticipation-building soundtrack elements, and so on) but the suspense is resolved by the startling shot of a non-monstrous character or object (see *The Innocents*, 1961; *The Cat People*, 1942; *Monster on Campus*, 1958). Pseudo-revelations provide small tension peaks which give the audience a taste of "the real thing," thereby enhancing viewer anticipation and insuring continued focus on the screen action. Partial revelations also provide the audience with a small taste of the eventual full revelation. Within the partial revelation some part of the creature is shown in order to give an indication of the nature and extent of the deformity. The most common types of partial revelations are hand/claw revelations (eg., *The Head That Wouldn't Die*, 1963; *Abominable Snowman of the Himalayas*, 1957), foot revelations (eg., *The Wolf Man*, 1941; *The Beast of Hollow Mountain*, 1956; *Snow Devils*, 1965), eye revelations (eg., *Attack of the Crab Monsters*, 1957), and shadow/silhouette revelations (eg., *The Unholy Three*, 1925; *Night of the Blood Beast*, 1958).

Revelation scenes are the major element toward which suspense is built and which resolve viewer anticipation. A particularly striking revelation scene is found in James Whale's *Frankenstein* (1931). After a series of partial revelations in Dr. Frankenstein's laboratory, tension builds to a medium shot of a heavy door which slowly creaks open to reveal the Karloff monster entering backwards (partial revelation). The creature slowly turns and the full extent of its monstrous disfigurement is lovingly revealed in a medium profile followed by three full-face close-ups (see Anobile, 1974:108-110). The *Frankenstein* revelation scene illustrates a common disclosure convention. Closed doors, boxes, and coffins cue audience anticipation in that they usually open to reveal the monster (see *Invasion of the Vampires*, 1962; *The Thing That Couldn't Die*, 1958; *The Pit and the Pendulum*, 1961; *Mark of the Vampire*, 1935; *Dr. Phibes Rises Again*, 1972. Compare these examples with the various coffin scenes in *The Serpent and the Rainbow*, 1988).

Another special form of the revelation scene—the transformation—is commonly employed. Transformation scenes entail the fully visible evolution of an apparent normal into a deformed creature. When handled with care and technical skill (as in the scene created by John Fulton in *The Werewolf of London*, 1935) the transformation sequence can be the sensational culmination of the special effect craft (see Brosnan, 1974; Schechter and Everitt, 1980). Transformation scenes are most commonly found in those films which deal with the werewolf and Jekyll/Hyde themes.

Conventions, Innovation, and the
Social Function of the Horror Genre

A central feature of contemporary horror cinema is the use of formulaic presentation and plot elements which are anticipated by viewers and manipulated by production personnel. Product conventions are, in short, the presentational norms which, when adhered to, form the emotional core of the horror film experience. As presentational elements arise they are conventionalized through consistent usage impelled primarily by the attachment of directors to creative tradition and by the ongoing ability of these formulaic elements to draw an audience (Gans, 1957; Hirsch, 1972). Conventions cue emotional response and are the familiar elements which assure the viewer that the presentation is taking place within the "safe" context of cinematic fantasy. Were horror film not so conventionalized, the graphic display would evoke revulsion rather than titillating fear.

While presentation conventions are an essential feature of the horror film aesthetic, innovation is of equal importance. Innovation of convention commonly has three major sources. First, the audience may become so accustomed to the conventions that they no longer call forth the desired emotional response. As Becker (1974: 773) observes:

Small innovations occur constantly, as conventional means of creating expectations and delaying their satisfaction become so well-known as to become conventional expectations in their own right (see also Brosnan, 1974: 192-193).

Development of audio/visual and special effect technology is the second major factor which impels innovation in the conventional elements of horror film. In all modes of cultural production, the technological resources employed shape the style and aesthetic of the product (cf., Fine, 1985; Kealy, 1982). New special effects techniques, for example, allowed the audience to witness the full-face transformation of a man into a monster (*Dr. Jekell and Mr. Hyde*, 1932) rather than having the alteration take place out of sight behind a laboratory table (*Dr. Jekyll and Mr. Hyde*, 1920). In contemporary examples of the horror genre, transformation scenes are overt, graphic, and drawn out in loving detail (see, for example, *The Howling*, 1981; *The Company of Wolves*, 1985; *Hellbound/Hellraiser II*, 1988).

Finally, change in horror conventions flows from the desire of production personnel to view their activity as creative and the product as innovative and aesthetically valuable (cf., Brown, 1968: 617; Hirsch, 1972; Kaplan, 1967; Cawelti, 1969; Kealy, 1982; Sanders, 1988). For example, special effects technicians form an especially significant subculture within the occupational world surrounding horror film production. Ongoingly aware of the effects produced by their fellow workers, special effects experts are engaged in an unofficial competition to create cinematic elements which outdo those previously produced. The visual consequence of this competition is that horror film effects have become increasingly realistic and overtly gruesome in the past decade. This escalation is most vividly apparent when contemporary remakes of classic horror films are compared with the originals (eg., *The Blob*, 1958 and 1988; *Invasion of the Body Snatchers*, 1956 and 1978; *The Fly*, 1958, 1986 and 1989 [*The Fly II*]).

As in the classic examples of the genre, horror film plot conventions continue to focus on modes of solving social problems—problems of disorder, threat, change, and ambiguity. Typically, the solution offered is one which emphasizes the value of cooperative social relationships. Adventure genre films generally, and horror film in particular, tend to reflect "quasi-theories" (ie., every-day, taken-for-granted explanations of the cause, consequences, and solutions to common dilemmas; see Hewitt and Hall, 1973) central to American culture. The value of individual creative achievement, the eventual triumph of good over evil, the effectiveness of violent responses to threat, and the utility of rational/scientific modes of problem solving are key quasi-theories promoted in horror film plot conventions.

In that horror cinema propounds these conventional explanations and solutions, it acts, even in its most violent form, as a significant mechanism of social control. Like other popular cultural materials which present deviant actors and behaviors (see Sanders, 1990), horror film reinforces the status quo by telling us that physical deformity indicates moral deformity, violence is legitimate and effective when directed by constituted authorities, difference is evil, and order is good (Gerbner, 1978; Wilkins, 1973). Once again we see the essentially conservative character of formulaic popular cultural products—conventions limit creative endeavors and "frame" social problems (Gamson, 1988) in ideological constraints that reinforce the social order in which those in positions of power have a vested interest.

Works Cited

Alloway, Lawrence (1972), "Monster Films," in Huss and Ross (eds.), *Focus on Horror Film*, pp. 121-124.

Amelio, Ralph J., (ed.) (1974), *Hal in the Classroom: Science Fiction Films*, Dayton, Ohio: Pflaum.

Anobile, Richard (ed.) (1974), *Frankenstein*, New York: Avon.

Aylesworth, Thomas (1972), *Monsters from the Movies*, Philadelphia: Lippincott.

Barthes, Roland (1980), "Upon Leaving the Movie Theatre," pp. 3-10 in Theresa H. K. Cha (ed.), *Cinematic Apparatus: Selected Writings*, New York: Tanam.

Becker, Howard (1974), "Art as Collective Action," *American Sociological Review*, 39: 767-776.

———— (1982), *Art Worlds*, Berkeley: University of California Press.

Brosnan, John (1974), *Movie Magic*, New York: St. Martin's.

Brown, Roger L. (1968), "The Creative Process in the Popular Arts," *International Social Science Journal* 10 (4): 613-624.

Cawelti, John G. (1976), *Adventure, Mystery, and Romance*, Chicago: University of Chicago Press.

Charney, Mark (1988), "Beauty in the Beast: Technological Reanimation in the Contemporary Horror Film," paper presented at the annual meeting of the Popular Culture Association, New Orleans, March.

Clarens, Carlos (1967), *An illustrated History of the Horror Film*, New York: Capricorn.

Derry, Charles (1977), *Dark Dreams*, New York: Barnes.

Dika, Vera (1987), "The Stalker Film 1978-81," pp. 86-101 in G. Waller (ed.), *American Horrors*.

Ebert, Roger (1981), "Why Movie Audiences Aren't Safe Anymore," *American Film* (March), pp. 54-56.

Edelson, Edward (1973), *Great Monsters of the Movies*, New York: Doubleday.

Evans, Walter (1984), "Monster Movies: A Sexual Theory," pp. 53-64 in Barry Grant (ed.), *Planks of Reason.*

Faulkner, Robert R. (1983), *Music on Demand: Composers and Careers in the Hollywood Film Industry,* New Brunswick, NJ: Transaction.

Fearing, Franklin (1947), "Influence of the Movies on Attitudes and Behavior," *The Annals* 254:70-79.

Fields, Echo (1988), "Qualitative Content Analysis of Television News: Systematic Techniques," *Qualitative Sociology* 11 (3): 183-193.

Fine, Gary A. (1985), "Occupational Aesthetics: How Trade School Students Learn to Cook," *Urban Life* 14: 3-32.

Fischer, Lucy and Marcia Landy (1987), "Eyes of Laura Mars" A Binocular Critique, pp. 62-78 in George Waller (ed.), *American Horrors.*

Frank, Alan G. (1974), *Horror Movies: Tales of Terror in the Cinema,* London: Octopus.

Gamson, W. (1988) "A Constructionist Approach to Mass Media and Public Opinion," *Symbolic Interaction* 11 (2): 161-174.

Gans, Herbert J. (1957), "The Creator-Audience Relationship in the Mass Media: An Analysis of Movie-Making," in Bernard Rosenberg and David Manning White (eds.), *Mass Culture,* New York: Free Press, pp. 315-324.

Geduld, Harry and Ronald Gottesman (1973), *An Illustrated Glossary of Film Terms,* New York: Holt, Rinehart and Winston.

Gerbner, George (1978), "The Dynamics of Cultural Resistance," pp. 46-50 in G. Tuchman, A. Daniels, and J. Benet (eds.), *Hearth and Home,* New York: Oxford University Press.

Gitlin, Todd (1989), "Postmodernism: Roots and Politics," pp. 347-360 in Ian Angus and Sut Jhally (eds.), *Cultural Politics in Contemporary America,* New York: Routledge.

Grant, Barry (ed.) (1977), *Genre Film,* Metuchen, NJ: Scarecrow.

———— (ed.) (1984), *Planks of Reason,* Metuchen, NJ: Scarecrow.

Greenberg, Harvey (1975), *The Movies on Your Mind,* New York: Dutton.

Harrington, Curtis (1952), "Ghoulies and Ghosties," *Sight and Sound* 3 (4): 157-161.

Hess, Judith (1977), "Genre Film and the Status Quo," pp. 53-61 in B. Grant (ed.), *Genre Film.*

Hewitt, John and Peter Hall (1973), "Social Problems, Problematic Situations, and Quasi-Theories," *American Sociological Review* 38 (3): 367-374.

Hirsch, P. (1972), "Processing Fads and Fashions: An Organization-Set Analysis of Cultural Industry Systems," *American Journal of Sociology* 77: 639-659.

Huaco, George (1965), *The Sociology of Film Art,* New York: Basic Books.

Huss, Roy and T. J. Ross (eds.) (1972), *Focus on Horror Film,* Englewood Cliffs, NJ: Prentice-Hall.

Jarvie, I. C. (1970), *Movies and Society,* New York: Basic Books.

Jensen, J. (1984), "An Interpretive Approach to Culture Production," pp. 98-110 in W. Rowland, Jr. and B. Watkins (eds.), *Interpreting Television: Current Research Perspectives,* Newbury Park, CA: Sage.

Kaminsky, Stuart (1974), *American Film Genres,* New York: Dell.

Kaplan, Abraham (1967), "The Aesthetics of the Popular Arts," in James B. Hall and Barry Ulanov (eds.), *Modern Culture and the Arts,* New York: McGraw-Hill, pp. 48-62.

Kaplan, E. Ann (1986), "Feminist Film Criticism: Current Issues and Problems," *Studies in the Literary Imagination* XIX (no. 1): 7-20.

Kealy, Edward (1982), "Conventions and the Production of the Popular Music Aesthetic," *Journal of Popular Culture* 16 (2): 100-115.

Kilday, Gregg (1989), "Why Movies Come in Bunches," *American Film* (April), pp. 14-16.

King, Stephen (1981), *Danse Macabre*, New York: Everest House.

Lazere, Donald (ed.) (1987), *American Media and Mass Culture: Left Perspectives*, Berkeley: University of California Press.

Lyon, Eleanor (1974), "Work and Play: Resource Constraints in a Small Theater," *Urban Life and Culture*, 3 (1): 71-97.

_____ (1982), "Stages of Theatrical Rehearsal," *Journal of Popular Culture* 16 (2): 75-89.

Manchel, Frank, *Terrors of the Screen*, Englewood Cliffs, NJ: Prentice-Hall, 1970.

Mauerhofer, Hugo (1949), "Psychology of Film Experience," *Penquin Film Review #8*, London: Penguin, 103-109.

McCarty, John (1981), *Splatter Movies*, Albany, NY: Fantaco.

Mendelsohn, Harold (1966), *Mass Entertainment*, New Haven, Conn.: College and University Press.

Modleski, Tania (1986), "The Terror of Pleasure: The Contemporary Horror Film and Postmodern Theory," pp. 155-166 in T. Modleski (ed.), *Studies in Entertainment*, Bloomington: Indiana University Press.

Moss, Robert F. (1974), *Karloff and Company: The Horror Film*, New York: Pyramid.

Needleman, B. and N. Weiner (1976), "Heros and Villains in Art,"*Society* 14: 35-39.

Peary, Dennis (1974), "Political Attitudes in American Science Fiction Films," pp. 49-59 in Ralph Amelio (ed.), *Hal in the Classroom: Science Fiction Films*.

Peterson, Richard A. (1976), "The Production of Culture: A Prolegomenon,"*American Behavioral Scientist* 19 (July): 669-684.

_____ (1982), "Five Constraints on the Production of Culture: Law, Technology, Market, Organizational Structure and Occupational Careers," *Journal of Popular Culture* 16 (2): 143-153.

Polan, Dana (1987), "Daffy Duck and Bertolt Brecht: Toward a Politics of Self-Reflective Cinema?" pp. 345-356 in D. Lazere (ed.) *American Media and Mass Culture*.

Powdermaker, Hortense (1950), *Hollywood, The Dream Factory*, Boston: Little, Brown.

Rosenblum, Barbara (1978), *Photographers at Work*, New York: Holmes and Meier.

Sanders, Clinton R. (1974), "Psyching out the Crowd: Folk Performers and their Audiences," *Urban Life and Culture* 3 (3): 264-282.

_____ (1982), "Structural and Interactional Features of Popular Culture Production: An Introduction to the Production of Culture Perspective," *Journal of Popular Culture* 16 (2): 66-74.

_____ (1988), "Organizational Constraints on Tattoo Images: A Sociological Analysis of Artistic Style," pp. 232-241 in Ian Hodder (ed.), *The Meanings of Things*, London: Unwin Hyman.

_____ (1989), *Customizing the Body: The Art and Culture of Tattooing*, Philadelphia: Temple University Press.

_____ (ed.) (1990), *Marginal Conventions: Mass Media, Popular Culture, and Social Deviance*, Bowling Green, OH: The Popular Press.

Schatz, Thomas (1981), *Hollywood Genres*, New York: Random House.

Schechter, Harold and David Everitt (1980), *Film Tricks*, New York: Harlin Quist.

Sobchack, Thomas (1977), "Genre Film: A Classical Experience," pp. 39-52 in B. Grant (ed.), *Genre Film*, Metuchen, NJ:Scarecrow.

Sontag, Susan (1966), *Against Interpretation*, New York: Dell.

Starker, Steven (1989), *Evil Influences: Crusades Against the Mass Media*, New Brunswick, NJ: Transaction.

Turow, Joseph (1982), "The Role of 'The Audience' in Publishing Children's Books," *Journal of Popular Culture* 16 (2): 90-99.

Twitchell, James (1985, *Dreadful Pleasure*, New York: Oxford University Press.

Waller, George (ed.) (1987), *American Horrors*, Urbana, IL: University of Illinois Press.

Warshow, Robert (1971), *The Immediate Experience*, New York: Atheneum.

White, D. L. (1977), "The Poetics of Horror: More Than Meets the Eye," pp. 124-144 in B. Grant (ed.), *Genre Film*.

Wilkins, L. (1973), "Information and the Definition of Deviance," in S. Cohen and J. Young (eds.), *The Manufacture of News*, Beverly Hills, CA: Sage, pp. 22-27.

Wright, Gene (1986), *Horrorshows*, New York: Facts on File.

Wright, Will (1975), *Sixguns and Society*, Berkeley: University of California Press.

Filmography

1920	*Dr. Jekyll and Mr. Hyde*	Dir. John S. Robertson
1925	*Unholy Three (The)*	Dir. Tod Browning
1931	*Frankenstein*	Dir. James Whale
1932	*Dr. Jekyll and Mr. Hyde*	Dir. Rouben Mamoulian
1932	*Dracula*	Dir. Tod Browning
1933	*Island of Lost Souls*	Dir. Erle Kenton
1935	*Mark of the Vampire*	Dir. Tod Browning
1935	*Werewolf of London*	Dir. Stuart Walker
1941	*Dr. Jekyll and Mr. Hyde*	Dir. Victor Fleming
1942	*Cat People (The)*	Dir. Jacques Tourneur
1945	*House of Dracula*	Dir. Erle Kenton
1953	*Beast from 20,000 Fathoms*	Dir. Eugene Lourie
1953	*It Came from Outer Space*	Dir. Jack Arnold
1954	*Them*	Dir. Gordon Douglas
1955	*Tarantula*	Dir. Jack Arnold
1956	*Beast of Hollow Mountain (The)*	Dirs. Edward Nassour / Ismael Rodriguez
1956	*Indestructible Man (The)*	Dir. Jack Pollexfen
1956	*Invasion of the Body Snatchers*	Dir. Don Siegel
1956	*Phantom from 10,000 Leagues*	Dir. Dan Milner
1956	*X-The Unknown*	Dir. Leslie Norman
1957	*Abominable Snowman of the Himalayas (The)*	Dir. Val Guest
1957	*Amazing Colossal Man (The)*	Dir. Bert Gordon
1957	*Attack of the Crab Monsters*	Dir. Roger Corman
1957	*Deadly Mantis (The)*	Dir. Nathan Juran

1958	*Blob (The)*	Dir. Irvin Yeaworth, Jr.
1958	*Earth vs. the Giant Spider* *(The Spider)*	Dir. Bert Gordon
1958	*Fiend Without a Face*	Dir. Arthur Crabtree
1958	*Fly (The)*	Dir. Kurt Neumann
1958	*Monster on Campus*	Dir. Jack Arnold
1958	*Night of the Blood Beast*	Dir. Bernard Kowalski
1958	*Thing That Couldn't Die (The)*	Dir. William Cowan
1958	*War of the Colossal Beast*	Dir. Bert Gordon
1958	*War of the Satellites*	Dir. Roger Corman
1959	*Angry Red Planet (The)*	Dir. I. B. Melchior
1959	*Horror Chamber of* *Dr. Faustus (The)*	Dir. Georges Franju
1959	*Return of the Fly (The)*	Dir. Edward Bernds
1960	*House of Usher*	Dir. Roger Corman
1961	*Innocents (The)*	Dir. Jack Clayton
1961	*Pit and the Pendulum (The)*	Dir. Roger Corman
1962	*Invasion of the Vampires*	Dir. Miguel Morayta
1962	*Tales of Terror*	Dir. Roger Corman
1963	*Diary of a Madman (The)*	Dir. Reginald LeBorg
1963	*Head (Brain) That* *Wouldn't Die (The)*	Dir. Joseph Green
1963	*Man With the X-Ray* *Eyes (The)*	Dir. Roger Corman
1965	*Planet of the Vampires* *(Planet of Blood)*	Dir. Mario Bava
1965	*Human Duplicators (The)*	Dir. Hugo Grimaldi
1965	*Monster A-Go-Go*	Dir. Herschell Gordon Lewis and Bill Rebane
1965	*Snow (Space) Devils*	Dir. Antonio Margheriti
1965	*Space Monster*	Dir. Leonard Katzman
1968	*Eye Creatures (The)*	Dir. Larry Buchanan
1968	*Rosemary's Baby*	Dir. Roman Polanski
1969	*Oblong Box (The)*	Dir. Gordon Hessler
1971	*Mephisto Waltz*	Dir. Paul Wendkos
1971	*Tower of Terror* *(In the Devil's Garden)*	Dir. Sidney Hayers
1972	*Dr. Phibes Rises Again*	Dir. Robert Fuest
1972	*Other (The)*	Dir. Robert Mulligan
1974	*Exorcist (The)*	Dir. William Friedkin
1974	*It's Alive*	Dir. Larry Cohen
1975	*Trilogy of Terror* [made for TV]	Dir. Dan Curtis
1978	*Invasion of the Body Snatchers*	Dir. Philip Kaufman
1981	*Howling (The)*	Dir. Joe Dante
1985	*Company of Wolves (The)*	Dir. Neil Jordon
1985	*Re-animator (The)*	Dir. Stuart Gordon
1986	*Fly (The)*	Dir. David Cronenberg
1986	*From Beyond*	Dir. Stuart Gordon
1987	*Lost Boys (The)*	Dir. Joel Schumacher

1987	*Near Dark*	Dir. Kathryn Bigelow
1988	*Blob (The)*	Dir. Chuck Russell
1988	*Hellbound/Hellraiser II*	Dir. Tony Randal
1988	*Serpent and the Rainbow (The)*	Dir. Wes Craven
1989	*Abyss (The)*	Dir. James Cameron
1989	*Fly II (The)*	Dir. Chris Walas
1989	*Leviathan*	Dir. George P. Cosmatos

Songs in Screwball Comedy

Rick Shale

Screwball comedy is a term often used but seldom defined. Any humorous film in which the characters exhibit a degree of zany behavior is likely to be labeled "screwball." But such a casual use of the term does a disservice to a unique body of films. Everyone, as James Harvey points out in *Romantic Comedy*, "knew in a general way what a screwball comedy was: both swanky and slapstick, slangy, irreverent, and skeptical—and powerfully, glamorously 'in love with love' " (287). Before exploring the use of songs in these films, let us first attempt a more precise definition of screwball comedy.

Nearly all critics agree that the screwball era began in 1934 and ended sometime in the early-to-mid 1940s. Frank Capra's *It Happened One Night* and Howard Hawks' *Twentieth Century*, both released in 1934, are always cited as the two films that inaugurated the genre, though some critics will also include in this seminal group another 1934 film *The Thin Man*, starring William Powell and Myrna Loy.

But why 1934? Andrew Sarris, in an important article titled "The Sex Comedy Without Sex," argues that the stricter enforcement of the Production Code which began that year, propelled romantic comedy into this new genre called screwball. Filmmakers, no longer able to show overtly sexual or romantically physical situations, turned to crazy behavior as a sex substitute. People seldom kiss in screwball comedies, but they often hit, wrestle, or fall down. Other critics remain skeptical of the Code's influence, but nearly all agree that screwball represented a melding of several traditions: *sophisticated comedy*, which Lubitsch had made popular in the previous decade; *the tough comedies* starring wisecracking women like Joan Blondell, Jean Harlow, or Mae West; *slapstick*, which had nicely weathered the crossover from silent films; and *the Broadway stage*, which already had an established tradition of romantic comedy. The hallmarks of this new brand of cinematic romance called screwball were verbal wit, daffy personalities, and often rather violent horseplay.

Wes Gehring, in his definitive study *Screwball Comedy: A Genre of Madcap Romance*, argues persuasively that these films are anti-heroic in nature. "The genre," he writes, "should be seen as part of the general movement taking place in American humor during the late 1920s from the capable to the frustrated character, a movement that has come to be associated

160

with the problems of coming to terms with an irrational modern world" (69). He adds that "while satire can and does exist, the screwball comedy viewer is generally allowed to grow fond of these wealthy wackos, in a superior sort of way, while also enjoying the escapism of beautiful people in beautiful settings" (154).

Gehring lists five characteristics that link screwball films to the tradition of the comic anti-hero: first is *abundant leisure time*. Characters in these films are seldom seen working (the notable exception being newspaper reporters, who became a screwball staple). A second characteristic is the *childlike nature* of these characters. These are films about people with few responsibilities. The emphasis is always on having fun or liberating a stuffy personality. As Sarris and others point out, screwball films are comedies of courtship; marriage, if it occurs at all, generally comes only in the final reel. Children are thus seldom present, but pets often serve as child surrogates. The dog Asta in several films or the leopard in *Bringing Up Baby* are examples. A third point is the *urban setting* of these films with an emphasis on elegant mansions and city life. At least one nightclub scene was practically obligatory for these "caviar comedies" as one critic dubbed them. In *Pursuits of Happiness* Stanley Cavell points out that many notable screwball films at their conclusion depart from the urban landscape, usually New York City, for the wilds of Connecticut. Here, in what Cavell terms "the green world," a phrase he borrows from Northrop Frye, the screwball lovers reconcile their differences. Gehring's fourth characteristic is the *apolitical outlook* of these screwball characters. It is this point that leads him and many other critics to label most of Frank Capra's comedies populist or political rather than screwball. Screwball films are rarely inspirational; Capra's almost always are. The final characteristic is the *frustration of the male figure*. Women usually displayed the screwball tendencies; men became their hapless victims caught in the illogical maelstrom of love. "Screwball," observes James Harvey, "was a special kind of women's game...." "Screwball heroines," he explains, "rarely miss the point. Screwball heroes, on the other hand, often do" (287). If the films have a strong, dominant male, it is usually because a second male, invariably Ralph Bellamy, is present to serve as the comic butt.

These films always paired a strong female and a strong male lead. This is why Marx Brothers movies do not qualify as screwball; the behavior is certainly zany enough, but—Margaret Dumont notwithstanding—the Marx Brothers films lack this male-female balance and were not really romantic comedies.

An interesting characteristic of many screwball films that has been overlooked by most historians is the frequent use of song. Two points are worth noting: about half of all the films that meet the definition of screwball contain at least one song. More significantly, in most cases these songs are sung by the stars of the film, not by secondary characters cast for their voices.

In Frank Capra's *It Happened One Night,* Clark Gable plays a temporarily unemployed newspaper reporter and Claudette Colbert a runaway heiress. Gable recognizes her and in return for the exclusive story agrees to help her get to her fiancé. Of course they will fall in love, but in the first few reels of the film they are quite antagonistic, he combatting her upper class snobbism with a macho middle class surliness. As they ride north on the night bus, a group of fellow passengers begins to sing "The Man on the Flying Trapeze." Capra has the cast sing three verses of the song, and during each the camera allows us to discover more people joining in. Gable sings along with the first chorus, as Colbert looks discomfitted and remains silent. By the second verse she has melted somewhat and joins in. In the third chorus we see the bus driver join in too, and the punch line is that the driver gets so involved with the song that he misses a turn and crashes the bus. The song serves to transform the strangers on the bus into a group. So binding is its force that we might instantly suspect anyone not singing of being anti-American. Capra, to use James Harvey's phrase, often "tries to blackmail us into a feeling of communality" (170). Despite the class differences—and the passengers clearly represent a range of classes, Colbert being at the upper end of the scale—everyone knows the words. Of course they do. Songs in screwball comedies are the songs America sings.

In *You Can't Take It With You* (1938) Capra uses the song "Polly Wolly Doodle" first to accentuate, then to melt class differences. When business tycoon Anthony Kirby, played by Edward Arnold, and the slightly daffy Vanderhof family are jailed after a fireworks explosion, kindly old Grandpa Vanderhof, played by Lionel Barrymore, turns to song to banish the gloom of incarceration. The other prisoners join in and respond appreciatively, but Kirby's refusal to take part in the festive merrymaking brands him an uncaring, unfeeling, selfish elitist. Later in the film the same song is used to effect a reconciliation between Kirby and his son, played by James Stewart. "Do you know 'Polly Wolly Doodle'?" asks Grandpa Vanderhof of Kirby. "Of course you do," he says, answering his own question. A few hot licks on the harmonica reveal Kirby's newly acquired feelings for others, and the problems of two families dissolve into thin air. The screenplay by Robert Riskin mentions no specific song, but Capra's choice of "Polly Wolly Doodle" was appropriate; the film audience would likely know it too. This traditional song of unknown authorship was a staple of minstrel shows and had been introduced to film three years earlier by Shirley Temple who sang it in *The Littlest Rebel* (1935). "Polly Wolly Doodle" has been used in at least half a dozen films. Capra used it again in *Pocket Full of Miracles* (1961), and it is also heard in films as wildly different as Sam Peckinpah's *The Wild Bunch* (1969) and Blake Edward's *S.O.B* (1981).

Screwball comedies are inherently aggressive—sometimes verbally, sometimes physically, but nearly always romantically. For Capra, though, when a song begins, the combat ceases and the opposing forces reconcile. Other directors use songs quite differently.

In *The Awful Truth* (1937), perhaps the quintessential screwball film, director Leo McCarey uses two songs to drive people apart. Irene Dunne and Cary Grant play Lucy and Jerry Warriner, a married couple who decide early in the film to divorce. The comic plot revolves around their separate romances and eventual reconciliation. After leaving her husband, Lucy takes up with wealthy Dan Leeson, an Oklahoma bumpkin played by Ralph Bellamy. When we first meet this character, he is humming "Home On the Range." McCarey clearly intends his audience to associate Dan with this song, which carries with it connotations of the west, open spaces, and home life. Midway in this doomed courtship Lucy and Dan together sing "Home On the Range." She sings beautifully and accompanies them on a piano, but Dan can't carry a tune. "Never had a lesson in my life. Have you?" Dan exclaims at the song's conclusion. Their failure to make beautiful music together adroitly signals to us that Lucy and Dan's relationship will not last.

A second song, "My Dreams Are Gone With the Wind," was composed specifically for the film by Ben Oakland and Milton Drake and is used twice. In the first instance it is sung by Jerry's date, Dixie Belle, played by Joyce Compton. She turns out to be a nightclub singer whose rendition of the song includes a "wind effect" which blows her skirt up above her waist at appropriate moments. This song too is about home, and it opens with the following lyrics:

> I used to dream about a cottage small
> A cottage small by a waterfall.
> But I wound up with no home at all.
> My dreams are gone with the wind.

Much later in the film, Jerry has left Dixie Belle and is about to marry a wealthy socialite. Lucy realizes the match will not work and more importantly realizes she wants Jerry back. She masquerades as Jerry's sister, crashes a party at the socialite's home, and, playing drunk, offers a scandalous reprise of Dixie Belle's song, all to the horror of the socialite's rather stuffy family and to the growing amusement of Jerry. That the song is an important subtext of the plot is revealed by a slight change in lyrics when Lucy sings it. In the second stanza, Dixie Belle had sung:

> All through my life I drifted with the tide.
> I let romance take me for a ride.
> I'm just a fool with nothing to hide.
> My dreams are gone with the wind.

Lucy alters the words and sings:

> I'll never forget the way I do my stuff.
> I do my stuff but you call my bluff.
> You call my bluff but sho' enuff,
> My dreams are gone with the wind.

Her comic, vulgar rendition succeeds. Jerry leaves with her, perhaps charmed by the zany performance, which was clearly staged to win him back rather than maliciously embarrass him. Soon they are off to the "green world" of Connecticut and a reconciliation.

McCarey had also used song in *Ruggles of Red Gap* (1935), a warm, entertaining film about the Americanization of Ruggles, an English valet played by Charles Laughton. Leila Hyams briefly sings "By the Light of the Silvery Moon" and teaches "Pretty Baby" to Roland Young, who plays Ruggles' former master. In the film's finale, the frontier citizens of Red Gap sing "For He's a Jolly Good Fellow" to Ruggles, who has renounced his servant status and has opened a restaurant.

In *Theodora Goes Wild* (1936), starring Irene Dunne and Melvyn Douglas, music is used as a metaphor for courtship and sexual uncertainty. After these two meet and have a pleasant night on the town, Dunne returns to her home in Connecticut with Douglas in romantic pursuit. In order to shut him up and avoid scandal, Dunne establishes Douglas as a gardener and gives him temporary quarters in a cottage behind the home she shares with her elderly aunts. As Dunne plays the piano and sings "Be Still My Heart," director Richard Boleslawski effectively cuts back and forth between close-ups of Dunne and Douglas as she sings such lyrics as: "Just read those eyes/Trembling lips that don't know where to start./Even though you know they're telling lies,/Be still my heart." When Douglas begins to whistle the song back to her, she pounds the keys furiously to drown him out. One aunt slams a door breaking the glass, and the other aunt shuts a second door on the cat's tail. Chaos reigns. A final close-up shows Dunne, head shaking, still pounding the keys; the cacophony effectively symbolizes her mixed emotions and romantic repression. Several other songs from "Rock of Ages" and "Onward Christian Soldiers" to "Pop Goes the Weasel" and "Three Blind Mice" are used to advance the themes of this film.

Topper (1937) opens with Cary Grant and Constance Bennett driving down the road singing "The Old Oaken Bucket." The plot will revolve around this couple's attempt to get their friend Cosmo Topper to be less formal, more fun-loving. His reputation for rigidity is introduced before he is when Grant and Bennett change the lyrics from "The iron-bound bucket/the moss-covered bucket" to "iron-bound Topper/moss-covered Topper." Later in the film Grant and Bennett join Hoagy Carmichael (who plays himself) for a rendition of Carmichael's "Old Man Moon."

Perhaps the most famous use of song in a screwball comedy is in Howard Hawks' 1938 film *Bringing Up Baby*. Susan Vance, played by Katharine Hepburn, has acquired a pet leopard named Baby. The animal will come only when it hears its favorite song "I Can't Give You Anything But Love, Baby." In the course of this screwiest of screwball comedies, the song is sung by Hepburn and Grant several times, the final rendition accompanied by a yowling leopard and a barking dog. Hawks based his film on a 1937 *Collier's* short story by Hagar Wilde, who originated the idea that the animal will answer only to this particular song. "I Can't Give You Anything But Love, Baby" was composed in 1928 for a Broadway review and has been used in several stage musicals and nine films (Ewen 157).

In *Ball of Fire* (1941), directed by Hawks from a script by Billy Wilder and Charles Brackett, Gary Cooper plays a shy, reclusive English professor, whose research on slang brings him into contact with a chanteuse named Sugarpuss O'Shea, played by Barbara Stanwyck. Her lusty rendition of "Drum Boogie" with the Gene Krupa band (lip-synced, according to Gerald Mast) arouses Cooper; later, as he struggles to make his romantic intentions known, Oscar Homolka and the others who play Cooper's fellow professors sing "Sweet Genevieve" and the fraternal drinking song "Gaudeamus Igitur." The effect is touching rather than comic, and the tone of the film is often more Capraesque than Hawksian (see Mast 356 and Wood 106).

Another director who used songs effectively was George Cukor, who directed Cary Grant and Katharine Hepburn in two film versions of Philip Barry plays, *Holiday* (1938) and *The Philadelphia Story* (1940). In *Holiday*, Grant plays Johnny Case, who is about to marry into the wealthy Seton family. The problem is he plans to marry the stuffy, formal Seton daughter, played by Doris Nolan, rather than the fun loving, spirited one played by Hepburn. The film becomes a working out of the ways to remove the barriers that separate Hepburn and Grant. Two of Johnny's pals, played by Edward Everett Horton and Jean Dixon, visit the Seton mansion and take refuge in an upstairs playroom where they are joined by Hepburn and Lew Ayres, who plays her alcoholic brother and fellow black sheep of the family. Cukor has the four of them sing "Camptown Races" as a means of showing who can bend or unwind a little. It is impossible to imagine any other members of the crusty Seton family singing such a folksy tune, much less having fun doing it, so when Hepburn rises to the occasion and wins over Johnny's friends, we clearly see *and hear* which Seton sister deserves Johnny.

In *The Philadelphia Story* (1940) Cukor employs two songs which had premiered a year earlier in separate MGM films. Tracy Lord, played by Hepburn, must choose between three men: her former husband C. K. Dexter Haven, played by Grant; a reporter named Macauley Connor, played by Jimmy Stewart; and her fiancé, played by John Howard. Connor and a photographer have crashed the Lord household under the pretext of being friends of a distant relative. Tracy sees through their ruse and strings them along for comic effect. Her precocious younger sister Dinah, played by Virginia Weidler, entertains these "guests" by singing a rousing rendition of "Lydia the Tatooed Lady," a song Groucho Marx had introduced a year earlier in MGM's *At the Circus*. The song functions nicely as a comic set piece, but its final line "You can learn a lot from Lydia," sung just as Hepburn enters the room, implies that we are to equate Lydia with Tracy Lord. The male characters, notably Stewart's, will indeed "learn a lot" from Tracy.

Later in the film, after a night of drinking and celebrating, Macauley Connor carries a wet and pleasantly drunk Tracy back from the swimming pool, and sings "Over the Rainbow." He has fallen for Tracy and with some fervor sings "Somewhere over the rainbow, way up high,/There's a land that I heard of once in a lullabye." As he comes to the line "And the dreams that I dare to...," he is jarred from his reverie by the presence of Tracy's fiancé and former husband, both of whom have come to check on her condition. "Over the Rainbow," which had been introduced only a year earlier in MGM's *Wizard of Oz*, fits well into this situation with Stewart's character temporarily off in a dream land of romantic euphoria. These songs also serve to humanize the characters who sing them and make them realistically contemporary. What could be more natural, more real, than to be singing songs from two recent MGM hits? They are songs everyone in the audience was likely singing too. Interestingly, "Over the Rainbow" and "Lydia the Tatooed Lady" were both composed by the same team of Harold Arlen and Yip Harburg.

Of all the screwball directors, none used songs in a more satiric or comically ironic way than Preston Sturges, whose best films were made for Paramount between 1940 and 1944. Sturges comes at the end of the screwball era, and his films serve as a transition between that genre and war time situation comedies. Sturges not only wrote his own scripts but sometimes composed the songs in his films. In *The Miracle of Morgan's Creek* (1944), for example, Betty Hutton does a hilarious lip sync to a Sturges composition, "The Bell In the Bay."

Hail the Conquering Hero (1944) stars Eddie Bracken as Woodrow Lafayette Pershing Truesmith, a would-be Marine whose dreams of battlefield honor have been dashed by a discharge for hay fever. Sturges opens the film with a song he composed after the screenplay had been completed. "Home to the Arms of Mother," sung by Julie Gibson and the Guardsmen, establishes the film's satiric target of motherhood and excessive sentimentality. The camera pans across the patrons of a waterfront bar and finally comes to rest on Woodrow, who is drowning the sorrows of his failed military career. He is soon adopted by a group of well-meaning Marines (led by William Demarest) and persuaded to return to his hometown. These men, like comic spirits of chaos, are not content to simply send Woodrow home; they dress him in medals and invent stories of war exploits. The homecoming scene allows Sturges to introduce additional themes through music. Several amateur bands have gathered at the train station for Woodrow's hastily arranged homecoming celebration. Their inability to hear their cues causes the prissy organizer of the event (played by Franklin Pangborn) to rush comically from one band to another in a futile attempt to control the cacophony. The overlapping sounds add to the general pandemonium, but the actual numbers these bands play relate to several themes that will be developed in the film. "Home to the Arms of Mother" is heard again, now with Woodrow's widowed mother present to greet him. "Hail the Conquering Hero" reflects the fraud that Woodrow unwittingly and unwillingly perpetrates on his hometown, a simple ruse that will escalate into a comic nightmare. "Mademoiselle From Armentieres" conjures up the memory of Woodrow's heroic father who died fighting in France as Woodrow was born, and the final song "There'll Be a Hot Time In the Old Town Tonight" foreshadows the snowballing chaos that will soon develop.

Small town politics is another comic target of the film, and the town fathers soon nominate Woodrow for mayor. Sturges' second original composition is the campaign song "We Want Woodrow." The lyrics are painted on a four-sided box sign and sung at a political rally. *Hail the Conquering Hero* is more a wartime situation comedy than a screwball film, but it is one of Sturges' most interesting works. The use of songs to provide subtle thematic cues to the audience is one aspect of the film's complexity.

In *The Palm Beach Story* (1942) Sturges uses several old standards for comic effect. The Ale and Quail Club, an improbable group dedicated to drinking and hunting, serenades Claudette Colbert on a train to Florida. They burst into her sleeping compartment and offer a raucous rendition of "Sweet Adeline." Sturges cuts from the group to Colbert cringing at the discordant sounds to a shot of the hunting dogs howling. The sounds of the latter are scarcely distinguishable from those of the singers. They then sing "Goodnight Ladies" and segue into "Merrily We Roll Along" before rushing off to investigate some fellow members who are shooting up the club car. The Ale and Quail Club is superfluous to the plot of the film, but their manic mischief and singing make an indelible impression.

The Palm Beach Story also includes perhaps Sturges' best use of song for ironic effect when Rudy Vallee croons his hit recording "Goodnight Sweetheart." Claudette Colbert has left her husband Joel McCrea and is being courted by Vallee, who met and fell in love with her when she accidentally stepped on his face. Vallee plays a millionaire, and near the end of the film he serenades her with his famous number, elaborately staging it with full orchestra on the lawn of his Palm Beach mansion. As he sings, Colbert is upstairs with McCrea and having second thoughts about leaving him. Vallee sings the song three times. During the first, Colbert and McCrea retire to separate rooms. They both shut doors and windows to drown out the song, which suggests that the lyrics are having an effect quite different from the one intended by the singer. The words, "Goodnight, sweetheart, though I'm not beside you/Goodnight, sweetheart, til my love will guide you," suggest separation and reconciliation, a nearly obligatory theme of most screwball comedies. As Vallee repeats the song, we see Colbert struggling with her dress and her conscience. She eventually goes to McCrea for assistance in extricating herself from her gown (and, one assumes, from the romantic mess she's created). During the third and final repetition of the song, she abandons all thought of Vallee and throws herself into McCrea's arms, interrupting the kiss only momentarily to moan, "I hope you realize this is costing us millions." Sturges cuts to Vallee singing the final "Good night" and then fades out on a shot of the reconciled lovers.

Songs clearly play an important role in a remarkable number of screwball films. Capra nearly always used songs to build a sense of community; Sturges almost always to poke fun. Hawks, McCarey, and Cukor employed songs for humorous and thematic effect. Though some tunes, such as Sturges' original compositions, were unknown prior to the film's release, most were popular contemporary songs or traditional favorites. Many times the songs themselves were less important than *who* was singing them and *why* they were being sung. During no other era of screen comedy have the stars themselves so often turned to song to express thematic concerns or to develop character. Any study of screwball films will be enhanced by careful attention paid to these songs.

Works Cited

Cavell, Stanley. *Pursuits of Happiness: The Hollywood Comedy of Remarriage.* Cambridge: Harvard U. Press, 1981.

Ewen, David, ed. *American Popular Songs From the Revolutionary War to the Present.* New York: Random House, 1966.

Gehring, Wes. *Screwball Comedy: A Genre of Madcap Romance.* Westport, CT: Greenwood Press, 1986.

Harvey, James. *Romantic Comedy In Hollywood: From Lubitsch to Sturges.* NY: Knopf, 1987.

Mast, Gerald. *Howard Hawks, Storyteller.* NY: Oxford University Press, 1982.

Sarris, Andrew. "The Sex Comedy Without Sex." *American Film* 3.5 (March 1978): 8-15.

Wood, Robin. *Howard Hawks.* Garden City, NY: Doubleday, 1968.

Filmography

1934	*It Happened One Night*	Dir. Frank Capra
1934	*The Thin Man*	Dir. W. S. Van Dyke II
1934	*Twentieth Century*	Dir. Howard Hawks
1935	*Ruggles of Red Gap*	Dir. Leo McCarey
1936	*Theodora Goes Wild*	Dir. Richard Boleslawski

1937	*The Awful Truth*	Dir. Leo McCarey
1937	*Topper*	Dir. Norman Z. McLeod
1938	*Bringing Up Baby*	Dir. Howard Hawks
1938	*Holiday*	Dir. George Cukor
1938	*You Can't Take It With You*	Dir. Frank Capra
1940	*The Philadelphia Story*	Dir. George Cukor
1941	*Ball of Fire*	Dir. Howard Hawks
1942	*The Palm Beach Story*	Dir. Preston Sturges
1944	*Hail the Conquering Hero*	Dir. Preston Sturges
1944	*The Miracle of Morgan's Creek*	Dir. Preston Sturges

The Culture-Clash Comedies of the 1980s

Roy M. Vestrich

In Wallace Stevens' complex narrative poem "The Comedian as the Letter C," the poem's protagonist, Crispin, is described as having served "Grotesque apprenticeship to chance event,/ A clown, perhaps, but an aspiring clown" (40). It is a description which is equally applicable to many of the disaffected and disenfranchised figures that populate a strain of satire and dark comedy in the cinema of the 1980s. This strain can be traced in some degree to the screwball comedies of the 1930s and to the social rebel and counter-culture films of the 1960s and early 1970s. But it is a distinctly 1980s brand of cinematic comedy which can appropriately be labeled *culture-clash comedy*. The proliferation of these films inarguably constitutes a cycle, and may indeed suggest the emergence of a new comic genre which will in time posit its own set of rules and audience expectations. At very minimum, these films share a number of plot devices which propel action and narrative, and may serve as frameworks for comic structures.

There are six common and popular, though not necessarily mutually exclusive, manners in which the culture-clash concept can be used as a basic, overarching plot device. First, the "clash" is one of class or socio-economic status as in *Trading Places* (1983), *Down and Out in Beverly Hills* (1986), *Educating Rita* (1983) and *Who's That Girl* (1987). Second, the clash occurs due to distinctive and apparently incompatible personality types as in *Neighbors* (1981) and *Outrageous Fortune* (1987). Third, the clash occurs between a sub-culture and either mainstream culture or another sub-culture as in *Desperately Seeking Susan* (1985) and *After Hours* (1985). Fourth, the clash is based in geographically determined and defined differences which can be either international in scope as in *The Coca-Cola Kid* (1985), *Local Hero* (1983), and *Moscow on the Hudson* (1984), or more narrowly focused on rural versus urban living as in *Funny Farm* (1988). Fifth, the clash may involve a fantasy figure, such as an alien, who interacts with a human character, and through whom the world can be seen anew, as in *Splash* (1984), *Starman* (1984), *My Stepmother is an Alien* (1989) and, in one of the oddest of all uses, *Who Framed Roger Rabbit?* (1988). The sixth manner in which culture-clash is used as a plot structuring device is in the so called "switch" films in which a child becomes an adult or vice-versa; films in this vein include *Like Father, Like Son* (1987), *Vice-Versa* (1988), *Big* (1988), and *18 Again* (1988).

Certainly, not all of the films mentioned could be successfully grouped as members of the same genre; however, some of them are similar enough in terms of plot structures, settings and character types to suggest that the culture-clash plot device is indeed fostering a new identifiable set of conventions, or formula, for film comedy. Of the six permutations on the basic premise described above, the first four uses are particularly interrelated: they provide filmmakers with an endless array of possibilities for achieving both comedy and social commentary. In the remainder of this essay, I will focus attention on some key films which use the first four culture-clash plots, and which are treatable as members of the culture-clash comedy cycle of the 1980s.

As the umbrella term "culture-clash comedy" implies, all the films which fall under it are related inasmuch as they thematically involve conflicting and clashing cultures or sub-cultural attitudes, perceptions and lifestyles. In many cases, their narratives are fully motivated by the problems encountered in the process of reconciling polarized cultural priorities and values. And in almost all cases, the comedy is rooted in the manner in which displaced protagonists come to terms with a new environment or cultural system: with how well or poorly they manage their frequently "grotesque apprenticeship to chance event." Most often, the central protagonists will be young, urban or suburban, established (or aspiring to a successful career), and importantly, a little naive and mildly malcontent. They are, in short, consummate "yuppies": Benjamin Braddocks who have grown up and taken their place in the world, whose wallets now bulge with the very plastic they once mocked. They are, like Benjamin, comic anti-heroes, but they are sometimes more capable, and their searching is not necessarily adolescent in nature.[1]

Despite some differences, screwball comedies and some lightweight, commercial "counter-culture" or subversion films of the sixties and early seventies, such as *There's Girl in My Soup* (1970), and *I Love You Alice B. Toklas* (1968), do contain many of the basic plot elements which give form and structure to this new brand of comedy, but they were not nearly as willing to develop and dwell on the dark side of comedy. Too, unlike the basic screwball comedies, this cycle is not limited to rigid, conservative males and eccentric women in a "topsy-turvy romance"; it makes fuller use of the spectrum of human lifestyles and character types (Gehring 178-185). Nor are these films primarily confined to the "civilized" cultural milieu of the affluent, but rather often weave in and out of fringe and mainstream cultures. In addition, though screwball comedies certainly satirized "traditional romance," they were tailored within the limits of a narrow social conscience, and seldom aspired to political or other deeper levels of social satire. Additionally, the dark comedies of the sixties such as Mike Nichols' screen version of Jules Feiffer's *Little Murders* (1971), or Tony Richardson's *The Loved One* (1965), bear a strained relationship in terms of plot and tone to these new films, though they may be seen as precursors of this contemporary film cycle from a broader sociological perspective.

In his study of subversive tendencies in film, Amos Vogel mused about the sixties: "it is possible that future generations will view the rise of the Counterculture movement—Woodstock, the Beatles, Zen Buddhism, the flower children, communes and free schools—as the beginning of a new radical politics of the latter twentieth century." And he further characterizes the period as a time when "the young declared their independence from received wisdom and 'immutable' patterns (such as competitiveness, violence, and the desire for bourgeois living) creating their 'alternative lifestyles' with a gusto and consistency that unites—as does the avant-garde in art—form and content and hence becomes doubly dangerous" (306). Vogel's forecast for the latter part of the century has, at least on the surface, proven false. Those patterns associable with bourgeois life and thinking are clearly still going strong. Many of the campus radicals of the era are now sitting in board room chairs instead of staging "sit-ins"; the communes have gave over to country clubs and fitness spas; and even the icons of protest rock and roll, such as the Beatle's "Revolution," have become part of the advertising world's attempt to capitalize on nostalgia. The movement has in many respects been depoliticized and synthesized into mainstream American culture. It has lost its *form*, and poses no real threat to either liberal remnants of the "Great Society," nor the agenda of right-wing administrations which have dominated the 1980s. However, the *content* of that age is still here, it is part of our cultural mythology and it may indeed provide the key to understanding the visions expressed in 1980s culture-clash comedies.

Despite a cast which included "Saturday Night Live" veterans Dan Aykroyd and John Belushi (his last film before his tragic death) and the intriguing Cathy Moriarity, *Neighbors*, John G. Avildsen's screen adaptation of Thomas Berger's novel, did not meet with either commercial or critical success at the time of its release. Earl Keese (Belushi), a timid suburbanite, finds the sanctity and a sanity of his suburban cul-de-sac home suddenly violated by a bizarre couple. Vic (Aykroyd) and Ramona (Moriarity), who move into the run-down house next door, manage to turn Earl's suburban mediocrity into a comically charged nightmare. Ramona is an attractive blonde who enjoys playing the vamp; she consistently teases the uptight Earl with both verbal and physical sexual suggestions. Vic is a cross between a fascist (of the neo-nazi order) and an anarchist. He has his own bizarre sense of order and morality which he then seeks to impose upon Earl. As a result, Earl becomes a displaced character within his own home.

As the film proceeds into the night, Earl attempts to regain a grip on his household. He tries to fight back against Vic, first with pranks and then with violence. But all attempts backfire. Still, the morning after the living nightmare, Earl realizes that he had "more fun than on any other Friday night" in his life. He even attempts to convince Vic not to move away. The couple eventually offer Earl a chance to join them on their adventures; and with only a brief second thought, he jumps at the chance to chuck it all. Rather than just leaving a note for Enid, Earl ends up setting fire to his house. As the film closes we leave the cul-de-sac, with its high voltage power lines sizzling above the burning house.

Though the film contains many truly dark-comic moments, the bleakness is somewhat undercut by the lightness of the musical score, which is often a tongue-in-cheek variation on recognizable themes from shows such as the "Twilight Zone," old horror films, and film noir. It is a particularly fitting score in the sense that many sequences in the film are also parodies and spoofs on these sci-fi and horror formulas. However, it may actually detract from the film's potential to brood, and strike its truest target, suburban life. For the track comes off almost as an afterthought, functioning to bring the offbeat humor into a more mainline comic style of parody (consistent perhaps with certain audience expectations of the cast) and lessen the dark edge of the satire. Still, the fact that the narrative of the film is propelled by a displaced character who finds his cultural values, as defined by his lifestyle, upset by a conflict with a couple who do not share his attitudes and value system, establishes this film as a culture-clash comedy. And like many films which follow in this cycle the resolution necessitates a reconciliation of the conflicting values through either a complete rejection, a compromise, or a complete surrender of one rules system to the other. In this case Earl's joining of the couple represents a surrender of sorts, with suburban life as the defeated party.

The term culture-clash should indeed suggest the more common phrase "culture shock." This, of course, refers to a psychological phenomenon which occurs when moving from one familiar culture (usually geo-culturally defined) to an unfamiliar one. It is something that many people have experienced when travelling abroad or within disparate regions of their own nations. It is also something we can experience when returning to our native culture after having spent an extended period of time living and adjusting to another culture. And though for the purpose of exploring these films I have taken a much broader view of the culture-clash concept, allowing it to account for collisions of sub-cultural lifestyles and social attitudes, some of the films under consideration are indeed about the problems of dealing with the customs and mores of a foreign land. Two films in particular, *Local Hero*, and *The Coca-Cola Kid*, utilize this theme to develop both their narratives and their satiric aim.

Though Bill Forsyth's *Local Hero* is a much gentler film than the others under consideration, it is an important film in that it can be used to help define the parameters of culture-clash as a plot device. The film derives its basic structure from a rather simple plot: a young, aspiring Houston-based Knox Oil company executive, MacIntyre (Peter Reigert), is sent to Scotland to buy some land for an offshore oil exploration and development. He arrives in the town of Ferness, and with the aid of a local accountant and hotel owner, Gordon Urquhart (Denis Lawson), the acquisition proceeds relatively smoothly. Little by little, Mac falls in love with both the town, which has a timeless simplicity, and with Gordon's wife, Stella (Jennifer Black). But complications with the sale arise when an eccentric beachcomber, Ben Knox, refuses to sell the beach which he legally owns. Efforts to persuade him are at a standstill until the head of the oil company, Happer (Burt Lancaster) arrives on the scene.

On the surface the plot would seem to indicate a Capraesque comedy for the Eighties: an attack on the dehumanizing and environmentally insensitive expansion of big business, and ultimately a vindication of simpler, old world community values. Even the title of the film anticipates a singular heroic figure who will challenge and overcome the American "invasion." But this is not the case; the film almost paradoxically humanizes the corporate characters and paints the locals as simple folk willing to sell their homes and lifestyles for the fantasies of wealth. In fact, in the film's one potentially darker moment, the members of the town assemble and march onto the beach to harass Ben, we assume forcibly if necessary, into selling his land, as he represents the only block between them and the realizations of their Rolls Royces, mansions and so on.

The key to understanding this film, however, does not really lie in the fantasies of the townspeople, nor even in Happer's eventual choice to discard plans for an oil refinery in favor of an astronomical and oceanographic research institute. Rather, the philosophical point of view is embodied in the changes that overcome the displaced character of Mac. The film begins with Mac in Houston content to cruise in his Porsche, remain emotionally uncommitted, and conduct business impersonally by telex conference. During his stay in Ferness he learns the pleasures of companionship and is "seduced by the notion of escaping the inhumanity of the urban sprawl for all the enveloping beauty of the Highlands" (Hunter and Astaire 92). It ends with him back in Houston, but now smelling seashells, hanging postcards of the Scottish coast and pictures of Gordon and Stella (the perfect couple) on his walls, and looking longingly into the empty night lights of the cityscape. How we get from point to point is clear, but the future of both the Scottish town and MacIntyre remain somewhat unclear. For though Ferness has altered Mac, it has also been altered by him. We must assume the purchasing deal will eventually go through and the institute, with a few offshore oil rigs as well, will change the character of the town. In a sense, there has been some reconciliation of cultural concerns; a happy medium has been struck between the aspirations of the corporate minds, both Happer's and Knox's eccentricities, the fantasies of the townspeople, and the environment itself. Perhaps a soviet sailor who frequently visits the town puts forth the practical view when he notes that life is hard for the locals because they "can't eat scenery." However both the pastoral cinematography and the attitude change in Mac suggests that the while the film redeems the basic goodness of the human spirit, it also laments the inevitable passing of the more simple way of life and the timeless character of the town.

As in *Local Hero*, the plot of Dusan Makavejev's *The Coca-Cola Kid* involves an American businessman sent to work on problems abroad. But this film is more akin to Forsyth's *Comfort and Joy* in that it is much darker and disturbing in nature and ultimately involves a business turf war. In *Comfort and Joy* a more or less innocent radio announcer is drawn into a frequently violent battle between feuding ice cream truck companies; in *The Coca-Cola Kid* a dynamic young company trouble shooter is sent to Australia to help increase sales and break into a territory controlled by an independent soft-drink manufacturer who does not hesitate to use force in maintaining his hold on the market. What ensues thereafter is an adventure down-under laced with Makavejev's usual mix of barbed wit, ironic twists, biting satire and eroticism. As with *Local Hero*, the philosophy of this film manifests itself less in the action than in the changes which overcome its protagonist. In this case, Becker (Eric Roberts) is the "whiz kid" sales troubleshooter out of "Atlanta, Georgia, USA." A company man to the hilt, he sees Coke as the symbol of American freedom, virtues and Godliness: he tells a rotary club crowd that they are not really free without Coke in their lives. In keeping with what one might expect from a man who holds a Harvard MBA in "theology and business," his rhetorical style is more closely related to a proselytising Southern preacher than an executive. His job is not a job but a mission.

Becker's style and rigid character is counterpointed by the rather easy-going Australian executives who have been instructed to placate his whims. He also finds elements of his character echoed in the equally driven and determined, but a little weathered, local soft-drink tycoon T. George McDowell. But most importantly he finds himself challenged by the rather spontaneous and intensely infatuating personality of his assigned secretary, Terry (Greta Scacchi). It is Terry (who is, unbeknown to Becker, T. George's estranged daughter) that brings about the main changes in Becker. Her volatile and often violent nature is combined with her free spirit, genuine caring and cunning sensuality. She leads Becker into self-confusion, by placing him in awkward and often compromising positions. Through his confusion and embarrassment he becomes more in touch with his own feelings and basic human passions and emotions. Eventually, after T. George blows-up his own factory in an effort to prevent a hostile takeover, Becker resigns his post with the corporation and submits to his role in Terry's life.

Though there are at times socio-political sub-plots (one important one involves a hotel waiter who is member or a subversive organization and mistakenly contracts Becker to deliver armaments), these are often brutally comic in nature. Yet, however comic and satiric in design, the film's condemnation of the corporate mentality goes unchecked. The fact that the film also displays an understanding of the secondary role that corporate thinking plays to higher values, even for its most vicious proponents, does not lessen the attack. Rather it is a part of the strategy. The changes which occur in Becker are unquestionably for the better. For though there is some immediate economic security—Becker has made off with twenty-five thousand dollars put up front by the waiter's organization for an arms shipment— the promising career has been replaced by the ambiguous future. And too, the gung-ho nationalistic pride, the narrow corporately empowered imperialism of the American seems to have been dampened and reduced, or perhaps broadened, to a healthier respect for international, or community sovereignty. Unlike Forsyth, Makajevev does not spend time lamenting the passing of traditions, but like Forsyth he does seem to hold forth, at least in this film, a view of the human spirit as redeemable.[2]

Down and Out in Beverly Hills moves us to both the material impoverishment of street-life and the spiritual impoverishment of affluence. Although Mazursky utilized the basic premise of Renoir's *Boudu Saved from Drowning* (1932), the film cannot be seen as true homage to Renoir in stylistic terms. Bazin wrote of *Boudu*: "in this film the scenario is tangential to the subject; the casting, incidental to the characters; and the plot oblique to the situation" (30). In Mazursky's film nothing could be further from the truth: for the scenario propels the subject; the casting defines the characters; and the plot creates the situation. In *Down and Out*, a street bum, Jerry (Nick Nolte), loses his dog, Kerouac, and consequently, we deduce, his desire to live. He loads his pockets with stones and throws himself into the backyard pool of coat-hanger tycoon Dave Whiteman (Richard Dreyfuss). Dave pulls him from the pool, and much to the disgust of his wife, Barbara (Bette Midler), administers mouth to mouth resuscitation reviving the unconscious bum. Obviously fascinated by the root causes of the desperate act, Dave invites Jerry to stay and recuperate. He is given clean clothes and room in the cabana; and almost immediately, his presence begins to change the Whiteman family in both profound and peculiar ways.

To be certain, the Whitemans are by no means the average American family. Dave is an uptight, easily aggravated but highly successful businessmen; Barbara with her gurus, meditating, chronic headaches and status displays is a parody of the California cult and fad following housewife; the daughter is a know-it-all college student who keeps her distance from the family; Max, the teenage son, is a videocam wielding rebel flirting with an adolescent identity crisis; and last, but not least is Maria, the attractive Mexican maid who is sleeping with her boss, and has on the surface the most stable personality and a strong sense of the importance of her role in the household. The introduction of Jerry catalyzes changes in each character that may be seen as extensions of their own neurosis, fears and anxieties. For Dave, Jerry provides a sense of freedom and abandon from the pressures of business and family. He also presents a kind of Pygmallion challenge, as Dave seeks to reform Jerry into a model citizen. For Barbara, Jerry is at first an aggravation, but eventually he becomes her lover, curing her headaches as well as her frigidity, and softening her rather hard-edged and obnoxious personality (played out with true Midler verve). For Max, Jerry becomes a big brother, or perhaps the father with whom he can communicate: he advises the boy to be true to himself, resulting in Max's identity crisis manifesting itself in an androgynous, à la Boy George, manner. For the daughter, Jerry becomes a romantic enigma and lover, who enables her to discard her expectations for a man like her father, in favor of someone "soulful" like himself. And for the maid, Jerry becomes both a lover and teacher, opening her eyes up to the manner in which she, as a Third World citizen, is being exploited by her capitalist boss.

As in *Neighbors*, the majority of action in this film takes place within the sanctity of the home; but Jerry does not seek to impose his lifestyle values on the Whiteman's, he merely forces them to confront and challenge their own. Mazursky clearly intends to satirize the empty affluence of Beverly Hills, but he does not in truth condemn it as harshly as Avildsen condemns suburban mediocrity. The upbeat Hollywood ending of the film—in which Jerry, having walked off in his original clothes with the Whiteman's dog, Matisse, finds himself acculturated beyond eating garbage, and so returns to the open arms of the family—is almost antithetical to the house burning in *Neighbors*. It rings of "and so they lived happily ever after," even with this stranger in their midst. Although there is some ambiguity as to the future, it may indeed be Jerry's life which will be the most drastically and deeply altered by the encounter. Once again, the film leans toward a view of people as redeemable: the cynical overtones are far outweighed by the resurrection of basic human kindness and caring at the end.

Mazursky's sensibilities to the problems of married life, family and relationships have been well documented in numerous films, and Susan Seidleman, in her second feature film, *Desperately Seeking Susan*, tackles many of the same issues in an innovative and at times daft way. The film juggles elements of romance, mystery, and high-spirited comedy. Unlike most of the other films discussed so far, the lifestyle-clashing characters do not interact directly: their confrontations are almost always mediated by a third party or convolutions of circumstance. The actions revolve around a bored suburban housewife, Roberta (Rosanna Arquette), who reads the personals for vicarious thrills. She becomes intrigued by particular notices involving a woman named Susan (Madonna) that appear in the paper on a regular basis. Roberta sets out to spy on Susan at a rendezvous in New York's Battery Park. Eventually, through a series of coincidences and plot contrivances, Roberta is mistaken for Susan.

But this is not a simple hip *Prince and the Pauper* update or reversal like John Landis' *Trading Places* (1983), rather it becomes both a mystery and journey into the recesses of Roberta's "good girl" imagination and Susan's "bad girl" lifestyle. Roberta, suffering from temporary amnesia, actually assumes she is Susan for a while. In turn, she finds herself pursued by a mobster; she takes employment as second-rate magician's assistant; she is arrested as a prostitute; and she becomes romantically entangled with a relative stranger. But though she wears Susan's clothes and dwells in Susan's Lower East Side cultural milieu, she maintains much of her natural innocence and purity. As Seidleman points out, Roberta "doesn't *really* become Susan, just a more interesting version of herself, a synthesis between the 'bad' and the 'good' girl" (Yakir 20). Though the film resolves itself too easily by pairing Susan and Roberta as heroic figures—having caught the thief and murderer, and returned a pair of priceless Egyptian earrings to the proper authorities—it doesn't undercut its own satiric side.

As is common to many of these films, suburban affluence is satirized with zeal. Roberta's unfaithful husband, Gary Glass (Mark Blum), the "spa King" of Fort Lee, New Jersey, is a two-dimensional, money-and-self-obsessed character. Roberta's emotional longing and penchant for romantic fantasies counterpoints his straightforward, matter-of-fact and shallow behavior. The shallowness of suburbia is further amplified by both our brief glimpses of Roberta's pre-Susan life, and the other incidental suburban characters we meet. Thus, we can fully accept Roberta's discontentment and are expected to feel no sympathy for the husband when she leaves him at the end for a Bleeker Street Cinema projectionist. The projectionist (Aidan Quinn), provides the gentleness, caring and adventure that Roberta was seeking; he also serves as a primary catalyst in helping Roberta to affect change within her own life. And though at film's close she has lost both material security and a clear future path, there is little doubt that she is better off.

Another film centered on the misadventures of an innocent in the world of lower Manhattan is Martin Scorsese's *After Hours*. But unlike the high-spirited comedy of *Susan*, the humor in this film is dark, cruel and unrelenting. Paul Hackett (Griffin Dunne, who also co-produced the film), is the likeable, young, straight, Upper East Side, New Yorker who finds himself amid the odd going-ons of Soho late night. The film first establishes Paul's character at his workplace, a sterile office complete with computers and co-workers who are only there until something better comes along. It then takes us to his apartment, which is characteristically small, simply furnished in neo-Bloomingdales, and where he is unquestionably alone. Bored by the prospect of another night prone on the couch, clicking the buttons on his cable TV box, Paul goes out to a coffee shop, where he meets a vibrant and kooky young woman, Marcy (Rosanna Arquette), who is on her way back home to SoHo. Later that night he goes to visit her, and his comic nightmare begins.

Although Marcy in a sense brings Paul into a new world, this film is not about a singular zany woman upsetting a conservative male's sense of order. Rather a series of bizarre and at times grotesque encounters, coincidences and circumstances evolve throughout the night. Paul in turn becomes partially responsible for Marcy's suicide; he is befriended by a barmaid who is a mid-Sixties anachronism and can't handle rejection (Teri Garr); he is mistaken for a thief and hunted by a group of angry vigilantes lead by a Mr. Softee ice-cream truck driver; he is brought home by a man who takes him for a gay pick-up; he is given a partial mohawk at a slam-dancing punk bar; and he is used as a living mold for a plaster sculpture by a emotionally disconcerting middle-aged barfly (Verna Bloom). This not so ordinary evening in Soho is at times satiric, ironic and horrific, but it always maintains its dark comic edge. The sparingly offbeat soundtrack, the almost non-stop camera movements (tracking shots and dolly-in shots abound), and the strong angular compositions balance the filmmaker's comic intent with the tensions of the scenario. In addition, numerous allusions in both the dialogue and the actions to the *Wizard of Oz* form a kind of sub-textual level of parody. The film is ultimately about a character whose only desire is to get back home alive; and he is fully dependent on others to help him achieve that goal.

Paul never does make it back home that night, but he is, still covered in hardened plaster, accidentally dumped from the back of the true thieves' (Cheech and Chong) van in front of his office building the next morning. And he returns to work a little worn and dusty, but not obviously damaged by the nightmare he'd just experienced. Perhaps the oddest thing about this film is that Paul's life does not really seem profoundly altered: he starts safely bored and innocent, spends most of the film frightened, and ends up at his desk facing the predictable safety of his computer terminal. The change in his character may be analogous to the change in Dorothy after her most peculiar dream: a new appreciation for the familiar people and objects of his day-to-day and banal life.

Perhaps the condensation of the action into one night, and the lack of weighty dramatic interaction and development warrants a return to normalcy ending. But such an end unfortunately, weakens any strong satirization of the yuppie lifestyle. Indeed, the Soho art world, and the punk communities are left to take the brunt of the film's satiric blows. For Paul, despite his shallowness, is intended as sympathetic character; we may at times laugh at the inept manner in which he serves his "grotesque apprenticeship to chance event," but we are always motivated to keep on rooting for him.

Paul's one wild night is no match for the fate of a similar male protagonist in Jonathan Demme's even bleaker comedy, *Something Wild*. Charlie Driggs (Jeff Daniels) is a tense, reserved and straight young businessman, content to appease his "closet rebel" nature by skipping out of a restaurant without paying the check. He is observed and more or less abducted by a kinky young woman, Audrey, who dresses in a melange of punk and "dynamatrix" chic, wears a Louise Brooks wig and calls herself Lulu (Melanie Griffith). Audrey quickly asserts her authority over Charlie; she introduces him to a little sado-masochistic bedplay, forces him to shirk his responsibilities at the office, and basically to obey her rather asocial whims as they journey from the city into small-town America. Audrey had chosen Charlie to masquerade as her husband before both her mother and her high school reunion primarily because he appeared a safe bet: a family man, who would go along with the ride for a little thrill without forming any attachments. But Charlie's motivations are not so simple. Like Audrey he tends to fabricate elements of his existence; he hides the fact that he is embittered by a divorce and the dissolution of his once happy suburban life, and he becomes a rather willing participant in Audrey's games more out of a genuine need for companionship than a need for adventure. Unlike an innocent caught in Audrey's webs of deceit, Charlie spins a few webs of his own.

Despite some matched qualities of the two, Audrey and Charlie do come from different worlds. Charlie's straight, clean, upper-middle class career orientation and former suburban aspirations run contrary to Lulu's criminal fringe and blue-collar small-town background. And though the film begins as a somewhat disconcerting but light-hearted romp, it turns dark and vicious with the introduction of this criminal fringe element, embodied in Audrey's estranged ex-con husband, Ray Sinclair (Ray Liotta). Ray is Charlie's antithesis, and perhaps his alter-ego. As John Powers has pointed out "dark haired and swarthy with biceps squeezing from his black T-shirt, Ray is the deadly mirror image of Charlie, the blonde fair haired and besuited square who has spent his life as a 'closet rebel.' " Powers goes on to note that Ray "becomes a physical expression of unconscious forces lurking beneath the sanitized surface of daily life" (50). Much as Audrey abducted Charlie in a self-serving yet playful manner that accords with her nature, Ray abducts Audrey in a violent effort to force a reaffirmation of a relationship she no longer desires. At this point the film's comedy does not cease entirely, but it is truncated by a dramatic violence vaguely reminiscent of Peckinpah's *Straw Dogs* (1971).

Charlie must confront not only his feelings for Audrey, whom he prefers to call Lulu, but must match Ray's violence in order to win her. And in a battle to the death raged within the innermost security of his suburban house, Charlie overcomes his foe and rival. Demme's decision to portray the brutality of the fight in a shocking and charged manner, has occassioned some reviewers to question the billing of this film as a comedy. And though the realism of the violence has a particularly dramatic poignancy, the actual death scene itself is played out by Liotta with some intentionally comic contrivance. Having been stabbed in the chest by walking into a knife held by Charlie, Ray looks across and exclaims in a rather perplexed tone "Shit, Charlie!" Like a dying cowboy in a bad western, he stumbles forth, mortally wounded, takes one last look at himself in a mirror, and then shuffles off the screen (we cut to a close up of his boots). This veritable and conscious cliché is further accentuated by the sparse and definitively comic tones flowing in the incidental soundtrack. Thus, this climactic scene, despite its tragic overtones, remains comic—pitch black, but comic nevertheless. Like many films we have discussed so far, an epilogue style ending follows, in which Charlie, having quit his job and made other changes in keeping with his new, deeper personality, is reunited with Lulu, and together they set forth into an ambiguous future.

Although there are numerous more examples of films which were produced within the decade that possess similar "culture-clash" scenarios, the truest measure of whether or not this cycle indicates a developing complex of filmic conventions may be the fact that in the late eighties a handful of extremely formulaic culture-clash comedies were produced. A film such as James Foley's *Who's That Girl* (1987), pits a fast-talking, hip-wiggling, volatile, petty thief (Madonna) against a be-spectacled, uptight attorney (Griffin Dunne) in a predictable comic-adventure, culture-clash farce. The nightmare world and the dark vision expressed in the most innovative of these films has been reduced to the level of a formulaic pre-teen comic fantasy. But the culture-clash premise is more than evident, however stereotypically perverted, in the formula: an innocent, conservative character (male in most cases), is shanghaied by a high-spirited fringe culture figure (frequently female), taken on a metaphorical or actual journey, and will ultimately either develop a strong attraction for the new life or reject it in full.

It is, of course, impossible to separate the proliferation of this cycle, which at its core subverts conservative values and aspirations toward self-indulgent affluence, from the political shift to the right that occurred during the Reagan years. Excepting perhaps the Eddie Murphy vehicle films such as *Coming to America*, these satiric, often politically left-of-center films were no match at the box office for the breed of right-wing, and often facistic cinema characterized by films in the *Rambo* (1985), *Red Dawn* (1984) vein. But their relative success may indeed be accounted for partially in terms of their appeal to both the rebellious spirit, and the spiritual questing of the Sixties counter-culture. They provide a new *form* for an old *content*; they reaffirm the counter-cultural imperatives on a smaller and more personal scale by attacking suburban mediocrity, empty affluence, and the ugliness of the rat race. Even at their darkest and most cynical, as a group they herald romantic visions, stress the value of human companionship, and the challenge of an adventurous and ambiguous, rather than pre-planned, future.

The staying power of this cycle, will undoubtedly rest on how effectively the basic premise, the rich array of plot conventions and thematic variations continue to strike a chord with future audiences.

Notes

[1]Not all films in this genre utilize a "yuppie" archetype; the culture-clash characters can both be members of fringe or non-mainstream cultures as in Jim Jarmucsh's offbeat film, *Stranger Than Paradise* (1985). The discussion here has been limited as means of defining the basic, mainstream tenets and plot characteristic of the cycle, but variations on clashing character types and cultures are already abundant in films that I would group under this heading.

[2]Some of Makajevev's other films are *Innocence Unprotected* (1971), *WR: Mysteries of the Organism* (1971) and *Montenegro* (1981). Though some have a satiric edge motivated by clashing cultures, not all present such an optimistic view of the human spirit.

Works Cited

Bazin, Andre. *Jean Renoir*. Trans. W. W. Halsey II and William H. Simon. New York: Delta, 1973.

Gehring, Wes D. "Screwball Comedy: An Overview." *Journal of Popular Film and Television* 13:3 (Winter 1986): 178-185.

Hunter, Allan and Mark Astaire. *Local Hero: The Making of the Film*. Edinburgh: Polygon, 1983.

Powers, John. "Bleak Chic." *American Film* 12:5 (March 1987): 50.

Stevens, Wallace. "The Comedian as the Letter C." *Poems by Wallace Stevens*. Ed. Samuel French Morse. New York: Vintage, 1959. 40.

Vogel, Amos. *Film as a Subversive Art*. New York: Random House, 1974.

Yakir, Dan. "Celine and Julie Go Lightly: Side-by-Side-by-Seidleman." *Film Comment* 21:3 (May-June 1985): 20.

Filmography

The following is a partial, chronological list of 1980s comedies that incorporate one or more basic culture-clash premises in terms of main or sub-plot structures.

1980	*Private Benjamin*	Dir. Howard Zieff
1980	*The Gods Must Be Crazy*	Dir. Jamie Uys
1981	*Continental Divide*	Dir. Michael Apted
1981	*Neighbors*	Dir. John Avildsen
1982	*Some Kind of Hero*	Dir. Arthur Hiller
1982	*Victor/Victoria*	Dir. Blake Edwards
1983	*Doctor Detroit*	Dir. Michael Pressman
1983	*Educating Rita*	Dir. Lewis Gilbert
1983	*Experience Preferred... But Not Essential*	Dir. Peter Duffell

1983	*The Flamingo Kid*	Dir. Garry Marshall
1983	*Local Hero*	Dir. Bill Forsyth
1983	*Mr. Mom*	Dir. Stan Dragoti
1983	*Reuben, Reuben*	Dir. Robert Ellis Miller
1983	*Trading Places*	Dir. John Landis
1984	*All of Me*	Dir. Carl Reiner
1984	*American Dreamer*	Dir. Rick Rosenthal
1984	*Goodbye New York*	Dir. Amos Kollek
1984	*Moscow on the Hudson*	Dir. Paul Mazursky
1984	*Protocol*	Dir. Herbert Ross
1984	*Splash*	Dir. Ron Howard
1984	*Starman*	Dir. John Carpenter
1985	*After Hours*	Dir. Martin Scorsese
1985	*The Coca-Cola Kid*	Dir. Dusan Makajevev
1985	*Back to the Future*	Dir. Robert Zemeckis
1985	*Bliss*	Dir. Ray Lawrence
1985	*Desperately Seeking Susan*	Dir. Susan Seidleman
1985	*European Vacation*	Dir. Amy Heckerling
1985	*Gung Ho*	Dir. Ron Howard
1985	*Lost in America*	Dir. Albert Brooks
1985	*Maxie*	Dir. Paul Aaron
1985	*Options*	Dir. Camilo Vila
1985	*Stranger Than Paradise*	Dir. Jim Jarmusch
1985	*Volunteers*	Dir. Nicholas Meyer
1986	*Crocodile Dundee*	Dir. Peter Faiman
1986	*Desperate Moves*	Dir. Oliver Hellman
1986	*Down and Out in Beverly Hills*	Dir. Paul Mazursky
1986	*Peggy Sue Got Married*	Dir. Francis Coppola
1986	*The Mosquito Coast*	Dir. Peter Weir
1986	*Something Wild*	Dir. Jonathan Demme
1986	*Shanghai Surprise*	Dir. Jim Goddard
1986	*Three Amigos*	Dir. John Landis
1987	*Adventures in Babysitting*	Dir. Chris Colombus
1987	*Baby Boom*	Dir. Charles Shyer
1987	*Blind Date*	Dir. Blake Edwards
1987	*Ishtar*	Dir. Elaine May
1987	*Like Father, Like Son*	Dir. Rod Daniels
1987	*Maid to Order*	Dir. Amy Jones
1987	*Planes, Trains, and Automobiles*	Dir. John Hughes
1987	*Outrageous Fortune*	Dir. Arthur Hiller
1987	*Sammi and Rosie Get Laid*	Dir. Stephen Frears
1987	*Walk Like a Man*	Dir. Melvin Frank
1987	*Who's That Girl*	Dir. James Foley
1988	*Beetlejuice*	Dir. Tim Burton
1988	*Bagdad Cafe*	Dir. Percy Adlon
1988	*Big*	Dir. Penny Marshall
1988	*Big Business*	Dir. Jim Abrahams
1988	*Coming to America*	Dir. John Landis
1988	*Crocodile Dundee II*	Dir. John Cornell
1988	*18 Again*	Dir. Paul Flaherty

1988	*A Fish Called Wanda*	Dir. Charles Crichton
1988	*Funny Farm*	Dir. George Roy Hill
1988	*Like Father, Like Son*	Dir. Rod Daniels
1988	*Moon Over Parador*	Dir. Paul Mazursky
1988	*Overboard*	Dir. Garry Marshall
1988	*Stars and Bars*	Dir. Pat O'Conner
1988	*Twins*	Dir. Ivan Reitman
1988	*Vice-Versa*	Dir. Brian Gilbert
1988	*Who Framed Roger Rabbit?*	Dir. Robert Zemeckis
1989	*The Accidental Tourist*	Dir. Lawrence Kasden
1989	*Back to the Future II*	Dir. Robert Zemeckis
1989	*Bill and Ted's Excellent Adventure*	Dir. Stephen Hereck
1989	*Earth Girls are Easy*	Dir. Julien Temple
1989	*Her Alibi*	Dir. Bruce Beresford
1989	*My Stepmother is an Alien*	Dir. Richard Benjamin

Contributors

Parley Ann Boswell teaches American Literature at Eastern Illinois University in Charleston, Illinois. Her interests include Colonial American culture and American film.

Carlos E. Cortés is a Professor of History at the University of California, Riverside. The recipient of two book awards, he is currently working on a three-volume study of the history of the U.S. motion picture treatment of ethnic groups, foreign nations, and world cultures. A former guest host on the PBS national television series, "Why in the World?", he received his university's Distinguished Teaching Award and the California Council for the Humanities' 1980 Distinguished California Humanist Award.

Ralph R. Donald (Ph.D., University of Massachusetts) teaches film and television in the Department of Radio-Television-Film at Howard University, Washington, D.C. Special areas of research include propaganda on film and television, and motion picture genres, especially the combat films of World War II and Vietnam, horror and science fiction films.

Linda K. Fuller, Co-editor of this series, (Ph.D., University of Massachusetts) is an Assistant Professor in the Media Department of Worcester (MA) State College. Author of "The Baseball Movie Genre: At Bat or Struck Out?" (*Play and Culture*, Feb., 1990), *The Cosby Show: Audiences, Impact, Implications* (Greenwood Press), and co-author with Dr. Lilless McPherson Shilling of *Communicating Comfortably: Your Guide to Overcoming Speaking and Writing Anxieties* (HRD Press, 1990), Linda has done extensive research and publishing on the Olympic Games, and teaches a course in sportscasting.

Gary Hoppenstand received his Ph.D. in American Culture from Bowling Green State University. He has written or edited several books dealing with popular culture topics, and is currently working on a book-length critical study of British horror genre author/director, Clive Barker. He is an Assistant Professor in the Department of American Thought and Language, teaching in the Film Studies track.

John H. Lenihan is Associate Professor of History at Texas A&M University, where he specializes in American cultural-intellectual history and film. He is the author of *Showdown: Confronting Modern America in the Western Film*, published by the University of Illinois Press.

Paul Loukides is a Professor of English at Albion College where he teaches courses in film, creative writing and literature. He is particularly interested in the conventions of popular film and is currently at work on *Beyond the Stars III*.

Greg Metcalf is with the Department of American Studies, University of Maryland, College Park, also teaches Government and Film courses when he's not writing about Mark Twain, Mary Cassatt, Philip Marlowe and the function of paratextual characters in contemporary American society.

Brooks Robards has a Ph.D. in Communication from University of Massachusetts, Amherst, an M.A. from University of Hartford and an AB from Bryn Mawr College. She does research on Film & TV and has published articles on the TV cop genre and on innovation in TV programming. She is Professor of Mass Communication at Westfield State College in Massachusetts.

Garyn G. Roberts received his Ph.D. in American Culture from Bowling Green State University in 1986. His recent works include the book *A Cent A Story!—The Best from Ten Detective Aces* and *Old Sleuth's Freaky Female Detectives From the Dime Novels* (co-edited with Gary Hoppenstand and Ray B. Browne). Works in progress include an edited collection of essays on dark fantasy grandmaster Clive Barker, and *Black Days, Grotesque Rogues, and Square-Jawed Justice: The World of Dick Tracy* (a book length study of the famous comic strip). Roberts is an Assistant Professor in the Department of American Thought and Language at Michigan State University, and among his interests number popular film and literature.

Clinton R. Sanders is an Associate Professor of Sociology at the Hartford Campus of the University of Connecticut. His areas of specialization include: cultural production, animal-human interaction, and social deviance. Temple University Press has recently published *Customizing the Body*, Sanders' ethnography of the tattooing subculture. The "armadillos" in the title of the paper refers to Tod Browning's innovative display of these animals in the early scenes of the classic *Dracula* (1932).

Rick Shale is an Associate Professor of English at Youngstown State University, Youngstown, Ohio, and an adjunct faculty member of the Department of Human Values in Medicine at the Northeastern Ohio Universities College of Medicine, Rootstown, Ohio. His publications include *Academy Awards: An Ungar Reference Index, 2nd ed.* (NY: Frederick Ungar, 1982) and *Donald Duck Joins Up: The Walt Disney Studio During World War II* (Ann Arbor: UMI Research Press, 1982).

Roy M. Vestrich holds a Ph.D. in Communication and an M.F.A. in English from the University of Massachusetts at Amherst, and an A.B. in Language and Literature from Bard College. He has served as vice-president and president of the Northeast Popular Culture Association, and is presently an Assistant Professor of English and Communication, and Coordinator of the Film studies program at Castleton State College in Vermont. He has published film, art, dance and theatre criticism, and is currently working on an anthology about television comedy, and a character convention study of the image of the artist in film.

DATE DUE